The Principle

of

Self-Determination
in
International Law

TO THE MEMORY OF MY FATHER

AND

TO MY MOTHER

The Principle
of
Self-Determination
in
International Law

W. OFUATEY-KODJOE

New York

nELLEn PUBLISHInG COMPAnY, InC.

International Standard Book Number 0-8424-0064-8
International Standard Book Number 0-8424-0070-2
Library of Congress Catalogue Number 75-16787

Printed in the United States of America

University Press of Cambridge, Mass. Series
Consulting Editor: Robert A. Nicholas

Distributed by   Frederick Fell Publishers, Inc.
                      386 Park Avenue South
                      New York, New York 10016

                      Published simultaneously in Canada by
                      Thomas Nelson & Sons
                      Don Mills, Ontario, Canada

CONTENTS

Preface

The term "self-determination" is used more frequently and with more passion than any other term in contemporary international relations. First exploding onto the international scene as the plea of European "oppressed nationalities," it later became the battle cry of colonial peoples struggling to free themselves from imperial domination: and recently, it has become the claimed right of groups all over the world and in such diverse circumstances as Northern Ireland, Biafra, and Bangladesh as they struggle to overthrow what they consider to be alien oppressive rule. Yet in spite of, or perhaps because of, its great importance, self-determination also has the distinction of being one of the most confused expressions in the lexicon of international relations.

Since the turn of the century, when the term "self-determination" gained wide currency in international political relations, there has emerged a substantial literature devoted to attempts to explain and clarify the concept. Unfortunately, the bulk of this literature has been fraught with conceptual and methodological problems. An analysis of the literature points to the conclusion that these problems can be traced to one fundamental flaw. *This fundamental flaw is that, with very few exceptions, these writers begin their analysis of the principle already equipped with their own definition of self-determination, which is derived not from the practice of the international community but deduced* a priori *from political doctrines.* Thus, what the writers have done is add to the general confusion about the meaning of the principle of self-determination. The result of this confusion is that it is very difficult to handle effectively the contradictory claims and counterclaims that are being advanced by various groups.

Some publicists have responded to this bewildering situation by advocating that the term be dropped altogether.

This suggestion is to us an unwise escape from reality. The reality is that as long as a group feels that it is laboring under alien and oppressive rule there is a good chance that it will at some time attempt to liberate itself on the basis of its right to self-rule. It was this motivation that led to the invocation of the principle of self-determination by the nationalities in eastern Europe prior to World War I, and by the Asians and Africans in the period after World War II. Furthermore, there is every indication, judging from the nature of the new states as "plural societies" with serious ethnic and cultural cleavages, that these demands for self-determination will continue with increasing frequency and seriousness. Nor is this situation limited to the *Tiers Monde*. A recent list of upheavals involving minority groups and separatist movements cuts across all geographic and ideological boundaries. Thus, the self-determination movements of the Montagnards of South Vietnam, or the Taiwanese, or the Buganda revolt of 1966 have their counterpart in the Flanders for the Flemish movement in Belgium, the Croatian liberation movement in Yugoslavia, and the violent French secessionist movement in Berne. Admittedly, at present, these conflicts are going on *within* states, and therefore, the demands made by groups for self-determination are as yet dormant on the international level. However, as in the aftermath of World War I, it is possible for political events to catapult these demands onto the international stage, at which point they become problems for the international community as a whole.

With the increasing frequency of conflicts involving the principle, what is urgently needed is the establishment and clarification of generally accepted rules and criteria that can be applied relatively uniformly. For while it is true that a clear definition of a principle does not always lead to the peaceful solution of a conflict, it is certainly safe to assert that the removal of confusion and uncertainty from the definition tends to heighten considerably the expectation of a clear and unambiguous application of the principle, and thus enhances the inclination of the parties to submit to peaceful settlement. The present imperative, therefore, is to attempt to develop a definition of the principle of self-determination with as much clarity and precision as is permitted by the exigencies of contemporary international political life.

The aim of this study is to define the scope and content of the principle of self-determination. In order to do this, we propose to assemble all elements of international practice pertaining to and involving all claims advanced on the basis of that principle, and to analyze this international practice in order to arrive at a clear definition based not on theory but on an interpretation of the principle that members of the international community may accept as binding.

This approach is based on two important considerations: first, the recognition that there exists a long record of international practice involving claims and counterclaims advanced on the basis of a right of self-determination; second, that any international practice of such long duration involves, *ab definitio,* an implied core, or nexus, that represents that part of the practice that the states accept as binding. It is this consensus among the states, as to the scope of an international practice they are willing to accept as binding, that constitutes the definition of the scope and content of the principle involved, in customary international law.

In order to be valid, an attempt to ascertain the scope and content of a principle of international law must be in accordance with certain criteria and procedural rules ". . . by which it [international law] distinguishes rules belonging to it." The most authoritative statement of these procedures is Article 38, paragraph 1, of the Statute of the International Court of Justice. On the basis of that statement, a conception of the requirements for defining rules of international law that are recognized as generally acceptable in the judicial life of contemporary international society has emerged out of the work of the International Law Commission, the jurisprudence of the International Court of Justice, and in the writings of many authoritative publicists. It is in accordance with these procedural rules and criteria that our attempt to define the principle of self-determination will proceed.

In this effort, I shall try to present my thoughts in a manner that I hope will be stimulating not only to international lawyers but also to those with a more general interest in international relations.

The original study from which this book grew was undertaken under the expert guidance of Professor Oliver Lissitzyn, Ambassador Arthur Lall, and the late Professor Wolfgang

Friedmann. I am most grateful to these great scholars for developing and sustaining my interest in international law and organization, for their encouragement and inspiration . . I have also received a great deal of help along the way, for which I would like to show my gratitude; to my colleagues Irving Markovitz, Harry Psomiades, and Benjamin Rivlin, who commented on various parts of the manuscript: to the City University of New York, without whose research grant the study could not have been done, and to the African Studies and Research Institute of Queens College, and the Ralph Bunche Institute on the United Nations who gave valuable research assistance. Also my gratitude goes to Thelma Collier who showed great skill and patience in deciphering my writing, to my editor, Robert Nicholas to my daughters Ayeki and Ofuakuor who helped with the indexing, and to wife Virginie, for her quiet, steady support.

Part One

SELF-DETERMINATION IN INTERNATIONAL RELATIONS LITERATURE

CHAPTER I

INTRODUCTION:

THE PROBLEM OF DEFINITION

The Significance of the Principle of Self-Determination in International Relations

There is probably no expression that is used as frequently and as passionately in contemporary international relations as "self-determination." For the past two decades, it has been the battle cry of colonial peoples everywhere in their struggle to extricate themselves from European imperial domination and to "emerge" into full political sovereignty and participation in international affairs. But this has not been the only process in which the right of self-determination has been invoked. Even now, there are groups all over the world, and in such divergent circumstances as Bangla-Desh, Northern Ireland, Quebec, and southern Sudan, who are involved in serious conflicts that are linked with the principle of self-determination, in both the popular mind and in professional diplomatic circles. Many of these conflicts have led to a widespread breakdown of public order and bloody confrontations that have come dangerously close to civil war. In one such case, in Nigeria, the conflict actually precipitated a civil war that was probably the most poignant tragedy of our time.[1]

The frequency and passionate commitment with which the expression is used indicates the increasing importance of the principle of self-determination in contemporary international relations. This is clearly acknowledged in the U.N. General Assembly, undoubtedly the greatest concentration of diplomatic activity in today's world, where, as recent debates show, issues

1

involving the principle are recognized as having the utmost urgency for the peace and security of the world, in that they have progressively received more agenda time than any other issue.[2]

Any principle of such importance probably deserves serious attention. In this case, however, the argument in favor of paying serious attention to this principle is even more compelling. For even now, over and above its general importance, this principle lies at the very heart of the two most serious international conflicts in the world today. For years, there has been a state of war and intermittent fighting in the Middle East, in which each side argues that it is engaged in the defense of its right of self-determination.[3] And in Vietnam, the United States has just gone through the process of painfully disengaging itself from its largest military involvement since World War II in a war in which both sides are claiming the right of self-determination.[4] These conflicts are the only wars of any magnitude), but more important, they are the only wars of any magnitude), but more important, they represent the gravest potential danger to the peace and security of the entire world.

The Controversy about Self-Determination

If self-determination is one of the most important concepts in contemporary international politics, it also has the rather dubious distinction of being one of the most controversial. Over the years, the right of self-determination has been claimed by diverse groups, in a variety of situations, and for the sake of realizing such apparently contradictory and incompatible aims that it has seemed as if the principle could not possibly be defined.[5] Nowhere is this problem more in evidence as it is in the United Nations, where the concentration and telescoping of diplomatic activity has led to such rapid-fire advancement of contradictory claims and counterclaims that observers have often been left quite bewildered. At least one of these commentators has suggested, in his frustration, that the expression "self-determination" should be completely discarded.[6]

Actually, this call for the total elimination of the expression is far from new. In fact, it is almost the exact echo of the attitude shown by most publicists when President Woodrow Wilson proposed it as the basis for world order and European territorial settlement at the end of World War I. This attitude is eloquently expressed in the following statement by Robert Lansing, who, significantly enough, was President Wilson's Secretary of State:

> Self-determination should be forgotten. It has no place in the practical scheme of world affairs. It has already caused enough despair, enough suffering and enough anarchy.[7]

In spite of this drastic admonition, the term "self-determination"'was not forgotten.[8] On the contrary, having been introduced into the realm of international affairs, it stuck there with remarkable tenacity.[9] Furthermore, it shows every sign of staying there for some time. Two decades after Lansing's warning, the principle of self-determination was still as potent as ever, and it showed every inclination of continued existence. In a 1943 study, Erich Hula surveyed some of the underlying reasons why various groups had made claims based on the principle of self-determination and offered the following comment on the continued relevance of the principle:

> Nor can we safely be sure that we shall not witness in some not too distant future a revival of ethnical groups also in Western Europe with the disruptive consequences we know from the history of that process in Central and Eastern Europe. Moreover, the ideas of nationality and national independence are no longer confined to Europe. They differ in actual strength from continent to continent, and from race to race, but like European nationalism they have become effective all over the world, both as unifying and as disintegrating forces. . . . Thus the principle of national self-determination is still one of the most potent political ideas of our time.[10]

This prophecy was vindicated with startling speed after World War II. Not only was the principle enshrined in the United Nations Charter, the most far-reaching international instrument of our time, but also, groups freshly awakened to national consciousness in the European colonial empires began to make vociferous demands for independence, propelling the United Nations to feverish activity in promoting decolonization based on the principle of self-determination.

Apart from liberation struggles in the few remaining European enclaves, the era of decolonization is almost over. But it would be idle to think that because the principle of self-determination has been linked mainly with decolonization that

3

it will fall into disuse and atrophy at the conclusion of this process. For one, the fact that the term was mainly associated with European national minorities in the period before World War II did not prevent its recurrence in its present mode. Therefore, there is no reason to think that after the era of decolonization the principle will not emerge in yet another variant. In this regard, the internal structure of the newly independent African and Asian states suggests that such a prediction is far from idle. Almost all of these new states are "plural societies" with serious ethnic or cultural cleavages[11] in which attempted secessions by minority groups have not only occurred with disturbing frequency,[12] but show every promise of becoming increasingly serious.[13] The situation in other parts of the world is not much different. A list of recent upheavals involving minority groups or separatist movements cuts across all geographic and ideological boundaries.[14] The self-determination movements of the Montagnards[15] of South Vietnam, the Taiwanese, the Buganda revolt of 1966, and the Somalia irredentist movement have their counterparts in the self-determination movements in Quebec, the revolt of the Catholic minority in Northern Ireland, the Flanders for the Flemish movement in Belgium,[16] the Croatian liberation movement in Yugoslavia,[17] and the violent French secessionist movement in Berne.[18] Even the Soviet Union, self-proclaimed champion of the right of self-determination, has not been able to escape the nationalist sentiment and separatist activity. Communist party officials have observed with some dismay that vestiges of nationalism ". . . are still tenacious among a certain segment of politically immature people . . . always ready to break out to the surface. . . ."[19] What these findings indicate is that worldwide separatist and nationalist movements are on the ascendancy, and the concept of self-determination will prove to be a permanent fixture in international politics.[20] Admittedly, almost all these conflicts are taking place within the various states, and, therefore, demands that these groups may make on the basis of the right of self-determination are dormant on the international level. Nevertheless, as we shall see,[21] it is possible for political events and conditions to catapult these demands onto the international stage, where they become problems not only for the individual states but for international society as a whole. Even now, West Germany is keeping alive her claim that the German nation be unified within her pre-1937 borders on the basis of her right of self-determination.[22] It is interesting to estimate the amount of national energy that Germany would put into this claim under favorable international political conditions.

What the above discussion indicates is that as long as groups feel that they are suffering under alien and oppressive rule there will be those among them who will want to liberate themselves and gain independence on the basis of what they believe to be their right to control their own destiny. It has happened in the past. It is happening now. And there is every indication that it will continue to happen in the future. Furthermore, the disapproval of writers and publicists has not been able to stop the attempts of oppressed peoples to gain their freedom[23] and it is quite unlikely that they will be able to do so in the future.[24] Therefore, the suggestion that the principle of self-determination be ignored or discarded is probably an unwise escape into fantasy.

The Urgency of the Need for a Definition

To advocate that the principle of self-determination be discarded is not only unwise, it is quite tragic. For it totally ignores the fact that some such conflicts have had the most tragic effects on the world. Arnold J. Toynbee puts this point very succinctly:

> However barren the controversy over the rights and wrongs of self-determination may be, it is certainly inexpedient to ignore its existence, for this controversy is one of those great permanent forces that have to be reckoned with in human affairs; in our historical retrospect we have already taken the measure of the havoc which it has caused; and it is evident that the recurrent outbreaks of the struggle have been as violent as they have been, just because the problem has usually either been left out of account of dismissed as insoluble.[25]

Up until quite recently, the only way by which a group could change its political status by secession or a declaration of independence was by revolution. The success of any secession attempts did not depend upon their advancement of claims based on the principle of self-determination, because no such right was recognized, but ultimately upon the success of their revolution. On the other hand, states are not ordinarily disposed to stand idly by and watch secessionist movements directed toward their dismemberment. As a rule, national representatives have attempted to forestall secessionist movements by such programs as enforced assimilation. But once such a separatist movement actually got under way, the solution invariably has been to crush it ruthlessly. As a result, in the overwhelming number of instances, attempted secessions have been accompanied by armed conflict and sometimes full-scale wars.[26]

In general, such conflicts were fought out and resolved within the confines of the state, usually at the expense of the secessionist movement. In the past, the legal norms of international society, based as they are on the concept of state sovereignty, have considered such matters to be exclusively within the jurisdiction of the state concerned. Given this situation, any states faced with such problems had been able to employ the full force of their coercive instruments against separatists or secessionists without fear of outside interference. Therefore, in general, the states were able to confine such conflicts within their borders. Until quite recently, whatever concern has been shown on the international level in internal wars of this nature has been based on humanitarian considerations. The absolute right of a state to treat insurgents in any way it desired was not questioned, for international law did not recognize the right of a people to revolt against established authority. Most important, there was no appreciation whatsoever that such conflicts had any implications for international peace and security.

This situation changed dramatically during World War I, when, as a result of the role played by the nationalist agitation in eastern Europe in precipitating the catastrophic war, it became increasingly recognized that controversies involving the principle of self-determination had very ominous implications not only for the states in which they might occur but for the peace and security of the entire world.[27] So strong was this recognition that, as the members of the international community began to accept some measure of responsibility for international peace after World War I and began to develop various structures and instruments designed to maintain the peace, they inevitably turned their collective attention on controversies involving claims based on the principle of self-determination as one of those issues that was particularly important for the preservation of international peace and security.

6

Since that time, the members of the international community have recognized the necessity to evolve rules and criteria for judging the validity of such claims and for resolving such controversies without permitting force to be the final arbiter.[28] Thus, the entire history of the development of international organization in the present century, specifically, the history of the European territorial settlement, the League of Nations' handling of the Aaland Islands dispute,[29] the work of the League Minorities Commission, and the Permanent Mandates Commission, and the huge mass of U.N. activities in the field of decolonization have all been parts of this process of the evolution of rules, principles, procedures, and techniques of dealing with this matter that has such serious import for the security of the world.

With the increasing frequency of conflicts involving the principle of self-determination, the necessity to establish generally accepted rules and criteria for the solution has become more urgent. It is in connection with this growing need for clarification of the principle that the present confusion surrounding the term deserves the serious attention of students of international relations. For while it is true that a clear definition of principles in itself does not always solve serious conflicts, it may be safely asserted that the persistence of a confusion of terms considerably lowers the expectation of unambiguous application of principles, and, therefore, tends to inhibit the inclincation of the parties to submit to peaceful settlement.[30] The present imperative, therefore, is not the elimination of the term "self-determination" but rather the attempt to develop a definition of the principle with as much clarity and precision as the exigencies of contemporary international political life will permit.

The Sources of Confusion

There are a variety of reasons that account for the confusion surrounding the concept of self-determination. For instance, there is the general problem of applying abstract principles to specific situations.[31] Then, there is the fact that it is the sort of term that easily lends itself to colloquial usage.[32] Furthermore, the connotative connection between the term "self-determination" and such ideas as "liberation" and "emancipation"[33] has given the principle a certain emotional appeal that makes it virtually impossible to oppose.[34] So that those opposed to some particular proposed application of the principle are forced into equivocations that further exacerbate the problem of defining it.

The most important reason for the present confusion surrounding the concept, however, may be attributed to the way in which writers and publicists have approached it. Since the turn of the century, there has been a dialogue on the international level concerning *inter alia* the question of defining the concept of self-determination.[35] Unfortunately, this effort has been largely unproductive, due mainly to the fact that most of the approaches have been afflicted by a variety of conceptual and methodological flaws. For instance, some publicists have attempted to dismiss the entire problem by simply asserting that the principle of self-determination is so vague that it has to be devoid of any legal effect.[36] This statement is based on a doctrinal error that is pointed out by Judge Lauterpacht in the following comment:

> ... although it may be admitted that the effective implementation of a rule is somewhat reduced by the lack of precision, there is no logical reason to say that the rule, therefore, does not exist, for, the existence of a rule of law, strictly speaking, is independent of the exactness of its definition.[37]

Indeed, there are several principles of international law, with acknowledged legal validity, such as the principle of nonintervention, the principle of diplomatic and consular immunity, and the right of self-defense, the exact definition of which are, on occasion, as controversial and confused as the definition of the principle of self-determination. Commenting on one of these principles, Professor Schwarzenberger noted that:

> ... the principle of diplomatic immunity emerged as a rule of customary international law by which State jurisdiction over sovereigns and envoys was excluded. Even so, on the level of international customary law, the exact scope of the rules governing State and diplomatic immunity and the legal principle into which they were abstracted remained, and remains controversial.[38]

Another contention that flies in the face of contemporary doctrine and practice of international law is the assertion that the principle of self-determination does not exist in law and has no legal effect, because it is not recognized as such by text writers.[39] This proposition is based on a general thesis that a principle or rule of international law cannot be deemed to exist unless it can be found in international legal textbooks. As one exponent of this view asserts, ". . . the literature of self-determination . . . would seem to be a necessary starting point . . . for finding the meaning of 'peoples' or 'nations.'"[40] The overwhelming weight of contemporary practice and doctrine support the contrary view: rules of international law are created not by textbook writers but by the states that are the subjects of international law.[41]

Many writers committed the methodological error of basing their analyses on the assumption that the nature of such entities as "peoples" or "nations" could be determined by deduction from a set of objective characteristics.[42] In view of the evidence of research, this view cannot be sustained.[43] But even if this assumption is correct, to deduce a legally valid definition from such characteristics would be to confess to being naive of the fact that in the theory and practice of international law the status of groups and entities is not decided by objective characteristics but by the general acceptance of their status by the states in their international practice. As Quincy Wright succinctly put it, ". . . the status of entities subject to international law is determined by general recognition."[44]

It is true, of course, that the objectivation of the will of the states in a matter of recognition may be difficult at a particular time; however, not even this difficulty may be used as an excuse to resort to such deductions. As Professor Schwarzenberger has so convincingly argued:

> If this were permissible, it would mean that whenever, owing to the lamentable state of research into State practice in international law, writers cared to allege that there was no clear line of state practice, they were free to resort to the lofty realm of general principles of law. In this case, contemporary doctrines of international law would become as eclectic and arbitrary—and as easily liable to abuse—as any straightforward naturalist and deductive treatment of the subject.[45]

Another erroneous line of approach to the problem of defining the principle of self-determination is exemplified in Dr. Kelsen's interpretation of Article 1, paragraph 2, of the U.N.

Charter. According to Dr. Kelsen, on the basis of the principles of sovereign equality of states and nonintervention in domestic affairs as expressed in Article 2, paragraph 1 and 7 respectively, it may be deduced that the expression "principle of equal rights and self-determination of peoples" in Article 1, paragraph 2, means the principle of sovereign equality of states.[46] Dr. Kelsen's reasoning raises some other questions that will be dealt with later.[47] At this point, it is sufficient to point out that this analysis commits the basic (and surprising) error of going against one of the basic canons of treat interpretation. Dr. Kelsen's analysis is the same one that is expressly rejected by the committee that drafted the article, as shown in the *travaux preparatoires*.[48]

A few of the writers have devoted some attention to the observation and examination of state practice. Unfortunately, however, even these writers have not been able to escape serious methodological errors. For instance, in their observation of state practice, most of their energies have gone into cataloguing the array of contradictory claims and counterclaims, vociferously condemning those claims they consider particularly irresponsible.[49]

The practice of making *de lege ferenda* formulations is, of course, recognized as a legitimate and useful function of international law.[50] It is generally agreed, however, that this function of legal planning should use the existing law, *lex lata,* as its point of departure, and that to the extent that it fails to do this, it tends to diminish its utility.[51]

The usefulness of unbridled condemnation of national claims is even more questionable. First, it represents a failure to recognize the fact that claims and counterclaims are the indispensable raw material for the development of customary international law,[52] and, therefore, they must adequately be examined for evidence of accepted law, whether or not they meet with the approval of the analyst.[53] Second, it tends to put too much inherent worth on the claims, thus, drawing attention away from the purpose of this type of international legal investigation, which is to place the focus of the analysis not on the claims that are advanced, *per se,* but on the acceptance of claims by the members of the international community. As Professor McDougal has noted:

10

> ...it is not, of course, the unilateral claims but rather the reciprocal tolerances ... which create the expectations of patterns and conformity in decision, of practice in accord with rule, commonly regarded as law.[54]

The glimpses of the analyses we have seen have provided some indication, in a preliminary way, that the real reason for the persistence of confusion surrounding the concept of self-determination has been the fact that the various attempts to analyze the concept have failed to clarify it and may even have added to the confusion because of their own inadequacies. The problems that we have seen, however, are only symptoms of the one basic flaw that all of these approaches share in some measure. *This basic flaw is that the writers have come to the analysis of the concept already equipped with definitions of self-determination derived from political theories or ideological principles.* In other words, the writings of these publicists invariable contain a definition of the principle of self-determination that is derived from a personal political principle. While some writers have consciously established these definitions, other writers are hardly aware that the definition they have adopted is only one of several doctrinal derivatives. Whether these theoretical definitions of the principle of self-determination are explicitly stated or inadvertently implicit in their works, their very presence has constituted the basic *problem of defining the principle of self-determination.* For they are in a sense the cause of all the other theoretical difficulties into which the various approaches have run.[55]

In general, the writers may be grouped into three categories, on the basis of the type of doctrine from which their particular definition of self-determination is derived. For want of a better name, and for the sake of brevity, we shall characterize these three groups as the advocates of the following interpretations of the concept of self-determination: *the national determinism theory, the plebiscite theory,* and *the national equality theory.* These theoretical formulations will be given some consideration in a later chapter. It is sufficient at this point to state in a general way what these formulations mean and to identify the leading publicists identified with each of them.

The *national determinism theory* may lay claim to being the first sense in which the term "self-determination," in its German form *selbsbestimmungrecht,"* was first used. Originating in mid-nineteenth-century German liberal nationalism, it meant in general that every nation should be constituted into a state, and every state should incorporate within it only people of the same nationality, a theory commonly expressed in the slogan "one nation: one state."[56] During the interwar period, it was mainly advocated by German and Austrian writers in support of the creation of a Greater Germany.[57] Since then, it has found very little doctrinal support, although it is probably the most popularly held notion of the concept of self-determination.

The *plebiscite theory* is the most popular doctrinal interpretation of the principle of self-determination among western European publicists. The advocates of this formulation of the principle of self-determination during the interwar period were Sarah Wambaugh, *Plebiscites Since the World War;* C. A. Macartney, *National States and National Minorities;* and Johannes Mattern, *The Employment of the Plebiscite in the Determination of Sovereignty.* For these writers, the principle of self-determination had its beginnings in the vindication of the concept of popular sovereignty in the Glorious Revolution, the French Revolution, and most emphatically in the American Revolution.[58] Thus, for them, self-determination simply meant the concept of government by popular consent.[59] In relation to international relations, it meant the application of the democratic principle to territorial cession, that is:

When a territory is transferred from one sovereignty of one state to that of another, the consent of the inhabitants of the territory thus affected is required to make the transfer valid.[60]

As a rule, they are committed to the use of the plebiscite in cases of cession of territory, because they are convinced that plebiscites provide the best way of applying the democratic principle.[61]

The avowed successors of the advocates of the plebiscite theory in the decolonization era have been Rosalyn Higgins, *The Development of International Law through the Political Organs of the United Nations;* and Harold S. Johnson, *Self-Determination within the Community of Nations.* Johnson's work is almost a conscious attempt to follow in the footsteps of Sarah Wambaugh. He acknowledges that:

> It is a major purpose of this study to examine the plebiscite activities of the international community in order to evaluate the usefulness of the plebiscite as an international means for self-determination.[62]

He notes further that "Miss Wambaugh accepted the plebiscite as a means for self-determination."[63] Something that he also claims to do.

Mohammed A. Shukri, *The Concept of Self-Determination at the United Nations,* undoubtedly wrote the most comprehensive and thorough work on the concept of self-determination in the charter and practice of the United Nations, and it is an indispensable source for research into the theoretical foundations as well as the international practice of self-determination in the decolonization era as a whole. To this extent, it is the decolonization era equivalent of Alfred Cobban's *National Self-Determination,* which also examined the VARIOUS CONNOTATIONS, CLAIMS, AND POLICIES THAT WERE BASED ON THE VARIOUS THEORIES OF SELF-DETERMINATION DURING THE INTERWAR ERA. Even Shukri's excellent effort is slightly marred by his unconscious adoption of the plebiscite theory. At the beginning of his study, he offers a tentative definitoin:

> In its over simplified connotation, self-determination means the right of a people to choose the form of government under which they wish to live or the sovereignty to which they wish to belong.[64]

He then continues by asserting that the task of his research would be to ascertain what that definition means more specifically.[65] Of course, the way in which the research task was framed predetermined the conclusions that could be drawn. It was this formulation of the principle of self-determination at the outset that led Shukri in the end to offer incomplete conclusions about the nature of the "recipient unit" of the right of self-determination and his characterization of self-determination as the process by which a group freely chooses its international status.[66]

The *national equality theory* was stated most systematically during the interwar period by the Bolsheviks. A typical statement is presented below:

> The right of self-determination means that a nation can arrange its life ac-

cording to its own will. It has the right to arrange its life on the basis of autonomy. It has the right to complete secession. Nations are sovereign and all nations are equal.[67]

One of the main ways in which this formulation differed from the others was that it was based on the concept of sovereign equality of nations. In so doing, it introduced a teleological aspect into the definition, asserting that the purpose of invoking the right was to achieve or to restore self-government, and, therefore, the validity of a claim of the right of self-determination could not be sustained unless the claimant groups were "oppressed" or "subject." This position was essentially the same that was advocated by many of the subject nationalities of Europe during and after World War I, such as the Congress of Oppressed Nationalities.[68]

In the decolonization era, the national equality principle was generally advocated by Soviet writers, such as S. B. Starushenko, *The Principle of National Self-Determination in Soviet Foreign Policy,* as well as many western writres, such as Clyde Eagleton, "The Excesses of Self-Determination;" Hans Kohn, "The United Nations and National Self-Determination;" Huntington Gilchrist, "Colonial Questions at the San Francisco Conference;" and Benjamin Rivlin, "Self-Determination and Dependent Areas." In spite of their general advocacy of this principle, some differences exist between these writers, such as, for instance, on the question as to whether, as the Soviet writers assert, dependent peoples may legitimately use force of arms to regain their independence on the basis of a plea of self-defense.[69]

Whatever the optical or ideological principle from which a writer's interpretation of the principle of self-determination was based, the definition was bound to lead to problems or at least inconsistencies in relation to other doctrinally derived definitions or actual international practice. Faced with this situation, some writers simply preferred not to pay any attention to state practice, staying in what was for them the more comfortable realm of logical deductions. As we have seen, these attempts to analyze the principle of self-determination without reference to state practice led some writers to commit such simple errors as disregarding *trauaux preparatoires,*[70] while interpreting articles of the U.N. Charter.

The efforts of those writers who felt compelled to deal with international practice have seldom gone beyond demonstrations of the discrepancies between their own doctrinal definitions and what seemed, from the standpoint of that definition, to be the confused and inconsistent way in which states were actually applying the principle. Surprisingly enough, the writers have not considered changing their definitions. On the contrary, some writers have attempted to establish a connection between their definition and international practice, with some strange results.[71] In other cases, writers have been content to declare that international practice was incorrect, or unwise, and simply wait for international practice to catch up with their definition.[72] The result of all this is that, while international practice concerning the principle of self-determination has grown at a fast pace, discussion of the principle by writers and publicists has not progressed since the interwar period, either in terms of the issues with which they seem to be concerned or in terms of methodological sophistication. Thus, there has developed a serious lag between international practice involving the principle of self-determination and the level of theorizing on it, which further exacerbates the confusion.

In the past few years, the insertion of the principle of self-determination in the U.N. Charter, the Human Rights Conventions, several multilateral treaties, and the practice of the United Nations itself has led a growing list of writers to the conclusion that the principle of self-determination can now be considered as having legal effect.[73] But not even these writers have been able to achieve a breakthrough in the clarification of what has become the right of self-determination.

Toward a Definition of Self-Determination:
Our Approach

The aim of this study on the right of self-determination is to attempt to bridge the gap, insofar as it can be done, between international practice and theoretical thinking. It is hoped that by analyzing the practice of self-determination in accordance with the procedures of ascertaining the scope and content of a rule of international law, rather than by reference to a doctrine, it might be possible to arrive at as clear a definition as acceptance by the states would permit. In order to do this, we shall attempt to gather together the elements of international practice pertaining to that principle and to examine the extent to which the practice, or some aspect of it, is accepted by states as legally binding, in accordance with the generally recognized rules of evidence outlined above.

As regards the element of practice, it has already been demonstrated above that the principle of self-determination has been not only the basis of recurrent claims and counterclaims in international relations since the beginning of the twentieth century but it continues to be one of the most frequently used expressions in contemporary international politics, and it plays an important role in some of the most serious controversies of our time.[74]

Any international practice of such long duration always, *ab definitio,* involves an implied core or nexus that represents the part of that practice that states accept as legally binding, for the process of forming rules of customary international law is part of the very flow of international relations.[75] This continuous process involves the extinguishing, changing, and redefinition of previous definitions of the scope and content of the rule in question. Thus, the nexus of consensus among the states as to the scope of the principle they are willing to accept as legally binding may be narrowed or broadened in accordance with the changing patterns of claims and acquiescence in international practice, thereby changing the definition of the scope and content of the principle. However, the fact of the existence of the principle itself is not denied by this procedure. The task of ascertaining a rule of customary international law, thus, amounts to a determination of the extent of the core of that particular practice that the states accept as legally binding, that is to say, a determination of the *scope* and *content* of the principle. This whole point has been eloquently made by Professor Schwarzenberger:

The significance of variations in the practice of States regarding the scope within which they recognize any particular principle cannot be determined in the abstract. It requires investigation in each particular case whether, and within what limits, . . . a general practice recognized as law can be established. If, on the periphery of a principle, evidence of such a general practice is lacking, the scope of the principle itself must be correspondingly reduced to the common denominator of the actual practice accepted as legally binding. To deny the existence of a principle in the face of a still verifiable common denominator would

16

mean to ignore that, within the narrower compass, the consensus required for a
rule of international customary law still happens to exist.[76]

It is thus possible to say that on the basis of over half a century
of international practice there is a strong presumption that
there exists in international .law a principle of self-determination, having an implicit and yet undefined (at least
not clearly) scope and content that states accept as legally binding.

In attempting to ascertain the range and content of the principle of self-determination, the procedure would be to apply to
this mass of international practice the procedures that contemporary doctrine indicates with regards to the requirements for
ascertaining rules of international law. What we are suggesting
is that international law, like other disciplines, has certain"
... criteria by which it distinguishes rules belonging to it."[77]
These criteria are the procedural rules without which evidence
of the scope and content of a principle of international law
would not be considered valid. What we have concluded about
the various approaches that we have considered is that they
were based on doctrinal definitions, causing their analyses of
the principle to contravene these rules of procedure. In order to
guard against this kind of error, it is important for us to state
explicitly those rules of procedure that are considered legitimate and proper, and that this study would attempt to adhere
to. The most authoritative statement of these procedures is Article 38, paragraph 1, of the Statute of the International Court
of Justice. It is according to the criteria established there that
our attempt to establish the scope and content of the principle
of self-determination must proceed. Out of the inexhaustible
list of works that have been produced on the "sources" of international law and Article 38 of the court's statute specifically,
there is overwhelming agreement that only international conventions and international custom are "sources" of international law, in the sense that they are actual processes by which
rules of international law are created[78] and as such, the texts of
international conventions and international custom are the
only real sources of evidence of rules of international law.[79]

The wording of subparagraph (b) of Article 38 of the Statute
of the Court, which deals with rules of customary international

law, has come under a great deal of fire from some of the most authoritative publicists of our time.[80] These writers agree, however, that in spite of its unfortunate wording the meaning of the text is in line with the authoritative and generally agreed upon doctrine that rules of customary international law include the two essential elements of (1) the general practice and (2) the conviction that the practice is required by law.[81]

Until recently, the consensus among writers as to the general nature of rules of customary international law did not extend to the essential qualities of the practice or of the *opinio juris* that would be required to prove the existence of such a rule. When this matter came under the consideration of the International Law Commission in 1950, the majority of the members of the commission rejected what was then considered to be the traditional formulation of the requirements that must be fulfilled for a customary rule of international law to exist.[82] In particular, they rejected as factually inadmissible and doctrinally unnecessary the requirement that the practice of an alleged rule be of long-standing and be consistent with pre-existing practice. On the contrary, they concluded that there should be no *a priori* way of determining what sort of practice may ripen into a rule of customary international law, nor any single way of determining the presumed acceptance of the practice as law. They asserted that this presumed acceptance, called "acceptance," *opinio juris sive necessitatis,"* "acquiescence," or "assent," could be determined any number of ways, including the "absence of protest against the practice."[83]

Not only the International Law Commission but an increasing number of publicists have since adopted the viewpoint that "the absence or protest will suffice as evidence of acceptance."[84] Furthermore, the jurisprudence of the International Court of Justice also supports this view.[85] So that it may now be said that there has developed a conception of the requirements for proving the scope of rules of customary international law recognized as generally acceptable in the judicial life of contemporary international society, as evidenced in the opinion of the International Law Commission, the jurisprudence of the International Court of Justice, and in the writings of many authoritative publicists; all of whom together are the most representative and authoritative opinion of contemporary doctrine in international law. According to this conception, a rule of customary international law exists when there is evidence to justify the presumption that the practice involved is generally accepted as law. Also, that such a presumption is ordinarily justified by the absence of protest against that practice, unless there is positive proof that the absence of protest was not meant to imply acquiescence.[86]

On the basis of the foregoing discussion, two premises are strongly suggested. The first premise is that the peace and security of the whole world urgently demand a clarification of the nature and scope of the principle of self-determination, the range of the rights and obligations it may give rise to; and the nature of the recipients of these rights and obligations. The second premise is that the wealth of diplomatic practice that has involved the principle of self-determination and, therefore, whatever mutual tolerances of claims that have been made on the basis of the principle have inevitably provided a consensual nexus among states as to the scope of the principle in international law, so that it is now possible, given the present level of the development of the science of international law, to eliminate some of the problems of defining the term "self-determination."

Of what follows, Chapters II and III will examine the doctrinal discussion of the principle of self-determination in the interwar period and the decolonization era respectively. It is hoped that this analysis will not only demonstrate the shortcomings of the doctrinal approach to the definition of the principle of self-determination but that it will also provide us with some important questions that may profitably be used as a focus for examining international practice. In Chapters IV and V, we shall examine the international practice of self-determination, with special emphasis on drawing some parallels in the application of the principle under those different conditions. We shall then conclude in Chapter VI by attempting to define the right of self-determination based on the totality of international practice, and the "... knowledge concerning international law" that that doctrine provides.[87]

CHAPTER II

THE HISTORICAL ANTECEDENTS OF THE CONTEMPORARY DISCUSSION

It was during World War I that the term "self-determination" made its dramatic and explosive entry into the lexicon of international politics.[1] As early as the 1840s, the word *"selbstbestimmung,"* from which the English term is derived, made its appearance in the writings of radical German philosophers.[2] And in 1896, it appeared as a *political concept* in the report of the Congress of the Second International,[3] thereafter becoming one of the most recurrent and hotly debated terms in the polemical pamphleteering of socialist and nationalist groups in eastern and central Europe.[4] Yet the use of the term was confined to those circles until it was thrust onto the international stage. From that time, a dialogue began on the principle of self-determination and its implications for international peace and order, which, with some modifications, still continues.

The Origins and Nature of the Debate

The initial character of this dialogue was shaped by two important factors: first, the process by which the question of self-determination was first raised on the international level, and second, the status in international law of the term as it was defined at its initial introduction. These factors, in combination, determined the initial definition of the terms of the debate and the issues on which most of the attention of the writers was to be focused.

President Woodrow Wilson is generally credited with the popularization of the expression.[5] Much of this credit is indeed his due, for it was he who proposed that the new world order should be constructed on the basis of that principle, thus lending a certain dramatic impact and putting a stamp of validity on it and the political demands that it represented.[6] It must be noted, however, that the emergence of the principle in international dialogue at that particular time was not due to Wilson's endorsement of it but to the fact that the political demands the principle articulated had suddenly become crucial issues in international politics.[7]

It was not accidental that there was a debate about the principle of self-determination among eastern European intellectuals in the latter part of the nineteenth century. Polemical debates are never conducted in *vacuo;* they invariably represent attempts by protagonists to underpin their concrete demands with theoretical or legal justifications. The entire debate was a product of demands by the subject nationalities for autonomy and independence, and it was out of these demands that the theoretical formulations of the principle of self-determination was developed.[8] The fact that these formulations began to emerge in east and central Europe at that particular time was because the principle became relevant to political realities. That was the area of great ethnic heterogeneity in which many nationalities were situated, and that was the time of great nationalist fervor in which some of these groups acquired enough national consciousness to demand independence.[9]

The debate about national self-determination was effectively "quarantined" within east and central Europe, because the struggle for national liberation in that area had not yet become relevant to international politics. At that time, the entire question of nationalities existed completely outside the scope of international regulation.[10] Therefore, the debate reflected attempts by the various nationalities to formulate demands and propose solutions that were limited in scope to the empires within which they themselves were located.[11] The demands of these nationalities for independence and autonomy could not have been and were not made on the international level. Therefore, at that time, the debates that these demands triggered were nonexistent on the international level.

The unleashing of the expression "self-determination" onto the stage of international politics resulted from the collapse of the four empires of east and central Europe under the joint impact of World War I, the Bolshevik Revolution, and the nationalist revolutions of the subject nationalities.[12] The fact that the principle emerged in the form of national self-determination was due to the nature of the groups that were then demanding the right. Because the war had been a general European war, the disposition of the territories belonging to the defeated empires became a general European international problem. This meant that at the end of the war demands for autonomy and independence, which had previously been seen and dealt with as internal problems of the various empires, were directed at the international community as a whole, *on the international diplomatic level*. Thus, the circumstance leading to the collapse of the empires of east and central Europe made the demands of the subject nationalities an international problem and therefore caused the internationalization of both the dialogue concerning those demands and the principle of national self-determination on which they was based. In other words, the dialogue about the meaning of the term "national self-determination" that had been carried on within the confines of central and eastern Europe became an international debate, because the demands that the principle stood for now had to be dealt with *on the international level*.

As suggested above, the process of internationalizing the dialogue on self-determination had an important effect on the initial definition of the terms of the debate. During and after the war certain politically organized groups, generally identified as "nationalities," had already taken steps to form governments, claiming that their independence be recognized by the powers on the basis of the right of national self-determination.[13] As claimants, they formulated their demands on the basis of *their* definition of the principle. Thus, the initial definition of the terms of the debate was the one provided by the subject nationalities themselves. In fact, the definition was a logical outcome of their demands. Because only nationalities were demanding independence on the basis of the right of self-determination, the principle was advanced in the form of "national self-determination" and defined as the right of every nationality to independent statehood.[14]

Thus defined, the right of national self-determination had no status in international law.[15] In fact, the discussion marked the first attempt by the international community to systematically regulate on the international level a matter that had previously been within the exclusive competence of the state. Therefore, the discussion that emerged had little relevance to the determination of the scope or content of the right of national self-determination as *lex lata*. On the contrary, the discussion took the form of *de lege ferenda* formulations in which the main focus was centered on whether or not the application of the principle would be supportive or detrimental to international peace and security.[16]

From the standpoint of the concern for world order, the introduction of the term in the form of *national* self-determination, defined as the right of a nationality to form a separate and independent state, posed two questions. The first question was whether or not self-determination implied the right to secession. Actually, this question presented no conceptual problems. Because most writers accepted the initial definition of the right self-determination as the right to form a separate state, they logically concluded that it would also mean the right to secede from the existing states of which they formed a part. In fact, the great antogonism of many writers for the principle was based on their acceptance of the conception that the right of self-determination meant the right of secession, which would in turn lead to Balkanization and international chaos and unrest.[17]

The second question concerned the meaning of the word "nationality." For if the principle of self-determination was to be applied at all, it was of the utmost importance to international peace and order to determine which units were to enjoy the right. As shown above, the units to whom the principle of self-determination was supposed to be applied were the nationalities. Therefore, the next question to be answered was, exactly what is a nationality? That is, what criteria should be used in attempting to determine the legitimacy or validity of a claim to be a nationality? What are the essential characteristics of a nationality? It is, of course, true that all the subject nationalities had one common characteristic—self-determination on a basis of ethnicity. However, it is equally true that beyond this common quality, they were vastly dissimilar from the point of view of size, level of national and political consciousness, and territorial concentration.[18] Therefore, unless every group with common cultural characteristics was the subject of the right, it was going to be necessary to differentiate between those nationalities that could legitimately claim the right and those that could not.[19] Establishing a minimum size that could qualify for separate national existence was particularly important, otherwise it was possible for individual households to argue that they had the right to independence.[20] To most writers, therefore, the meaning of nationality seemed to provide some analytical problems, and thus it was the question to which they chose to give their attention, in the belief that the solution of the whole problem of defining self-determination lay with the explicit formulation of the meaning of that word.[21]

In accordance with general expectation, all attempts at formulating the term "nationality" were faced with formidable logical and practical problems. So that in all of the immense literature that was produced on the subject in the aftermath of World War I, there never emerged a generally agreed upon definition of the term "nationality" as it was used in reference to the right of national self-determination.[22]

Competing Definitions of Nationality

Reviews of the origins of some of the theories of self-determination, as well as theoretical analyses of the available formulations, have been impressively accomplished elsewhere,[23] and they do not need to be added to here. Furthermore, such an excursion into the realm of the history of ideas is outside the scope of this work. As we have already stated, one of the major contentions of this study is that the definition of a principle as it has been understood in long and established international usage is based not in its theoretical foundations but on the meaning that the states choose to give it. Therefore, what we shall attempt is not a complete survey of all the theoretical formulations of the principle but a presentation and examination of those major theories that were actively advocated in European international political practice during the interwar period. We shall critically examine some of the problems encountered by these formulations, especially with reference to their practical application. By identifying those definitions of self-determination that were actually being used by states in their diplomatic activity, we will be able to determine which of these formulations were, or nearly were, accepted as the actual definition of self-determination, after the distillation and systematization of the relevant international practice.[24]

The question then to be answered was, what is a nationality? Logically, the first response to receive attention on the practical level was that of the groups who were saying that "we are a nation: therefore, we have a right to national self-dedermination." According to this concept, a nationality is a group of people characterized by common language, ancestry, or culture.[25] One of the earliest formulations of this concept of nationality, which developed out of the nationalism of the German radical philosopher Gottfried Herder,[26] is to be found in Fichte's famous statement, "Whenever a separate language is found, there is also a separate nation which has the right to maintain its affaris independently and rule itself."[27] The use of language as the determining criterion of nationality, proposed here by Fichte, was subsequently widened to include such characteristics as common historical tradition, common culture, common racial characteristics, and sometimes common religion.[28] One particular variation of this concept of nationality is of special interest because of the role it played in the polemical debates among the Social-Democratic parties in east and central Europe prior to World War I. This concept, which is attributed to the Austrian Social-Democrats, suggested that "A nation is the aggregate of people bound into a community of character by a common fate.[29] Yet among the adherents of this concept, language was always considered preeminent among all the criteria of nationality, and by the end of the nineteenth century, most of the nationalities of east and central Europe were using this criterion to distinguish themselves.[30]

Another view of nationality that was given serious consideration in practice was advocated by such groups as the Congress of Oppressed Nationalities and the Bolsheviks, an explicit statement of which is to be found in Josef Stalin's important work, *Marxism and the National and Colonial Question,* first published in 1913 as a Bolshevik position paper on the national question.

> A nation is a historically evolved stable community of language and territory, economic life and psychological make-up manifested in a community of culture.[31]

It may seem, at first glance, that the Bolshevik definition of nationality is just another variation of the ethnographic definition. On closer inspection, however, it becomes clear that there exists a difference of some importance between the two types of definitions.[32] According to Stalin, for an entity to constitute a nationality, it *must* have "a combination of all these characteristics taken together." (1) Community of language; (2) community of territory; (3) community of economic life; and (4) community of psychological makeup.[33] But he goes much further than that, to state explictly that ethnic affinity is irrelevant to his definition of nationality. In fact, he strongly denounces Otto Bauer, who defines nationality as a "community of character," for "confusing *nation,* which is a historical category, with *tribe,* which is an ethnographical category."[34] For Stalin, the important points to be made about nationality in contradiction to other definitions were that (1) a nation was a historically evolved community and was therefore "subject to the laws of change"[35] and (2) that it existed quite regardless of ethnic affinity.[36] But most important of all, it was important to understand that a nation was a territorial entity. Again, Stalin comments:

Bauer's point of view, which identifies a nation with its national character, divorces the nation from its soil and converts it into an invisible, self-contained force. The result is not a living and active nation, but something mystical, intangible and supernatural.[37]

For the Bolsheviks, the definition of nationality, as used in reference to self-determination, applied not only to the oppressed nationalities of east and central Europe, but also to overseas colonies. In his essay on national self-determination, Lenin outlined what he thought should be the Socialist program of self-determination in relation to three different types of countries; the advanced capitalist countries of western Europe, the countries of eastern Europe, and the colonies.[38] In his analysis, he stated that in

the semi-colonial countries, like China, Persia, Turkey, and all colonies which have a combined population amounting to 1,000 million . . . Socialists must not only demand the unconditional and immediate liberation of the colonies without compensation—and this demand in its political expression signifies nothing else but the recognition of the right of self-determination—but they must render determined support to the more revolutionary elements in the bourgeois-democratic movements for *national* liberation in these countries and assist their uprising—and if need be their revolutionary war—against the imperialist powers that oppress them.[39]

Lenin's statement that "in these countries the bourgeois-democratic movements have either hardly begun, or are far from having been completed"[40] seems to suggest that, for him, these colonies were not yet full-fledged nations, but were on the way to being full nations.

However, this did not seem to Lenin and the Bolsheviks to be enough reason not to put the oppressed nationalities and the colonies in the same category as recipients of the right of national self-determination.[41]

The theory of nationality that follows is relevant, not because it was advanced by those claiming the right of national self-determination but because being the dominant theory in the political thinking of the victorious states and the major architects of the peace settlement, it could be an important influence on the definition of nationality that the international community was willing to adopt at that time. In western Europe, the idea of national sovereignty had developed as a formulation of the locus of sovereignty in a given political community,[42] therefore, the definition of nation that emerged was eminently political, as is shown in the following statement by the famous Abbe Sieyes. "What is a nation? A body of associates living under one common law and represented by the same legislature."[43] Out of this concept of popular sovereignty developed what has been described as the theory of "political nationality" in which there is a virtual equation of the nation with the state,[44] as the following statement indicates: "The people are the state and the nation; the people are soverign."[45] Therefore, when the Peace Conference was sitting, the western Europeans were generally defining nationality as a group of people with a common allegiance to the same state.[46]

Competing Theories of Self-Determination

Different theories of nationality imply different theories of national self-determination, and, therefore, it was not long before the focus of the debate changed to an examination of the meaning of self-determination. At the outset, the definition of national self-determination based on the ethnic theory of nationality had been accepted by even those who disapproved of its application, because it would be inconsistent with international order. However, as the focus of the doctrinal debate

28

changed from an examination of nationality to the meaning of self-determination, this theory of national self-determination came under fire as being incorrect. Thus developed in the early twenties some writing with theoretical statements and rebuttals about the proper definition of the term "self-determination." Out of this dialogue emerged three general theories of self-determination that were actively advocated by political groups on the international scene, so they can be said to have received some attention on the level of international practice. These theories were based, as we have tried to show above, on the three types of definitions of nationality, namely, the territorial, ethnological, and political. For convenience, we shall refer to these theories of self-determination as the *national equality theory,* the *national determinism theory* and the *plebiscite theory*.

The first of these theories of self-determination to be tested in practice was the national equality principle which was advocated by some of the minority nationalities of east and central Europe, and the Bolsheviks. This theory became the basis of the official nationality policy of the Russian state after the Bolsheviks seized power in the October Revolution, and it became internationally important as the operating principle of the Treaty of Brest-Litovsk in March 1918. It also became the basis of the demands of such groups as the Yugoslav Committee.[47] An authoritative statement of this definition, as presented by Josef Stalin, is as follows:

> The right of self-determination means that a nation can arrange its life according to its own will. It has the right to arrange its life on the basis of autonomy. It has the right to enter into federal relations with other nations. It has the right to complete secession. Nations are sovereign and all nations are equal.[48]

From this and other statements, it is clear that for the Bolsheviks the key to the definition of self-determination was the idea of achieving the sovereign equality of all nationalities.[49] According to their view, the exercise of the right of national self-determination meant the establishment of full control over itself and, therefore, the equal status with other nationalities. In their view, this could result in one of three ways: (1) by the achievement of a position of regional autonomy within a state; (2) the establishment of a federal union with other nationalities (in which all the member nationalities would be equal); or (3) the establishment of an independent state.[50]

The Bolsheviks also introduced a restriction on the type of nationalities that could exercise the right of self-determination to territorial communities that were *oppressed,* in the sense that they were collectively under the imperial control of another nation.[51] These communities, according to Bolshevik doctrine, could be of essentially two types: (1) the variety generally called *"subject nationality"* or *"oppressed nationality,"* common in eastern Europe; and (2) those overseas territories called *colonies.* According to the Bolsheviks, therefore, a full statement of the right of national self-determination is that all nonsovereign communities with a common territory, language, economy, and psychology have the right to sovereign equality with other nationalities, either by territorial autonomy within a state, by federation, or by complete independence. In their view, these qualifications were met by the subject nationalities of Europe as well as the colonies over which the European countries ruled.[52] The actual timing of the demand for the exercise of the right (whether by autonomy or by secession) was exclusively the decision of the nationality.[53]

Two types of theories of national self-determination emerged out of the ethnological definition of nationality. One of these was known as *national-cultural autonomy.* This rather interesting theory, which was developed by the Austrian Social-Democrats, received no attention on the level of international practice due to the circumstances of history, and, therefore, it is outside the scope of our discussion.[54] The theory of self-determination that we have called the *national determinism theory* was seriously advanced by the German government and was actually one of the basic drives of German foreign policy throughout the interwar period. As such, it had to be dealt with by the international community, and, therefore, it was the definition that was exposed to the possibility of the acquiescence, acceptance, or rejection by the international community.

As we have already seen, this theory, based on Fichte's formulation, defined national self-determination as the right of each nationality to constitute an independent state. Stated as such, this theory implies that each ethnic group has the right to secede from the state of which it is a part and form a separate state. But the principle goes much further than that; it postulates the principle of "one nation: one state"[55] which meant not only that each nation should form a state but also that each state should be ethnically homogeneous.

For the advocates of the theory of self-determination that we have called the *plebiscite theory*, the notion of "one nation: one state" was merely a tautology. For them, the nation *was* the state. Therefore, the idea of self-determination could not be anything more than the continuing political consent of the inhabitants to be members of the state. As C. A. Macartney put it: "Thus, national self-determination comes to mean simply self-government, the realiztion of the political ideal of freedom."[56] Accordingly, they defined national self-determination as the application of the principle of democracy to matters of transfer of territory. The principle of popular sovereignty holds that within the nation, which is also the state, the people are sovereign, and, therefore, they have the right to decide collectively all matters affecting the state and the nation. Applied to changes in territorial sovereignty, this principle means that no transfer of any territory is valid unless it is undertaken with the concurrence of the people who form the nation.[57] This principle had been honored in the past, notably during the French Revolution. And it is this practice, as it occurred in the past, that this group of writers retroactively defined as manifestations of the principle of national self-determination.[58]

As the above discussion has indicated, there were three main types of theories of national self-determination that were vying for recognition as the proper interpretation of the principle that should be applied in the territorial settlement in Europe at the end of World War I. Of course, whichever formulation of the principle would be accepted by the states in international practice was a matter to be decided by the states either by express agreement or in the development of international custom. But before this verdict was forthcoming, that is, before international practice could be clarified, the international debate on which was the "correct" definition continued. This doctrinal debate was essentially irrelevant to the practice of the states with regards to the principle of self-determination. However, it is important to give some attention to the debate. First, the debate reveals some of the internal inconsistencies of all attempts at theoretical formulation of the principle. More important, it illustrates the inherent fallacy of attempting to define the prin-

31

ciple of self-determination by deducing it from a political doctrine instead of defining it on the basis of international practice.

Analysis of the Discussion

Of the three theories of national self-determination under discussion the national determinism principle was the first to draw the attention of doctrinal opposition. The reason for this is not entirely clear, but it seems to have been due to the western European publicists' mistaken notion that the demands that the organizations of oppressed nationalities were making toward the end of the war were for the international recognition of the national determinist principle of "one nation: one state." At this time, most of the publicity was centered on some of the larger national groups that were requesting international recognition on the basis of their right to secede. This demand was interpreted as national determinism. Actually, their demand was based on the principle of national equality. Furthermore, a great many of the smaller groups were formulating their demands for self-determination in terms of cultural autonomy.

To the adherents of the *plebiscite theory*, the idea of *national determinism* was unacceptable as a definition of self-determination.

> To claim, there,fore, that every nation must form an independent state is to substitute for true self-determination a very different thing, which could rather be called national determinism.[59]

One of the reasons why the advocates of the *plebiscite theory* found national determinism objectionable was on the grounds of its impracticability. According to them, the application of the principle of "one nation: one state" was based on the totally erroneous assumption that there existed clear-cut boundaries between ethnic groups that could be transformed into political boundaries.[60]

It is important to note, however, that the main objection to the *theory of national determinism* was not based on its impracticability or unacceptability to states; *their main objection to the principle was that it was incorrect.* And it was incorrect, because it was contradictory to what they understood to be the only proper philosophical foundation of the principle of self determination, which, for them, was based on the idea of popular sovereignty. As such, it was of necessity a principle of democracy as it is applied to the settlement of territorial problems.[61] In the exercise of this principle, each individual uses his democratic right of indicating his personal wish concerning the cession of the territory on which he lives, through the plebiscite. Thus, self-determination is the democratic right of the individual to determine where he shall live by casting a vote. The consequence of his individual act of voting results in either making him a part of the majority or leaving him with a choice of passively accepting the delineation of the territorial boundary on the basis of the ruling of the majority or of exercising his *right of option*, a right that is recognized under international law.[62]

On this basis, they argued that the *theory of national determinism* cannot be accepted as a correct definition of the concept, because it is undemocratic. As they saw it, under that principle, the recipient of the right of self-determination was not the individual, as it should properly be, but a collectivity know as the nationality. By so doing, the principle assigns legitimate control over a person's action to his nationality and to that alone, thus anticipating his free decision as to the sovereignty under which he wants to live. Thus, the principle, at the very least, assumes something that ought to be proven, that a person's attachment to his ethnic group is by nature stronger than any other loyalties, a proposition that has been found to be untrue in many cases.[63] Thus, on the basis of the contention that the collective will of a people rather than their common nationality has primary importance in the formation and maintenance of the national state,[64] they agrued that unlike the so-called democratic self-determination, the principle of national self-determination based on personal nationality condemns people, contrary to their own desire, to live in states merely on the basis of their ethnicity.[65]

On behalf of the advocates of the nationality theory, it could of course, be argued that because common political allegiance had been more important than common nationality as a factor in the formation and maintenance of nation-states, it did not mean that common nationality could not also be the basis for nation-states. The Bolsheviks, in particular, with their conviction that nationalism was a historical force of temporary importance,[66] were quick to point out that the significance of the nationality question in eastern Europe at that time was due precisely to the fact that there were nationalities in that area who desired to use their common nationality as the basis for the formation of states.[67]

The seriousness of the second objection to the nationality principle depends on the type being advocated. For those who favored the theory of national equality, like the Congress of Oppressed Nationalities or the Bolsheviks, the prospect of intermingling ethnic groups presented no particular problems. As we have seen, at no time did they advocate a "one nation: one state" principle based on an ethnic definition of nationality. In fact, Lenin and Stalin both stated explicitly that what they were interested in was not the encouragement of secession but the acievement of national equality within a multinational state, and the Congress of Oppressed Nationalities always anticipated an association of many ethnic groups within the states for which they demanded independence. And as we have already seen of the nationality as defined by them, all that was required was a common territory, psychology, economy, or language.[68] For the advocates of the principle based on an ethnic definition of nationality, there seemed to be no way out of this problem, except through the process of mapping out the political boundaries to coincide as much as possible with the ethnic composition and to supplement the process by the exchange of population.[69]

On the other hand, the theory of national self-determination advocated by western Europeans was not devoid of its share of conceptual problems. As we have seen, this theory was essentially an extension of the theory of "no annexation without consultation," which had been discussed in international law literature in the latter part of the nineteenth century as the plebiscite principle.[70] The use of the plebiscite in matters of change of sovereignty raises several problems, such as the control of voting eligibility, establishment of residency requirements, and the drawing of postplebiscite boundaries.[71] While admitting the existence of these problems, the advocates of the *plebiscite theory* point out that these problems merely raise important questions in the execution of the plebiscites, so as to ensure that the results would be accurate reflections of the actual

34

choices of residents of those areas who will continue to live there. In their view, however, these problems do not negate the validity of the principle of self-determination. As Sarah Wambaugh states:

> If we are to continue in our belief in self-determination for places of less economic or political consequence, the plebiscite, however faulty, is the only tool we have. Our problem is to perfect it.[72]

One of these practical problems in particular highlights the serious conceptual problem of developing criteria for the delimitation of the plebiscite area. One such problem that is likely to be raised, for instance, is whether all the inhabitants of an area that wishes to secede should register its choice as one unit or whether smaller units within that area should also be allowed to register their choice, on the basis of which they might secede from the original seceding unit. This problem is of fundamental importance to this theory, because it is based on an extension of the idea that the sovereign people should decide. But while it is conceptually simple to say with President Wilson, "Let the people decide," it becomes infinitely more complex when an attempt is made to establish who these people are. As Sir Ivor Jennings appropriately noted, "The people cannot decide until somebody decides who the people are."[73] For this problem, even the perfect plebiscite in itself provides no solution. For in all these cases where plebiscites had been used involving a cession of territory, the institution of the plebiscite had been brought into play after the plebiscite area had already been carved out by treaty of cession or by conquest. In the light of these facts, it must be concluded that although the institution of the plebiscite may be used effectively as a way of determining the wishes of a group of people it cannot be used in the determination of the nature or size of the group that is to be consulted. Thus, plebiscites can do no more than express the will of the people within a territory that has already been delineated. Whether plebiscites have any effect at all depends on the validity of the principle of self-determination. For if the principle of self-determination is not accepted, then the desire of the people in that territory, whatever it is, is totally without effect, and, therefore, the result of a plebiscite taken in that area is void.[74]

Conclusion

As the above discussion shows, the international debate about the principle of self-determination that occurred in the aftermath of World War I yielded three basic theories or formulations that were advanced as definitions of the principle of self-determination. They each had an opportunity to be adopted by the international community as the acceptable definition of the principle, in the sense that they were all advocated in the international political arena. In this study, these three basic theories have been termed, for the sake of convenience, the *plebiscite theory*, the *national determinism theory*, and the *national equality theory*. As we have seen, the *plebiscite theory* is based on the definition of a nationality as a group of peoples with a common subjective attachment to the same state. The other theories are both based on the definition of a nationality as a group of people who share certain objective characteristics. However, there is a crucial difference between them. For while the *national determinism theory* is based mainly on nationality defined as an ethnic community, the *national equality theory* is based on nationality defined essentially on the basis of a common territory and nationalistic outlook.

These theories contain interesting statements on the nature of the principle of national self-determination. However, none of them is completely free of logical or practical problems. The advocates of the *national determinism theory* could not really cope with the totally justified objection to their theory that, due to the existence of great areas of extensive ethnic mixture, their prescriptions would be impossible to implement without recourse to the undemocratic procedure of elaborate population exchanges.[75] It seems, therefore, that the advocates of the *plebiscite theory* were correct in objecting to the definition of nationality on the basis of objective criteria. However, the definition of nationality based on subjective criteria also faced some problems, one of which was its inability to deal with the following question: granted that the people, being sovereign, should decide on changes in their political status, could not this right be extended to towns or even households? On the basis of the above discussion, it is clear that to answer this question in the affirmative would be a *reductio ad absurdum*.[76] Yet to answer it in the negative leaves the question unsolved as to whether or not *any* part of a state has the right to decide its own political future, and, if so, which parts have this right. The advocates of the principle of national equality attempted to solve the problem exclusively by rejecting both the definition of nationality on the basis of ethnic community and subjective political unity. Instead, they insisted on both objective and subjective criteria, the most basic of which were common territory and common psychology. This definition of nationality based on both objective (common territory, language, and economy) and subjective (common psychology and nationalist commitment) went a long way to solve some of the problems faced by the other two types of theories.[77] In addition, they introduced the idea that the *aim* of a theory of self-determination was to achieve the equality of the nationalities. And, therefore, *the question of the application of the principle of self-determination does not arise unless there is inequality existing between two distinct communities within the same political framework.* In other words, a nationality cannot validly invoke the principle of self-determination unless it were being oppressed by or under the subjugation of another distinct nationality. Under such circumstances, a successful application of the principle of self-determination should eradicate the subject status by either making it autonomous within the existing political framework or by seceding and becoming an independent state. In solving the problem this way, the advocates of the *theory of national equality* opened up another problem that they were unable to solve effectively. Granted that national self-determination could be achieved by either territorial autonomy or by independence, what objective criteria were to be used to differentiate easily between those nationalities that were to be granted independent status and those that were to receive only territorial autonomy, and, furthermore, who was to be authorized to make the decision?[78]

All the theories that were advanced dealt essentially with the same basic questions. Which units had the right to national self-determination? What did the right entail? Or more specifically, did the right of national self-determination include the right of secession? In terms of the first question, the search boiled down to the three subquestions concerning: (1) the nature of the group; (2) the relation between the group and other groups; and (3) the size of the group. As we have seen, writers made many attempts to provide answers to these questions on the theoretical level. Their formulations were derived from the political philosophies of democracy, nationalism, or Marxism. Most of the problems with these formulations of the principle of self-determination may be ascribed to the fact that they were derived from these political doctrines. Whatever consistency any of them could achieve was only within the closed purview of the particular doctrine from which they were derived, with little ability to deal with theoretical queries originating from outside their own systems, and certainly with no ability to deal with international political realities. Due to these shortcomings, none of the theories was able to provide a clear-cut definition of the concept of national self-determination that the international community as a whole was willing to adopt without reservation. In the meantime, the publicists were so committed to their doctrinal biases that they continued to ignore the growing repertory of international practice of the principle of self-determination, and their debate continued around much the same issues throughout the interwar period, to be revived and continued after the formation of the United Nations.

CHAPTER III

THE CONTEMPORARY DISCUSSION

Contemporary discussion of the principle of self-determination in international law literature has been diminutive compared to the volume during the interwar period. What is even more interesting is that the existing discussion has not been a conscious debate, as before, but rather it has taken the form of unrelated commentaries on the principle of self-determination as it has evolved in the charter and practice of the United Nations. The obvious reason for this is the incorporation of the principle of self-determination in the U.N. Charter, and the fact that as a result the United Nations has been the principal arena in which the claims and counterclaims of the principle of self-determination have been advanced. Thus, the U.N. Charter was the principal vehicle by which the principle was reintroduced into international dialogue.

Toward the end of the interwar period, international claims based on the principle of self-determination had drastically diminished, and, therefore, there was very little discussion of the principle in international law literature. To be sure, important demands for independence and autonomy were being made on the basis of the right of self-determination, and it seemed that more of these demands would be forthcoming in the not too distant future.[1] However, except in the mandated territories, which were already an international concern, these demands were not being made on the international level, but within the confines of the various colonial empires. It was the incorporation of the principle of self-determination in the U.N. Charter that brought it out of the exclusive domain of the empires and into the sphere of international relations by making the United Nations the arena within which such claims could be presented for the judgment of the entire international community.[2]

The Origins and Nature of the Discussion

As it had happened in the period immediately following World War I, the mode of introducing the principle of self-determination into international dialogue had a great effect on the nature of the discussion, and the issues on which the initial attention of the participants came to be focused. First, the U.N. Charter, in which the principle was written, is an international instrument. As such, it is, and is considered, binding.[3] Therefore, the writers who dealt with the question were obliged to consider whether or nor the principle of self-determination as it appears in the U.N. Charter gives rise to a right of positive international law.[4] Thus, the question of the existence of a right of self-determination as *lex lata* was seriously raised for the first time. Second, the actual expression used in the charter was "the principle of equal rights and self-determination of peoples." Therefore, in attempting to determine the nature of the group that would be entitled to the right of self-determination,[5] most of the publicists decided that they needed to ascertain what the framers of the charter meant by the term "peoples."[6]

Thus, two differences emerged between the discussions on the principle of self-determination as they developed at the end of World War I, on the one hand, and at the end of World War II, on the other. One difference concerned the status of the principle in international law. It may be recalled that in the aftermath of World War I there had been general agreement that the principle was not recognized in international law, and, therefore, the discussion had been carried on mainly on the basis of *de lege ferenda* formulations. By way of contrast, the post-World War II period saw some serious discussion of the possible legal character of the principle of self-determination resulting from its incorporation into the U.N. Charter. Even though the writers disagreed about self-determination as a principle of positive international law, at least the principle was within the realm of serious consideration. The other difference pertains to the discussion about the groups entitled to the right of self-determination. In this case, while the earlier discussion had focused on an investigation of the meaning of the term "nationality," the discussion during the era of decolonization was concerned mainly with the term "peoples" because of the wording of the U.N. Charter, and also in a probable attemtp to avoid the many problems connected with earlier attempts to define the term "nationality."

In spite of these differences, the writers of both periods were all basically concerned with the same problem, that is, defining the principle of self-determination. In fact, the introduction of the discussion of the legal nature of the principle of self-determination tended to intensify the necessity to define it. This was particularly the case for those writers who claimed that the principle had legal standing character. They were constantly faced with the argument that the vagueness of the principle precluded it having any legal content.[7] Frequently, their inability to define the principle forced them to make the valid, but nevertheless not too comfortable, assertion that the vagueness of the principle does not necessarily detract from its legal nature.[8]

Proposed Theories of the Principle of Self-Determination

The earliest commentaries on the principle of self-determination came very soon after the formation of the United Nations. Consequently, the attempts to define the principle that are made in such works are based on interpretations of the articles of the charter considered relevant to the principle by the writers.[9] Most writers agreed that it was extremely difficult to get a precise definition of the principle from a reading of the relevant articles.[10] Therefore, as the United Nations developed an increasing number of cases with regard to the application of the principle, later commentators began to emphasize the practice of the United Nations in their analysis of the principle.

In all this growing discussion, very few writers attempted to derive a definition of the principle of self-determination by systematic reference to the *proces verbaux* at the San Francisco Conference (as the canons of treaty interpretation suggest) or by deductions from the positions of the various states as revealed in U.N. practice. On the contrary, in most cases, writers began their analysis with their own set definitions of the principle of self-determination and then proceeded to evaluate the accuracy or wisdom of the U.N. Charter and practice in light of their definition. In most of these cases, the definition a writer brought to the analysis seemed to be inherited from the inter-war period. In this regard, most writers were either successors of the adherents of the *plebiscite theory* or the advocates of the *national equality theory*. Only the advocates of the *national determinism theory* had no apparent successors, probably because of the notoriety that that theory had acquired as a result of the use that the German Nazis had made of it in their expansionist aggression that precipitated World War II.[11]

Some new interpretations of the principle of self-determination began to emerge at this time. However, most of these new formulations were also based on doctrinal derivations, not on international practice. Perhaps due to the discussion on the legal nature of the principle that had started, many of these new interpretations were deduced from those principles of international law on which writers thought they should properly be based. Dr. Hans Kelsen's definition of the principle of self-determination, which is based on an interpretation of Article 1, paragraph 2 of the U.N. Charter, illustrates the nature of these formulations and how they may be derived from international legal principles.[12]

> The term "nation" in the formula of the Preamble probably means states; the term "peoples" in Article 1, paragraph 2, may have a different meaning, for in its connection with self-determination it may not mean the state, but one of the elements of the state; the population. *Self-Determination of the people usually designates a principle of internal policy, the principle of democratic government.* However, Article 1, paragraph 2, refers to relations among states. Therefore, the term "peoples" too—in connection with "equal rights"—means probably states, since only states have equal rights according to general international law. . . .
>
> That the Purpose of the Organization is to develop friendly relations among states based on respect for the principle of self-determination of the "peoples" does not mean that friendly relations among States depend on democratic form of government, and that the purpose of the Organization is to favor such form of government. This would not be compatible with the principle of "sovereign equality" of the Members; not with the principle of non-intervention in domestic affairs established in Article 2, paragraph 7. If the term "peoples" in Article 1, paragraph 2, means the term "nations" in the Preamble, then *"sefl-determination of the peoples" in* Article 1, paragraph 2, *can only mean "sovereignty" of the states.*[13]

Phrased in the simplest terms, Dr. Kelsen is saying the following: usually, the principle of self-determination is the same as the principle of democratic government, that is, government by consent of the governed, also known as the principle of popular sovereignty. However, to sustain this definition would be incompatible with general international law and the principles of the U.N. Charter. Therefore, Article 1, paragraph 2 would have to be read in such a way that the expression "equal rights and self-determination of peoples" would mean the sovereign equality of states. Thus, in effect, Dr. Kelsen rejects the plebiscite principle, which he calls the usual designation of the concept as the proper interpretation of Article 1, paragraph 2. In its stead, he introduces a new definition of self-determination that is, according to him, consistent with international law.

Of the post-World War II statements on the *plebiscite theory,* the definition of self-determination introduced by Dr. Rosalyn Higgins comes closest to the classical presentation of the concept of popular sovereignty. According to her, "Self-determination refers to the right of the majority within a generally acceptable political unit to the exercise of power".[14] Dr. Higgins introduces the reservation that the principle as she had outlined it does not have to imply "the Western system of parliamentary democracy".[15] However, there is no doubt that, for her, the principle of self-determination was synonymous with the principle of self-government. Stripped to its barest essentials, her formulation means no more than the assertion that self-determination for a "generally acceptable political unit" is the principle of majority rule within that particular unit. In fact, she herself explicitly acknowledges that her interpretation is "a departure from the traditional use of the terminology"[16] which she describes as ". .desire of a race for independence, to the desire to take over the goals of government and remove the foreign ruling groups."[17] This definition of self-determination is not even concerned with the whole problem of the established of territorial boundaries or the application of the democratic principle in cases of cession of territory.

However, other adherents of the plebiscite principle did not define self-determination as the principle of popular sovereignty, but as the application of that principle to matters of transfer of territory. In such a situation, the principle of self-determination was deemed to mean, as it had meant for their doctrinal ancestors, that no transfer of territory could be considered valid unless it was with the approval of the people. Thus, for such adherents of the *plebiscite theory* as Mohammed A. Shukri, self-determination ". . .is an act through which a people are called upon to choose self-government"[18] or as Harold S. Johnson puts it, "self-determination is the process by which a people determine their own sovereign status."[19] It is "first and foremost a method (by free democratic choice) to attain sovereignty."[20] Thus, as a claimable right:

> . . .self-determination means the right of a people to choose the form of government under which they wish to live or the sovereignty to which they wish to belong.[21]

The people who could claim this right, according to these writers, were identified as people who live under one government and live in the same territory.[22]

In contrast to the position of the advocates of the *plebiscite theory,* some writers approached the examination of the principle of self-determination in the U.N. Charter and practice with the view that the *national equality theory* is the correct interpretation. This assumption led them to associate the principle of self-determination with the program that had been outlined in the charter for dependent peoples. Therefore, in their investigation of the meaning of the principle as it appears in the charter, they did not concentrate only on Article 1, paragraph 2, and Article 55, in which the term actually appears, but also on Chapters XI and XII, in which the U.N. systems for decolonization and trusteeship are outlined.

In their analyses, these writers identified the groups that are entitled to the right of self-determination as nonsovereign, or dependent. In the words of one advocate:

> The first item which needs comment is the category of territories affected: those "whose peoples have not yet attained a full measure of self-government." This is perhaps the most satisfactory definition of dependent peoples that has yet been found. . .[23]

The point that bears noting is that those entitled to the right of self-determination, according to these theorists, are a group of people with a common territory that has the status of being non-self-governing. The right of self-determination that this group was to enjoy was defined by these writers as the right to self-government, which they defined as including (but not necessarily synonymous with) political independence. As Huntington Gilchrist notes:

"Independence" was not mentioned as a goal. . . . Nevertheless, had not the controversy over the use of the word "independence" arisen, it would be clear that the language of the Declaration actually includes independence (or, as the precisionists would say, was patent of that interpretation) when it refers to "progressive development of their free political institutions." What is the meaning of the phrase "free political institutions" if it does not at least include potential independence?[24]

In all respects, the position of these writers bears remarkable resemblance to the theory originally advocated by the Bolsheviks and the Congress of Oppressed Nationalities.

As U.N. practice developed, other writers also advocating the national equality principle presented commentaries analyzing the activities of the United Nations on the basis of their theory. One of these writers is Professor Eagleton, who defined the principle of self-determination in the following terms:

More broadly, self-determination has been defined as the right of a people to determine their own political destiny; this might mean incorporation into a state, or some measure of autonomy within a state, or somewhat larger degree of freedom in a federation, a commonwealth or a union; or it might mean complete independence.[25]

Again, this formulation bears a remarkable resemblance to the theories advocated by Lenin and Stalin in the interwar period. Of course, writers who even more systematically followed the thinking of the Bolsheviks and openly claimed the latter as their doctrinal ancestors were the publicists from the Soviet Union. The following passage, which is representative of their views, is almost an exact echo of Stalin's statement of the fundamental basis of the Bolshevik version of the principle of national equality: "nations are sovereign and all nations are equal"[26]

. . . every nation *qua* cohesive and distinct social unit is inherently seized of the quality of "national sovereignty." This "national sovereignty" is the quintessence of what constitutes a nation, both spiritually and materially; it corresponds to the sum total of those inalienable rights of a given human group which stamp it as a nation. This core element is the source from which flow all the secondary rights—that accompany this "national identity"—*inter alia* the right to political, economic and cultural autodetermination.[27]

According to this view, the political unit that is entitled to the right of self-determination is a nation, defined as a "cohesive and distinct social unit." Like the old Bolshevik definition of nationality, this formulation is based on criteria of social and territorial cohesion rather than on a criterion of ethnic community. Also, in both the old and the new formulations, the right of a nation to self-determination was derived from the concept that all nations were sovereign and equal, and, therefore, all nations had equal right to determine their own political status.

It may be recalled that Lenin had asserted that the right of self-determination extended to "all oppressed nations," which included not only the minorities of eastern Europe but also the inhabitants of colonial territories in Asia and Africa. Soviet writers maintained the same position and included colonial territories in their descriptions of the groups that were entitled to the right of self-determination. For instance, in discussing the international character of the problem of self-determination, one spokesman of this group notes that

> the non-consummation by the colonial peoples of their right of self-determination . . . is not the internal business of the home state. . . .[28]

The right of self-determination that they evisaged for the colonial territories was the right of national equality, including the right of national liberation and independence.[29]

As we have shown above, the doctrinal successors to *the national equality theory* were to be found among both Soviet and western publicists. However, Soviet writers went quite a bit further than their western counterparts. In their view, the right of self-determination did not only mean that all peoples had the right to an independent statehood but that they had the right to acquire this independence by force if necessary. As one advocate notes:

> . . . the peoples of the colonies are fully entitled with arms in hand to seek liberation from the yoke of the colonial power evading a peaceful settlement of said question, and be the first to start military action against it with the object of destroying its military forces stationed in their countries.[30]

For them, the attempt of such a group to liberate itself by initiating military action is no more than an act of self-defense against imperialist aggression. As one writer explains:

> The national liberation war of a dependent people against the colonial

power will always be a just, defensive war from the political as well as the legal standpoint, independently of who initiated the military action.[31]

This description of national liberation wars as self-defense is a logical development of the Soviet conception of national sovereignty. According to this conception, the sovereignty of a nation is permanent and, therefore, does not evaporate with the defeat of the nation or its political subjugation.

> Once possessed of "national sovereignty," a nation can be deprived of it only if the community itself is totally destroyed. Otherwise, a nation always retains this attribute, regardless of its technical juridical status at a particular moment in history. Thus, a community reduced to subject stature, though not politically sovereign, on the plane of "national sovereignty" remains the equal of its independent counterparts, notwithstanding the loss of its facilities for self-government.[32]

This contention, with the addition of some concept of permanent aggression leads easily to the conclusion that colonialism is a manifestation of aggression. If the concept of permanent national sovereignty is accepted, it should follow that the initial act of conquest by which the colonial territory was originally acquired was an act of aggression. In other words:

> ... the state of dependency and disenfranchisement of the colonial peoples is the result of an imperialist aggression committed earlier; expressing itself in the annexation of the territory.[33]

The point they make is that this initial act of aggression does not and cannot erode the "national sovereignty" of the group, and, therefore, the group retains its right to defend itself against the aggression that continues as long as the colonial subjugation continues. Thus, anytime that the group feels that it has developed the capacity to defend itself, it has the right to launch a defensive national liberation war against the imperialist state.

> Such a struggle will be just and legitimate, since, in the first place, neither aggression nor annexation enjoy the benefits of a statute of limitations, and, in the second place, international law forbids aggression and consequent annexation puts it outside the law.[34]

Furthermore, not only the initial subjugation of the colonial territory is classified as aggression but also any attempt by the imperial power to retain its hold on the colony by military action against the national liberation movement.

> ... armed intervention aimed at preventing a people from realizing the right of self-determination is aggression, that is, the gravest international crime.[35]

Some writers in this group have even suggested that national liberation wars are a form of international sanction against the international delict of imperialist aggression.[36]

Examination of the Proposed Theories

As the above discussion indicates, the theoretical interpretations of the principle of self-determination presented by these writers were derived from doctrinal principles. In adopting these formulations, the writers' main concern was that the formulations be consistent with other principles, such as the principle of popular sovereignty, antiimperialism, "sovereign equality" and "nonintervention in domestic affairs."

As we have seen, Dr. Kelsen's main concern in interpreting Article 1, paragraph 2 of the charter was to avoid a reading that would be contrary to Article 2, paragraph 7 and other principles of international law. It was his desire to reach this predetermined conclusion, which led him into an extremely tortuous bit of argumentation. Dr. Kelsen's approach is open to serious question on at least two points. First, it is untenable to read one principle of the U.N. Charter in such a way as to render another principle completely meaningless.[37] Second, as Professor Schwarzenberger has noted, in determining the scope of principles of international law, the possibility always exists that two principles might clash. In such cases, however, there is no reason to presume in favor of one or the other. A balance between the conflicting principles can be reached only be referring to the rules that underlie each one.[38]

For us, the point that has to be noted is that his definition of the principle was diametrically opposed to the intent of the drafters of the U.N. Charter. It is clear that if his conclusion that the principle of self-determination as it appears in Article 1, paragraph 2 was really supposed to mean the sovereign equality of states, then the drafting committee was guilty of extremely poor drafting or an oversight. "The principle of equal rights and self-determination of peoples" is certainly a bizarre way to express a principle that was specifically incorporated in Article 2, paragraph 1 of the same instrument as "the principle of sovereign equality of all its Members." The possibility of an oversight on the part of the drafting committee is complete dispelled by reference to the *proces verbaux,* which deals with the formulation of Article 1 of the charter. During the discussion of the principle of self-determination in Committee 1, Commission 1 of the San Francisco Conference, the Belgian delegate, Mr. Rolin, had proposed an alternative wording of Article 1, paragraph 2, different from the wording that was eventually adopted, on the grounds that the principle of equality could only apply to states. In rejecting this proposal, the committee reasoned that "the equality of states was dealt with and accepted under Chapter II, Principles, so that it was irrelevant here to the point at issue."[39]

The most serious problem with the plebiscite principle is graphically illustrated in Dr. Higgins' definition of self-determination as majority rule in a "generally acceptable political unit." Dr. Higgins probably uses this expression rather than the usual term "state" because it would have been impossible to deny that the issue of the principle of self-determination has arisen and continued in the United Nations because of claims by certain "peoples" that they had a right according to that principle to change their political sovereignty and achieve political independence. U.N. practice has shown *inter alia* that the principle of self-determination is concerned not with the promotion of any particular brand of democratic government within political units but with the determination of what political units are, or should be, generally acceptable. That is, whether or not a dependent people should become generally accepted as an independent sovereign state. As Professor Jennings had suggested, what was needed was a decision on who the people are that are supposed to be designated a unit for the purpose of democratically deciding whether or not they wished to establish a new sovereignty. Just as the original advocates of the *plebiscite theory*, Dr. Higgins' analysis is unable to deal satisfactorily with this query. For the principle of self-determination in U.N. practice has been concerned with establishing the criteria to determine which of the claims by groups to the status of statehood (the generally accepted politi-

49

cal unit) are indeed acceptable to the community of states.

In their formulations of the principle of self-determination, both Shukri and Johnson recognize the problem of designating the unit to which the principle of self-determination should be applied. In particular, Johnson, who is more consciously committed to the plebiscite principle, is acutely aware that "The most difficult question relating to self-determination is the identification of the unit for which a claim may be justified."[40] Shukri attempts to solve this problem by recourse to the practice of the United Nations. His account of which, on the issue of decolonization, is both thorough and accurate.[41] So is his description of the process by which the General Assembly established its competence to make the final decision on both the nature of non-self-governing territories and the point at which they may be deemed as fully self-governing.[42] However, Shukri's conclusion is "that territory, in the legal sense, is a main factor in deciding who is and who is not a people with a right to self-determination."[43] Although this conclusion is consistent with the *plebiscite theory*, it is certainly not consistent with U.N. practice, which he has so laboriously traced. No mention is made anywhere of the crucial qualification that for a claim of the right of self-determination to be considered valid the claimant group must be subject to alien jurisdiction, although this is spelled out in, *inter alia,* Resolution 1541 (XV), to which he alludes.

Perhaps due to the scantiness of international practice regarding his main purpose, to examine the plebiscite as an international means for self-determination,[44] his response to the problem of establishing the unit to which the principle should be applied was more doctrinal. According to Johnson, the question of applying the principle comes up when the sovereignty of an area is already in question, such as in a situation of impending annexation by conquest.[45] This assertion is exactly the same as that made by the original proponents of the *plebiscite theory*. Johnson also attempted to explain the international practice of self-determination in the decolonization era as a situation in which the sovereignty of an area is in question, but this time, due to an "ideological challenge,"[46] the issue is separated from the alleged solution, which is the settlement of the territorial dispute by applying the principle of self-determination, that is, the democratic principle of popular sovereignty by plebiscite. In the case of pending annexation, it has already been noted that the application of the plebiscite is not in itself self-determination, for the plebiscite becomes a useful and meaningful exercise only if the principle of self-determination has already been accepted. The plebiscite only records the will of the people; whether or not this expressed will is given effect depends on the prior acceptance of the validity of the concept of self-determination. This theory fails even more dramatically when viewed in light of the practice of the United Nations. First, plebiscites have been used only in the case of the trust territories, as he rightly admits.[47] Furthermore, U.N. practice clearly indicates that self-determination is not the process by which dependent peoples choose their sovereignty. On the contrary, it is the right that is used to validate what he has called the "ideological challenge." That is, it is by reference to the right of self-determination that a dependent people are deemed to be able to become independent.

In the case of both Shukri and Johnson, their theory of self-determination is unable to determine the nature of the unit to which the principle should be applied, either within the logic of the theory itself or in terms of making explicit the criteria that have been established in international, specifically the practice of the United Nations, by which such units would be recognized. The statement by Johnson that, "The plebiscite serves directly as the means by which to determine the national status necessary for self-determination . . ."[48] completely and erroneously ignores the simple fact that a plebiscite cannot be held unless the plebiscite area has already been demarcated on the basis of some form of national status.

The question of the transfer of sovereignty was rightly considered by the adherents of the national equality principle as the crux of the whole matter. In grappling with the problem of definition, most of these theorists settled on the peoples of colonial territories as groups entitled to the right of self-determination. They derived their initial proof from the wording of the charter which in Chapter XI refers to "Non-Self-Governing Territories."[49] However, their most important evidence was that as U.N. practice developed the peoples in the colonial territories were the ones demanding their independence on the basis of the right of self-determination, not only in direct dealings with the imperial powers but, most significantly, within the organs of the United Nations, and thus in international political affairs.[50] Like their doctrinal predecessors, the advocates of the *national equality theory* in the United Nations had the advantage of being the theorists whose formulation of the principle of self-determination came closest to the claims that were actualy being made on the international level on the basis of that principle.

The new version of the *national equality theory* still had to cope with some logical problems. One such, which was raised by Professor Eagleton, was the familiar argument that unless the principle were more carefully defined "it would seem to give each individual human being a right to be an independent country."[51] Professor Eagleton admits that if seriously advanced, this argument would be a *reductio ad absurdum* and would have no chance of being accepted in practice. In reviewing the available practice, he conceded that according to the United Nations the right is allowed to only colonial peoples, but he denied that this fact alone solves the problem of defining the principle:

> In sum, we have this limitation: only "colonial" peoples are to be allowed to base claims on the Charter term "self-determination." But we still do not know what a people or a nation is; indeed we do not know what a colony is.[52]

What Professor Eagleton was really disapproving of, with regard to the activities of the United Nations in the realm of self-determination, was based on his dissatisfaction with the criteria that the United Nations had apparently accepted as evidence of the legitimacy of a claim based on the principle. He accepted the usual criteria established by the advocates of the national equity principle, who seemed to be making headway in U.N. circles. He argued, however, that they were not enough grounds for the granting of independence to the peoples of the colonial territories. He queried:

> Assuming all this—desire, unity and territorial basis—is this enough to justify the United Nations in saying that independence—or whatever is called for in the name of self-determination—should be granted?[53]

And in response to his own query, he suggested that other criteria—economic viability, the ability to protect certain human rights, and assurance of the ability and willingness to be a responsible member of the world community—should be satisfied before a group is granted the right of self-determination.[54] All the points that have been raised by Professor Eagleton seem to be directly or indirectly connected to the size of a territory that is being considered for the right of self-determination. His comments are, therefore, directed at the one problem that the *national equality theory* is still unable to solve entirely satisfactorily, that is, the establishment of a minimum size of a nation entitled to self-determination.

The Soviet advocates of the *national equality theory* share their western colleagues' problem of establishing a minimum size. They face an even more formidable theoretical problem that emanates from their advocacy of national liberation wars as legitimate means for enforcing the right of self-determination. As we have already noted, the Soviet argument, that armed struggle by nationalists against imperial governments is a legitimate exercise of the right of self-determination, is based on the contention that colonialism is aggression, and, therefore, wars of national liberation are a means for the nationalists to exercise their inherent right of national self-defense. This argument raises some questions.

The first problem with the Soviet view is that it is really no more than a plea for the international recognition of the right of a group to initiate a nationalist revolution. Such a legal right to revolution is not only unrecognized, it is illogical.[55] But even if this argument were to be allowed, it would only result in putting the group's goals (which presumably would be the reason for the revolt) at the mercy of the success or failure of the revolution, rather than on its inherent legitimacy. For if the right of self-determination were recognized, then the right of the people to autonomy or independence should not have to depend on the power of their weapons. Thus, paradoxically, the right to revolt is not really concerned with the principle of self-determination at all; in fact, it represents a negation of that principle. It was precisely the realization that the solution of issues involving the principle of self-determination should not be left up to the result of armed conflict, which accounts for the development of one of the most important aspects of international organization. Since the end of World War I, one of the most important developments in international organization has been the growth of institutional structures for establishing the validity of the claims of various groups to the right of self-determination. One of the major impetuses for this has been the desire to discourage the use of force in solving problems involving such claims, thereby eliminating what was recognized as a great potential threat to general international peace and security. This was quite apart from any consideration of the justice or the legality of the principle. In fact, at the time that the principle was being developed in international practice, there was a general agreement that the principle had no status in positive international law. It was still this concern for taking such issues out of the realm of violent resolution that caused the incorporation of the principle in the charter of the United Nations.

Therefore, while the practice of the United Nations seems to suggest that the status of dependency gives a group the right to claim before the bar of the international community that it has the right of self-determination, it is impossible to sustain the conclusion that the United Nations would endorse as general policy the initiation of national liberation wars as legitimate exercises of the right of national self-determination. Furthermore, this definition of national liberation wars may run into conflict with the meaning of self-defense according to Article 51 of the U.N. Charter. Admittedly, the meaning and scope of Article 51 of the charter is a matter of some controversy.[56] However, the meaning of the term as it is applied to national liberation wars is quite different from the usual meaning in the practice of the United Nations, or in the interpretations now being debated. Considering that the United Nations has generally given its backing to a restrictive interpretation of Article 51, it seems unlikely that the application of the term "self-defense" to such wars will find general acceptance, even though a growing number of newly independent countries, particularly in Africa, now subscribe to it.[57]

The most serious problem with the definition of national liberation wars as the exercise of the right of self-determination is that it fails to provide a way of identifying the group on whose behalf the claim to the right is being made. In such cases, while it is not especially difficult to define the limits of the territory in question, it is virtually impossible to determine whether or not the majority of the people within that area support the national liberation movement and may, thus, be considered the "group" on whose behalf the claim is made. While the leaders of the revolutionary movement always argue that they indeed represent the majority of the people within that territory, the representatives of the imperial government maintain that the members of the revolutionary movement are a minute group of unrepresentative fanatics, or even a clique of gangster terrorists.[58] In the duration of such a war, the veracity of either side is virtually impossible to establish. At the end of the conflict, it is easy for the group that wins by dint of superior force to assert that their claim had been valid all along. Some writers have claimed that the fact that the leaders of national liberation movements participate in international agreements, such as the Geneva Accords of 1954, means that the international character of national liberation wars and the status of national liberation movements as subjects of international law is recognized.[59] In opposition to this view, it must be said that the recognition of the belligerency of a national liberation movement, or any other group involved in hostilities, has nothing whatever to do with the principle of self-determination. For the recognition of the belligerency is not based on the claims of the groups engaged in the conflict, but on the fact that they are fighting. There have been many cases of the recognition of the belligerency of groups involved in civil wars in which the issue of self-determination was irrelevant. But even if the recognition of the national liberation movement were to be allowed, it still leaves unanswered whether or not the claim of the national liberation movement to represent a majority of the people in that territory is valid. This problem is hopelessly compounded when there are rival national liberation movements who all claim to speak for the majority of the people as we have in Southern Africa at present. It is clear that exception must be taken to this theory on the grounds that it does not provide any clear criteria for determining the validity of claims by revolutionary movements to represent the majority of the people of a dependent territory.[60]

Survey of the Discussion of the Legal Character of the Principle of Self-Determination

The definition that writers have attributed to the principle of self-determination has had a significant effect on their investigation into the legal nature of the principle. For instance, the question that the advocates of the *national equality theory* were investigating was whether or not under international law dependent people with a territorial community have the right to acquire full sovereignty by associating with another sovereign state or by achieving political independence? On the other hand, for the advocates of the *plebiscite theory*, the question was whether or not under international law the population of a state has a right to have democratic government.

For instance, Professor Kelsen defined the principle of self-determination as synonymous with the concept of sovereign equality of states. And on the basis of that definition, he declared that the principle of self-determination has no legal validity, because the concept of sovereign equality ". . . means that everybody has the duties and rights which the law confers upon him, or that everybody shall be treated as the law provides; *which is an empty tautology*."[61]

Similarly, Professor Eagleton's definition of the principle was an important factor in his analysis. As shown previously, self-determination means, for him, the right of peoples to political independence. The question that he was posing, therefore, was whether or not such a right indeed existed in positive international law. His answer was a firm negative.

> The textbooks of international law do not recognize any legal right to self-determination, nor do they know any standards for determining which groups are entitled to independence; on the contrary, international law holds that a state which intervenes to aid a rebellious group to break away from another state is itself committing an illegal act.[62]

He then responds to the question of whether or not the United Nations has any authority to institute such a right by virtue of the powers acquired under its charter. Again his answer is a negative.

> The United Nations has no authority in the matter, in a legal or constitutional sense it is not authorized to issue a ukase freeing a people from a state, and setting up a group as independent; it cannot establish rules or criteria for self-determination which are legally binding on anyone.[63]

Indeed, he considered the actions that the United Nations had taken with regard to self-determination to be contrary to the provisions on domestic jurisdiction in the charter and, therefore, illegal.[64]

The approach used by another group of theorists in ascertaining the legality of the principle of self-determination in the U.N. Charter was to understand the intent of the framers with regard to the articles that are relevant to that principle. The rationale for this type of analysis was that the mere presence of a term in the charter gives no indication as to whether or not the framers intended it to be legally binding.[65] And, therefore, an examination of the *travaux preparatories* was needed. Like the other theorists, their definition of the principle of self-determination shaped their investigation to a considerable extent, for it determined which articles of the charter they considered relevant. As already explained above, their commitment to the definition on the basis of the national equality principle led them to the conclusion that the sections of the charter that contained the programs designed for the non-self-governing peoples were concerned with the principle of self-determination. Therefore, in choosing the charter articles, they considered not only Article 1, paragraph 2, Articles 55 and 56 relevant to the legal nature of the principle of self-determination but also Article 73. The conclusion of their analysis, as expressed in the words of Professor Quincy Wright, follows:

> It seems clear that Members of the United Nations by ratifying the Charter have undertaken legal obligations in respect to the self-determination of peoples within their territory.[66]

He goes on to assert that the legal obligation that the members of the United Naitons undertook was international in nature and was thus outside of the scope of unilateral and final interpretation by any of the signatories.[67] because a state "cannot finally interpret and apply its own obligations under international law."[68] With regard to the argument that the application of the right of self-determination is inadmissible, due to Article 2, paragraph 7 of the charter Wright asserted that:

> The issues of whether or not a matter is "essentially" within the domestic jurisdiction is itself a question of international law. It belongs to the sovereignty of states to make treaties, and consequently to eliminate an obligation which has been undertaken would be itself an invasion of sovereignty.[69]

It is clear from the above discussion that Professor Wright's analysis was based on the nature of the U.N. Charter as in international instrument of binding force. What needs to be noted is that it was also based specifically on Article 73 of the charter. As he states:

> Articles 73 is also clearly an obligation. Whether the "salt-water" theory was intended to apply to this article is a matter of interpretation . . . Clearly, determination of what are the non-self-governing territories with respect to which obligations are undertaken is not a matter within the domestic jurisdiction of any state.[70]

In Wright's judgment, the establishment of criteria for determining whether a group claiming the right of self-determination falls within the category of "dependent peoples" within the meaning of the relevant articles of the charter, or whether the status that is being claimed (such as independence) falls within the factual definition of self-determination can only be done by the concurrent action of the great majority of the members of the international community. In other words, the determination of the validity of claims for the right of self-determination is a matter of internatonal, not unilateral, decision. In this respect, he sees as legal the position taken by the U.N. General Assembly that it can decide which territories come under Article 73, on the grounds that such action would amount to no more than "general recognition."[71] He argues that under international law the status of entities is determined by general recognition, which means that if a large majority of members of the international community recognize an entity as a state, a government or a belligerent, a protectorate or a colony, "that status is objectively established."[72] Therefore,

> While the General Assembly's action as agent of the United Nations cannot go beyond recommendation, it would appear that a resolution asserting that status of an entity under international law would, if supported by most of the Members, constitute general recognition by the concurring Members objectively establishing the fact under customary international law.[73]

As the practice of the United Nations regarding self-determination increased, more attention was given in the literature to the implications of the practice for the legal nature of the principle. In most of the literature, the discussion was carried out in terms of the possibility that the practice itself may be creating a right of self-determination in customary international law. However, even in this area of discussion, writers analyzed the actions of the United Nations from the vantage point of their own preestablished definitions of the principle of self-determination. For instance, a large part of Professor Eagleton's analysis is an examination of the various claims that were being made and the trend of U.N. practice against his definition of the principle of self-determination. It was from the standpoint of his definition that he deplored those claims he considered outrageous.[74] On the same basis, he considered the criteria of the United Nations as a "sad comedown" for what, in his opinion, was the proper definition of the principle of self-determination.[75]

Other writers have taken a more charitable view of these activities of the United Nations. For instance, in 1955, Benjamin Rivlin held the view that the principle of self-determination had no legal validity. However, he saw the activities of the U.N. General Assembly as a "drive to convert the principle into a binding legal doctrine."[76] In 1960, Rupert Emerson went as far as to suggest that the activities of the United Nations might indeed make self-determination a right under international law.[77] Four years later, he stated that the "exercise of the right of self-determination has been asserted with a triumphant flourish against colonial overlordship. . ."[78]

Recent statements on the legal nature of the principle of self-determination concur with Emerson's position. For instance, Mohammed A. Shukri notes that:

> . . . the collective view of the United Nations coincides with the acceptance of states in recognizing self-determination as one of the principles of international law.[79]

And after examining the leading cases of U.N. activity with regard to the principle of self-determination, numerous General Assembly resolutions, and especially the Declaration on the Granting of Independence to Colonial Countries and Peoples, Dr. Higgins arrived at the following conclusions:

> . . . that Declaration, taken together with seventeen years of evolving practice by the United Nations organs, provide ample evidence that there now exists a legal right of self-determination.[80]

East European and Russian writers also agree with the conten-

59

tion that the principle of self-determination exists in positive international law. As one of their spokesmen asserts:

> ...the principle of self-determination of peoples is one of the most important principles of contemporary international law.[81]

However, they do not base their assertion only on the U.N. Charter and the subsequent practice of the organization. They see the charter as the affirmation of a principle of general international law that was already in existence. Thus, for them, the incorporation of the principle of self-determination in the charter was an example of the well-established practice of expressing in treaty form concrete statements of long-existing rules of customary international law.[82] Again, their analysis, like those of others, is based on their doctrine of the principle of self-determination; this, what they claim as a principle of international law is their own definition of the principle of self-determination, which, as we have seen, includes the idea that "national-liberation wars by which peoples realize their right to self-determination, as just wars, are from the standpoint of international law legitimate wars."[83]

Appraisal of the Discussion

As the foregoing discussion indicates, there are many discrepancies between the definitions of the principle of self-determination that have been advanced by writers and what U.N. practice might suggest. For instance, the current practice of the United Nations and the practice of the allied powers during the interwar period do not support a definition of self-determination as a process of choosing the sovereignty in which a group would want to live, or a definition of self-determination that includes a justification of the use of force against colonial powers on grounds of self-defense. Therefore, when these writers assert that the principle of self-determination is, or is becoming, a principle of international law, they are probably referring to a principle, the definition of which is different from one based on international practice. For instance, if the practice of the United Nations has evolved a legal right of self-determination, then the correct definition of that legal right is one that has to be established on the basis of that practice, not on the doctrinal commitments of writers. But this is not the case at the present time. The result is that there is confusion surrounding the principle of self-determination created mainly by writers and publicists, which has continued to exacerbate the problem of ascertaining its scope and content.

The error has been in attempting to analyze the definition and the legal validity of the principle of self-determination from the vantage point of a preestablished definition based on the political philosophy of writers, not on the consensus of the members of the international community (expressly stated in conventional form or from the legal acceptance of general practice). It is this imposition of a doctrinal definition on the analysis of the scope and content of a principle of international law that introduces the discrepancy, for it leads to a condition in which the definition emanates from the mind of a theorist rather than from the consensus of the states from which its legal validity has to come.

This problem is most graphically illustrated in the analyses of the advocates of the *plebiscite theory*. For instance, the assertion by Dr. Higgins that a legal right of self-determination exists is based on the evidence of U.N. practice, which, for her, amounts to ". . . the practice of states as revealed by unanimous and consistent behavior."[84] However, the source of her definition of the principle was not the behavior that she claims as the basis of the legality of the principle, although this is what seems to be suggested by the rules of evidence of customary international law. On the contrary, she supplied her own definition, probably due to her concern that ". . . without this qualification, all is in flux."[85] She then proceeded to match her definition with the activities that U.N. organs had undertaken under the rubric of self-determiantion. Her definition of the principle of self-determination as the "right of the majority within a general accepted political unit to the exercise of power"[86] is not even concerned with the same issues as the numerous U.N. resolutions on the principle of self-determination and the Declaration on the Granting of Independence to Colonial Territories and Peoples that she cites as an important source of the legal authority behind self-determination. As the title of the declaration plainly indicates, it and all the other U.N. resolutions concerning the principle of self-determination defined the principle as the right of the peoples of dependent territories to full sovereignty, either by associating with another sovereign state on a noncolonial basis or by attaining political independence. In spite of the discrepancy between the United Nations' definition of self-determination and Dr. Higgins', she attempts to apply her definition to some leading U.N. cases, including those of Morocco, Tunisia, Algeria, Cyprus, Angola, and Rhodesia. It is clear, however, that this imposition of a definition was a misfit. As Dr. Higgins herself notes, all these cases were concerned with the claim of nationalist movements for independence, and, furthermore, all the resolutions introduced or adopted during the consideration of these cases define the principle of self-determination as the right of dependent territories to achieve full self-government. (See, for instance, General Assembly Resolutions 1514 (XV), 1573 (XV), 1747 (XVI), and Security Council Resolution S/4835, just to name a few.) She solved the problem by asserting that only in the case of Southern Rhodesia could the term "self-determination" be used, because it was the only case in which the issue concerned the principle of majority rule. It may be recalled that for her, self-determination is tantamount to majority rule.[87] She argues that the other situations should properly be described as involving the issue of independence, because the concern in those cases was the elimination of foreign rule.

While Resolution 1747 (XVI) includes the principle of "one man, one vote," it is important to point out that the principle was mentioned in that context because it was relevant to the principle of self-determination in a very specific way. According to the trusteeship principle embodied in Chapter XI of the charter, dependent peoples could exercise their right of self-determination by attaining full self-government. Dependent people could attain full self-government by choosing *"by democratic processes"*[88] to become independent, integrated into another sovereign state, or associated with another state on the basis of freedom and equality. The granting of independence to Southern Rhodesia under a constitution that was rejected by a "vast majority of the people," through the denial of equal political rights and liberties, is clearly a contravention of the requirements of the right of self-determination outlined in Resolution 1541 (XV). It must also be noted that the situation was not one involving the principle of majority rule in a homogeneous society. Southern Rhodesia is a society in which the African population fits into the category of dependent peoples under alien jurisdiction of whites, as outlined in the annex to Resolution 1541 (XV).

In terms of Resolution 1747 (XVI), the real issue in Southern Rhodesia, as far as the United Nations was concerned, was in relation to Great Britain as an administering power. In this sense, it was also a matter of getting rid of foreign control. However, U.N. provisions stipulate that in such cases of cessation of the period of tutelage power be handed over democratically to the people as a whole. If, as was assumed, the African population was not ready for independence, then the United Nations by resolution was calling on Great Britain to continue to execute its responsibilities as an administering power by continuing to report on the territory in accordance with Article 73, subparagraph e of the charter. The basic problem with the explanations offered by Dr. Higgins emanates from the fact that she insists on using a definition of the principle of self-determination that is derived from the doctrine of popular sovereignty, matching it to whatever U.N. practice seems to be.

The methodological problem that the above example points to is shared by almost all the publicists who have dealt with the principle of self-determination, for it is the result of an approach that they all use; that is, the analysis of the principle on the basis of an assumed definition of the principle, emanating out of the political or ideological commitment of the writer. The advocates of a definition based on the *national equality theory* are not exempted from this problem, because their definition also springs out of their political philosophies. However, because their definition is closer to the demands that are actually being made, their attempts to make their definition fit international practice have not exhibited discrepancies of as glaring a magnitude as those of the advocates of the *plebiscite theory*. This is more attributable to coincidence than to superior analytical techniques. Indeed, the magnitude of the discrepancy between the practice and the definition of the advocates of the *national equality theory* is determined by their deviation from the basic version of that formulation thus, the discrepancy between the definition suggested by the consensus of the international community and the one advocated by Soviet writers has widened as a result of the latter's inclusion of the concept of the legitimacy of national liberation wars.

Conclusion

At the time of this writing, the international discussion of the principle of self-determination had been going on for almost seven decades and a few thousand pages. When the term was suddenly hurled into international affairs at the turn of the century, many prominent writers declared that the principle was no more than an abstract dictum that had serious definitional flaws, and at that time, almost all writers who had given the subject any attention had agreed with this initial observation. Indeed, some writers had gone so far as to assert that the term was so confused that the very existence of the principle was in serious doubt. In spite of the inability of the expression to satisfy the requirements of precision set up by these writers, the importance of the principle of self-determination in international politics has, if anything, increased considerably.

The reason for the continued importance of the principle in international political and legal affairs is that political groups continue to make such claims on the international level. In the main, the demands that groups have made on the basis of the principle of self-determination have been for the recognition of their right of political independence. From time immemorial, groups that have identified themselves as distinct communities have agitated and fought for their independence from what they considered foreign political domination. This phenomenon, the struggle for independence, played an important role in precipitating World War I, which in turn, created the conditions under which, for the first time in history, a conscious effort was made to apply a principle to the demands of groups for political independence as a matter of international concern.

Propelled by the necessity for the advocates of the claimants to base their demands on general theoretical formulations, a theoretical dialogue emerged, into which publicists were naturally drawn. In the doctrinal dialogue that ensued, there emerged three basic formulations of the principle of self-determination called, mainly for convenience, the *national determinism theory*, the *plebiscite theory*, and the *national equality theory*. As the dialogue continued, the *national determinism theory* was soon found to have the most logical deficiencies. So that by the end of World War II there were practically no theorists who were advocating that approach to the definition. Of the other two, the *national equality theory* began to emerge as the theory that was closest to the actual demands that political groups were making on the basis of a right of self-determination.

None of the three formulations, however, was without logical and practical problems. As presented, these theories emanated from the political doctrines of nationalism, democracy, and antiimperialism, or their derivatives. Consequently, their definitions of the principle of self-determination emphasized the necessity for ethnic homogeneity, majoritarianism, or national liberation. Aside from the logical problems that such one-sided formulations had to cope with, none of the formulations were able to explain by recourse to doctrinal deductions a phenomenon of such overwhelming subjectivity.

However, although these theoretical formulations have not solved the problem of defining the principle of self-determination, the development of the dialogue has in itself been of great importance, for the debate has exposed with some clarity the questions that will have to be answered if the principle is ever going to be defined with legal specificity and consistency. The most important fact that was revealed by the discussion is that there are two basic questions that require answers: (1) what is the *unit recipient*[89] or beneficiary of the right of self-determination; and (2) what is the *right of self-determination* to which this unit is entitled. With regard to the first question, it became clear that it would be necessary to establish the *size, internal nature,* and *relationship with external units* that a political entity should have to enable it to qualify for the right of self-determination. Concerning the second question, it has to be established what factual conditions can be considered as valid evidence of the successful exercise of the right of self-determinism, what international persons have the obligation to effect this factual condition, and by what means.

While the publicists were attempting to find answers to these questions by theoretical deduction, the international community was developing a respectable collection of cases in which the principle of self-determination was brought into play. Starting with World War I and continuing to the present, the international community has been faced with hundreds of claims based on the principle. During the interwar period, the groups that were making the demands were the "subject nationalities" of eastern Europe, while in the period after World War II the main claimants of independence have been the peoples inhabiting the European imperial territories in Asia, Africa, and the West Indies. All these add up to an impressive collection of claims that have been presented before the community of states. The reactions to these claims have come in the form of counterclaims, protests, tacit acquiescence, and expressed consent. Thus in the piecemeal way in which rules of customary international law have often been formed, the international community has dealt with these claims in such a way as to create a consensual nexus that provides an implicit definition of the principle of self-determination as well as the accepted interpretations of its application.

What seems to have happened, then, is that in attempting to solve the problem of defining self-determination the publicists based their analyses on theories deducted from various political philosophies instead of from actual diplomatic practice. Even in the instances where some attention was paid to international practice, it was often for the purpose of demonstrating that the practice was not in agreement with what the writer thought it should properly be according to his theory. So that, as time went on, there developed a serious lag between the theories of the principle of self-determination and the international practice to which the principle related.. In order to bridge this gap, it will be necessary to systematize international practice concerning the principle in order to extract the answers to the questions revealed in the doctrinal discussion, which have indeed already ebvolved. It is to the task of systematizing the international practice of self-determination that the next two chapters will be devoted.

Part Two

SELF-DETERMINATION IN INTERNATIONAL PRACTICE

CHAPTER IV

SELF-DETERMINATION IN THE INTERWAR PERIOD

The first conscious and systematic attempt to apply the principle of self-determination in international politics came in the aftermath of World War I, when it emerged as what was then considered the leading principle of European territorial settlement and the foundation of international peace. Before the end of the war, the principle had already captured the attention of all Europe in a most spectacular manner, when the newly installed Bolshevik government in Russia declared in the Decree of Peace of November 8, 1917, its desire for an immediate peace based on the principle of self-determination of all peoples.[1]

The Soviet peace declaration, and the German response had a considerable effect on the course of international affairs. Not only did it strengthen the national liberation movements in Europe and turn them directly against the central powers,[2] but it also "contributed to the Allied cause that final and essential degree of co-operation and oneness of purpose which was necessary for victory."[3] Of course, the declaration also had the lasting effect of boosting the independence movements in the Baltic states, leading to radical changes in the political map of eastern Europe.[4] In spite of all these effects, the Soviet declaration was seen essentially as an action of basically national consequence, rather than something of general international significance. Given its stature at that time, the Soviet Union quite clearly did not have the capacity to speak on behalf of the international community as a whole. And so it was the Paris Peace Conference that, both by the leaders themselves and a wide range of enthusiastic public opinion, was considered as the site of the formal international debute of the principle of self-determination.

The emergence of the principle as fundamental to the peace

settlement was a logical outcome of the political condition of Europe at the time, particularly the circumstances surrounding the origin and development of the war. As the victors of the war, the allied powers had also acquired the responsibility for establishing and maintaining the peace. In discharging this responsibility, the allies in some cases sought to realize their own selfish national interests. But it must be said in their favor that they never completely lost sight of their belief that the way to achieve peace was not by following their own interests but by eliminating the kinds of conflicts and frictions that had caused the war. What the allied powers were attempting to do was to create an international system in which the incidence of conflict would be minimized, and in which such conflicts that arose could be solved by accepted principles of justice. As they envisaged it, the system would have to be based on certain indispensable principles, and it was these that the allies, under the prodding of President Wilson, published as the principles for which they were fighting. Thus, the so-called war aims of the allies were, in this important sense, their peace aims, for it was these same principles that they were going to try to establish after the war.

The overriding aim of this new system of international relations was to be the maintenance of a just and durable peace. In order to achieve this aim, the allied powers envisaged a program with a set of political principles that would be applied in the most practical and coherent combination to specific conflicts as they emerge in the future. In establishing such general principles, the allies had to anticipate the kinds of political conflicts that were likely to occur. Naturally, they depended on the lessons of history and experience and looked for types of conflicts that had occured in the past, especially those that had contributed to the world war. So that each of the principles that were enunciated in President Wilson's famous speeches, as the foundations of a new world order,[5] was designed to provide a solution or a method for solving one of the types of conflicts that had been known to have disturbed the peace in the past. One of these general principles was the principle of national self-determination.

The inclusion of the principle of national self-determination in the program was entirely legitimate and logical. First, the principle was the focal point of one of the most virulent and

70

unrelenting political struggles in Europe throughout the entire second half of the nineteenth century.

During this period, one of the most pressing issues in the internal politics of European states, as well as in their relations with their neighbors, was what was then called the nationality question. In many parts of Europe, there were national groups that were suffering under the imperial rule of other nations. Such national gropus were generally considered "oppressed," for they were deprived of rights and privileges enjoyed by other national groups within the same state, and more often, they suffered actual persecution. With the development of nationalism in Europe, many of these groups began to organize for the purpose of liberating themselves from alien oppression. This problem was naturally most acute in east and central Europe, where most of these "oppressed nationalities" were situated. So that by the beginning of the twentieth century, that whole area ". . . was occupied, to the exclusion of almost any other subject, with an unremitting and unrelenting national strife. . ."[6] The groups that were struggling to liberate themselves from oppression had consistently defined national liberation as national self-determination; for them, the exercise of national self-determination was tantamount to national liberation from foreign subjection. In other words, the principle of national self-determination came to be regarded as the theoretical formulation of the demand for national liberation.

Second, the national liberation struggle with which the principle of national self-determination was associated was not only the basic underlying condition that had led to the war, but more than that, it was this struggle that had most conspicuously precipitated the conflict. For it was the determination of the dual-monarchy to crush Serbian nationalism that led to the famous Austrian ultimatum and, finally, the war.[7]

The Evolution of the Allied Commitment to the Principle of Self-Determination

The emergence of the principle of self-determination as the leading principle of the peace settlement was a slow and often imperceptible process. As we have seen above, the principle found its way into the list of peace principles. However, nowhere in the initial statements of the allied powers was there a suggestion that it was meant to have more importance than any of the other principles. In fact, up until about the middle of 1918, it seems to have been considered less important than some of the other principles. The term "self-determination" is conspicuous by its absence from both President Wilson's Fourteen Points and all the other principles of peace that he enunciated.[8] To be sure, Wilson's statement that self-determination is an imperative principle of action appears in the February 11, 1918, speech, in which he presented his Four Supplementary Points, but it is significant that the term appeared not in one of the four points but in the preamble of his speech.

Furthermore, up until the end of 1918, whatever commitment the allied powers might have had to the liberation of oppressed nationalities was extremely tentative. To be sure, they had committed themselves in the Fourteen Points to the independence of Poland and the "autonomous" development of the peoples of Austria-Hungary and the nationalities under Turkish rule. However, they had been careful to avoid a general endorsement of the idea of national liberation. Only once, in Wilson's speech of February 11, 1918, is the suggestion made that national aspirations should be respected; but even there, the paramount concern of the allied powers was for peace, and what they had in mind was something far less than a full endorsement of national liberation. That is, they had a commitment to accommodate the desire of nationalities to be liberated *provided these aspirations did not create any antagonism*. It is extremely difficult to imagine a desire for national liberation that would not generate some antagonism, at least on the part of the state from which the group wishes to be liberated.

Between mid-1918 and the time of the peace conference, all this changed dramatically, so that by the time the conference actually met, the principle of self-determination had clearly emerged as the leading principle of the peacemaking effort, and the informed public both believed and expected that it would be scrupulously implemented by the victorious allies.[9]

Soon after the beginning of the war, allied propaganda started to make tentative attempts to convince many people that one of the most important reasons why they had entered the war was to liberate small nations.[10] The fact that the principle of national liberation was of crucial interest to many national groups who considered themselves oppressed provided a good opportunity for the propaganda machines of both sides, and attempts were made by both the central powers and the allied powers to weaken the enemy by fanning the nationalist ambitions of the groups within enemy held territories byu propaganda and intrigue.[11] Right at the outset, the allied powers had the advantage in this propaganda war, for, at that time, the most nationalistic and organizationally sophisticated national groups were not only located within the territory of the central powers but they were also actually engaged in struggles to liberate themselves. On the other hand, the national groups to which the central powers could direct their propaganda were, with the exception of those in the Russian Empire, outside of the mainstream of European politics and either poorly organized or still unaffected by the desire for national liberation.[12] Furthermore, the central powers had territorial designs that prevented them from unequivocally supporting the independence of the minorities in Russia.[13] The allied powers thus began to emerge as the champions of all oppressed nations, and most of the subject nationalities in central Europe began to believe that the realization of their nationalist ambitions was contingent upon the defeat of the central powers.[14]

The dramatic breakthrough in the development of self-determination as the leading principle of the allied policy came with the collapse of the Russian Empire and the subsequent institution of a new Russian government avowedly committed to the principle of national self-determination. This situation significantly enhanced the posture of the allied powers as the champion of oppressed nationalities, for it removed what had been a major factor tending to retard the development of a forthright and general allied commitment to the idea of national liberation—the apprehension that by so doing they would embarrass their Russian allies. The Russians had their own minorities which they had no intention of freeing, and so, as long as the allies were tied to them, no general recognition of the principle of self-determination even confined to Europe, could be expected from them.[15]

The final catalyst in this development was the entry of the United States into the war. First, it ushered in President Wilson, who immediately set out to develop the diffuse commitment of the allied powers into an official policy endorsing the principle of national self-determination.[16] It was under Wilson's pressure that they make their war claims public that the allied powers formally declared that their aim was to liberate the subject nationalities in central Europe and the Balkans, and to reorganize Europe on the basis *inter alia* of respect for nationalities.[17] More important, President Wilson elevated the principle to the position of preeminence that it had reached by the time of the peace conference, for he indicated in his statements not only his conviction that the aspirations of the subject nationalities were entirely justified, but also his firm belief that this was the most important reason for which the war had been fought.[18] Second, the American entry into the war added the powerful prestige of the United States to President Wilson's endorsement of the application of national self-determination as a general principle of peace based on justice. When Wilson spoke, he spoke with the authority of the United States, untarnished by prewar political deals and free of the desire for territorial aggrandizement, that had saved the allied cause. This is what made it clear that Wilson as president of the United States was the leading spokesman of the allies, and that in outlining his policies, he was speaking of and committing the allied powers as a whole.[19] The result of all this was that within the span of a few months the principle of self-determination rose from relative unimportance to preeminence as the leading principle of allied policy for the postwar reconstruction of Europe.

As we have stated above, the task in this chapter is to ascertain the way in which the principle of self-determination was generally defined, on the basis of the way in which it was implemented. As we have seen, before the end of the war the allied powers had committed themselves to the proposition that the leading principle that they were going to apply in the peace settlement was the one of national self-determination. By virtue of their victory, they acquired the authority to implement this declared aim, and they believed while they were discharging this responsibility that, except in a few cases, they were indeed applying the principle. This means that during the peace settlement they believed that *they were implementing what they understood to be the principle of self-determination,* that is, the principle *according to their definition of it.* Therefore, the principle of self-determination that emerged from the peace settlement and its aftermath was based on the allied policy of self-determination, as it was defined by them, and as it was implemented on the basis of their authority. Thus, in order to fulfill our task of ascertaining the general definition of the principle, we must first find out the nature of the allied policy on it.

What, then, was the allied policy of self-determination? As we have seen, although the policy was implemented after the war, the statements outlining the policy itself were being made by spokesmen of the allied cause long before the war ended. It seems logical, therefore, to start the investigation with statements in which the term "self-determination" was actually used. It seems appropriate to take as our starting point the pertinent statements of President Wilson, who, as we have argued above, was recognized as the chief spokesman of the allied powers.

The Allied Definition of
Self-Determination

Perhaps the most celebrated statement made by Woodrow Wilson in which he actually mentions the term "self-determination" and outlines his Four Additional Principles appears in the following passage from his February 11, 1918, speech to Congress:

> Peoples are not to be handed about from one sovereignty to another by an international conference or an undertaking between rivals and antagonists. National aspirations must be respected; peoples may now be dominated and governed only by their own consent. "Self determination" is not a mere phrase. It is an imperative principle of action which statesmen will henceforth ignore at their peril.[20]

In the above passage, the principle of self-determination is associated with two concepts: namely, (1) boundaries between sovereignties should be changed only with the consent of the population; and (2) that the aspirations of national groups should be respected. These same two principles were formally put forth in the same speech as two of the Four Additional Principles that were to supplement the Fourteen Points as the basis of the peace, as follows:

> Second, that peoples and provinces are not to be bartered about from

sovereignty to sovereignty as if they were mere chattels and pawns in a game. . . .

Fourth, that well defined national aspirations shall be accorded the utmost satisfaction that can be accorded them without introducing new or perpetuating old elements of discord and antagonims that would be likely in time to break the peace of Europe and consequently of the world.[21]

On the basis of the above discussion, it may be concluded that for President Wilson the principle of self-determination was associated with both "principles" outlined above. But, also, that the "principles" themselves were considered by their author to be sufficiently different from each other that they were presented as two separate and distinct policy directives. What this conclusion suggests is that these two directives, although different from each other, both spring from the same general and fundamental principle, so that they represent specific applications of this more general principle. The nature of the connection between the principle of self-determination and these two prescriptions is that the principle of self-determination is the general principle and the two prescriptions are specific applications of it.

As already noted, in presenting his peace program, Woodrow Wilson was formalizing and systematizing some of the opinions and policies that the allied powers had been developing in the course of the war.[22] Therefore, an examination of some of the nationality policies of the allied powers as they developed in the earlier phases of the war might provide some understanding of the nature of the principle of self-determination, the specific applications of which President Wilson presented later in his Four Additional Principles.

In a statement on allied war aims, presented on January 10, 1917, in response to President Wilson's Peace Note, the allied powers declared that their aims were *inter alia:*

> . . . the reorganization of Europe, guaranteed by a stable regime and based at once on *respect of nationalities.* . . . the *liberation* of the Italians, as also of the Slavs, Roumanians and Czecho-Slovaks *from foreign domination,* the *setting free* of the populations subject to the blood tyranny of the Turks. . . .[23]

The key concept in the above passage is the idea of liberating nationalities from alien rule; that is, the principle of national liberation, which, as we have already observed, was generally considered at that time to be synonymous with the principle of national self-determination. So that when the allied powers in their statement of war aims committed themselves to the principle of national liberation, they were committing themselves, by definition, to the principle of national self-determination. Conversely, when the allied powers spoke of a policy of self-determination, they meant by it a policy of national liberation. President Wilson's principles were thus meant to be specific applications of the more fundamental principle of national liberation.[24]

By what logic, one might ask, was the principle of national liberation transformed into the two specific prescriptions? Actually, the logical connection between the principle of national liberation and the directive that national aspirations should be respected is easily apparent. As it was manifestly obvious at the time, the subject nationalities were aspiring to—and indeed fighting for—their liberation. Under those circumstances, respecting the aspirations of nationalities was tantamount to liberating the nationalities.

The connection between the principle of national liberation and the other principle—the right of people to choose their own sovereignty—is less obvious. In fact, the principle did not begin to develop until the final stages of the war, when the allies suddenly began to realize that territorial changes of great magnitude would unavoidably have to be made. It was true indeed that allied powers had officially committed themselves to the principle of national liberation as early as January 1917. However, by liberation, they meant in general the achievement by the nationalities of a status of autonomy within existing political boundaries.[25] They certainly did not intend to affect sweeping changes in territorial sovereignty by extricating the subject nationalities from their states making them independent, except in the case of Poland. In fact, up until the beginning of 1918, the relationship between the principle of self-determination, or national liberation, and changes in territorial sovereignty was only dimly recognized by the allies.[26] Not only did the allies not desire sweeping territorial changes and the creation of many new independent states but also they did not anticipate such an occurrence, for the subject nationalities themselves were at that point far from demanding total political independence. Most of them seemed to convey the impression through their propagandist literature that the satisfaction of their nationalist aspirations could be achieved by various formulas of political or cultural autonomy short of total independence. Under those circumstances the expression of the principle of national liberation and self-determination in the form of the directive that national aspirations should be respected seemed to satisfy the subject nationalities, the allied powers, and the conditions of the international situation.

In the last phases of the war, the entire situation changed drastically. First, some of the subject nationalities began to adopt the notion that their national aspirations could no longer be acheived by mere autonomy but rather by the attainment of full political independence.[27] As part of their national existence, these nationalities had organized national provisional governments; some of them had even become members of the alliance and were making a creditable contribution to the defeat of the central powers.[28] Also, as part of their national existence, they laid claims to what they considered to be their national territories. At this point, it became clear to the allied powers that their original desire to see the empires maintained was fast becoming irrelevant and that these nationalities were going to attempt to make those changes in territorial sovereignty that they considered necessary for their national existence.[29]

Second, the allies won the war, and as a result, those territories that were being claimed by the allied nationalities and some neutrals were ceded by the central powers to the allied powers. Therefore, the allied powers collectively acquired sovereignty over those territories. As a result, the responsibility for disbursing these territories among the various claimants fell to the allies. Of course, the allied powers had already committed themselves to the idea that the principle of self-determination was the most important principle for which they were fighting. Therefore, as it became increasingly clear that the allied powers would have to preside over territorial changes of such magnitude, it became urgently necessary for them to develop an operative principle, consistent with the principle of national self-determination, that would provide the guidelines for determining the validity of the expected territorial claims.

The directive that appeared as the application of the principle of self-determination was basically Woodrow Wilson's, and the logic by which it was developed shows the American origins of Wilson's political philosophy and the close integration and consistency with which he deduced his policy proposals from this philosophy.

According to Wilson, what the problem called for, like all other problems of practical politics, was the application of the basic tenets of his political philosophy. The principle of self-determination as it had been formulated did not anticipate sweeping territorial changes. But as they began to seem inevitable, he basically saw the problem of how to settle the new territorial boundaries in a way consistent with the requirements of the principle of self-determination. Or conversely, how can the principle of self-determination be applied to the task of establishing new territorial boundaries? To respond to the problem, Wilson went back to the philosophical foundations of this theory of self-determination, which, for Wilson, was direct derivative of the principle of popular sovereignty that is expressed in the Virginia Bill of Rights as "A people has a right to do anything they please with their own country and their own government,"[30] on which the constitution, the independence, and the very existence of the United States was based, and which Wilson proudly advanced as the creed of all free men. So final was the derivation of the principle of self-determination from the idea of popular sovereignty that for Wilson the two concepts were almost synonymous.[31] Therefore, the application of the principle of self-determination to the settlement of territorial boundaries would require a policy based on the principle of popular sovereignty. In other words, the application of the principle of self-determination to territorial settlement requires that the boundaries be established on the basis of popular sovereignty, that is, on the wishes of the population. As he clearly indicates in the following statement, his directive that people should not be handed from one sovereignty to another like property, without regard to their own wishes, was based on his concept of the principle of government by the consent of the governed, or popular sovereignty:

> ... no peace can last or ought to last which does not recognize and accept the principle that *governments derive all their just powers from the consent of the governed,* and that no right anywhere exists to hand peoples about sovereignty to sovereignty as if they were property.[32]

An even more explicit formulation of this application of the principle of popular sovereignty was presented by Woodrow Wilson in his famous Mount Vernon speech of July 4, 1918, in which he asserted that:

> ... the settlement of every question, whether of territory, of sovereignty, of economic arrangement, or of political relationship, upon the basis of the free acceptance of that settlement by the people immediately concerned. . . .[33]

It is important to note that, consistent with the classical conception of popular sovereignty evidence in the French and American revolutions, President Wilson was insisting on the requirement of the consent of the people not only for settling territorial questions but for deciding all questions affecting them.

The Application of Allied Policy

At the time the peace conference met, the principle of national self-determination was expressed by the allied powers as two policy directives, namely, (1) national aspirations should be respected; and (2) changes in territorial sovereignty must be based on the consent of the population of the area in question. However, by the time the conference met, most of the "well-defined nationalities" that were going to be liberated had already achieved independence.[34] Therefore, the problem facing the conference was not one of liberating nationalities but was one of drawing the territorial boundaries of the new states created by the liberated nationalities. Under these circumstances, the principle of respecting national aspirations was largely irrelevant to the work of the conference. The problem was basically one of settling territorial claims, and it called for the application of the principle that the people had the right to choose their own sovereignty. Thus, the second application of the principle of self-determination, that is, that any disposition of territory should be based on the population, became the keynote of the allied policy of self-determination at the peace conference. This keynote is reflected in the resolutions by which the Council of Ten established the five territorial commissions that were authorized to "consult the representatives of the people concerned.[35]

In the application of this principle, it was necessary to establish guidelines for determining the wishes of a given population. At the outset, there seems to have been divided opinion among the allied powers about what constitutes a valid method of deciding on the wishes of the people. British official opinion seemed to support the thesis that the way to ascertain them was by holding plebiscites.[36] The French delegation seemed to be in general accordance with the. British view that the application of the principle of self-determination should be by free and secret vote, with certain reservations.[37] However, U.S. delegation was entirely opposed to the idea of using plebiscites or any other similar method of consulting the people. In the view of the American delegation, the application of the principle required the demarcation of territorial lines on the basis of nationality. Therefore, in general, they advocated that information pertaining to nationality of peoples be acquired by "impartial census" or "impartial investigation" and that the territorial boundaries be based on the statistics thus acquired.[38] The Italian delegation was most categorically against the use of plebiscites.[39]

These differences of opinion expressed in allied memoranda about acquiring evidence about the wishes of a population were inconsequential. In dealing with the cases, the allied powers developed a practice that cumulatively established policy. The allied policy, as indicated in the cases in which they did apply the principle of self-determination, although it was not used in all cases, was that the nationality of a border population was the valid indication of their wishes and that a plebiscite was therefore generally unnecessary. The only cases in which the allies were willing to suggest or countenance plebiscites were those in which there was an extreme mixture of national groups, or in cases in which the allied powers were having difficulty deciding between the counterclaims of their own allies and thought they could escape the dilemma by using a plebiscite. A total of twelve plebiscites were written into the various peace treaties. In all these cases, and in the case of others that were proposed during the peace conference, the plebiscites were proposed as compromise solutions to save the allied powers from having to make politically difficult choices. As Sarah Wambaugh asserts:

> It is true that the Allies avoided a plebiscite in every region of first importance save that of Upper Silesia and that when they resorted to a plebiscite

it was as a method of comprise to escape from a dilemma rather than a deliberate choice.[40]

The acceptance by the allied powers of the nationality of peoples as evidence of their wishes with regard to territorial disposition was not accidental but was a conscious allied policy, and it received explicit formulation in several official allied statements. for instance, after the allied powers had decided to cede the Burgenland to Austria, the Austrian government had requested that a plebiscite be held in the area so that they could be sure of the loyalty of the population there. The allied powers refused to conduct the plebiscite on the grounds that:

> ... the ethnic character of the population too clearly indicated their attachment to Austria for the Powers to think it necessary to resort to a plebiscite. . . .[41]

Again, in response to Hungarian protests over the cession of Hungarian territory without Plebiscite,[42] the allied powers in their Coventry letter of the draft treaty presented to the Hungarian delegates, May 6, 1919, stated:

> As regards the question of plebiscites the Allied Powers considered them needless, when they perceived with certainty that this consultation, if surrounded with complete guarantees of certainty, would not give results substantially different from those at which they had arrived *after a minute study of the ethnographic conditions and national aspirations.*[43]

In short, the allied powers were contending that the will of the population could be established simply by ascertaining the nationality of the border populations. This was based on their belief that the nationalities wanted to join the state that was controlled by members of their own nationality, thereby liberating themselves and losing their former position as an "oppressed" or "subject" nationality. On this basis, the allied powers concluded that the application of the principle of national self-determination to the territorial question called for the demarcation of the territorial boundaries along lines of ethnicity, or nationality. Thus, as it finally emerged, the method by which the allied policy of self-determination was applied was, in the words of Woodrow Wilson himself, ". . . to make an equitable distribution of territories according to the race, the ethnographic character of the people inhabiting those territories."[44]

82

This drawing of territorial boundaries on the basis of ethnographic data was not, however, the only method by which the allies applied the principle of self-determination. Even before the conference met, it was generally realized that this particular method of applying the principle could not be suited to the actual conditions of all the subject nationalities that were desirous of being *liberated*. First, it was fairly obvious, as David Lloyd George asserts, that "no matter how frontiers may be drawn or redrawn, even considerable minorities must in all cases remain on the wrong side of every one of them."[45] Also, "not only on frontiers but far into the interior where there existed an inextricable mixture of races and a confusion of tongues which rivalled Babel.[46] Under these conditions, it was clearly impossible for the allies to draw up state boundaries that would coincide with nationality lines, even if they wanted to. Nevertheless, the allied powers felt that this kind of difficulty did not and could not exempt them from their pledge to *liberate* all subject nationalities. Indeed, the very same condition of extreme ethnic mixture demanded that they proceed on the basis of "self-determination and the consent of the governed" if they were going to achieve a just and lasting peace.[47]

In the early days of the war, many peace organizations and nationality organizations had been formulating proposals by which some scattered nationalities could achieve self-determination within existing territorial boundaries.[48] And just prior to the peace conference anticipated territorial problems began to force the attention of the allied governments toward similar speculations. Of the many proposals that emerged, the Smuts Plan deserves our attention, because it provides some insight into what the allied powers meant by the principle of self-determination.

The Smuts Plan called for the League of Nations to be the reversionary with regards to the "peoples and territories formerly belonging to Russia, Austria-Hungary and Turkey," with the responsibility for their "ultimate disposal." In the performance of this function, the league was to apply the principle of self-determination.[49] The plan goes on to indicate that in the application of this principle consideration must be given to the fact that "when these territories and peoples come to be considered individually it will be found that their conditions for self-determination and autonomy or self-government vary considerably." The plan delineates three general types of territories and then recommends the method of applying the principle most suited to each type. First, there were territories capable of statehood (such as Finland and Poland) for which the recommended method of application is the recognition of its independence. The second type is a territory that is capable of some sort of autonomous existence but incapable of full independence (such as Transcaucasia or Georgia). For this type, the plan recommended that the league guarantee its autonomous existence within another state. Finally, there is a type of territory wherein, "owing chiefly to the hexterogeneous character of the population and their incapacity for administrative cooperation, autonomy in any real sense would be out of the question." The plan recommended that this type be administered as a mandated territory under the authority of the League of Nations, but a mandatory power chosen by the league with the consent of the population, if possible, according to the principle of self-determination.

For the purpose of this work, the chief value of the Smuts Plan lies in the fact that it highlights the allied powers' attitude that the principle of self-determination could be applied in a number of ways depending on the political realities of each situation. In so doing, it helps to separate conceptually the principle from its mode of application. Furthermore, it focuses attention on the fact that all these modes of application were intended to achieve the same goal of self-determination, which can then be seen, in general terms, as the elimination of the subordinate or "oppressed" status of the nationalities or groups in question. The Smuts Plan had only a limited influence in the development of the entire conference and the league. Even in the evolution of the mandates system, where it had the most influence, it underwent several critical changes before the final version.[50] It is clear, however, that the basic rationale that went into the formulation of the Smuts Plan also inspired the system of minority guarantees, the mandates system, and other subsequent actions of the League of Nations.[51]

The Minorities Protection System

When the allied powers decided on the system of guaranteeing minority rights as an alternative way of applying the principle of self-determination to the nationality problem, they were in fact returning to the definition of self-determination that they had held earlier; that is, that "The requirements of self-determination might be met by assuring autonomy and self-government to every people as a component member of a regional federation."[52]

There was no systematic statement of the general purposes of the peace treaties, however, it seems from the discussions preliminary to the drafting and the nature of the treaties that the intent of the allied powers was to guarantee to some national minorities a measure of autonomy within the new states. According to the various instruments that established the minorities protection system,[53] those whose rights were to be guaranteed were designated as "persons belonging to racial, religious or linguistic minorities."[54] There is no doubt that this designation was meant to apply to national minorities.[55] However, it was meant to apply to all known minorities[56] and from the standpoint of the minorities protection system, no further differentiation was made between national minorities on the basis of territoriality, minimum size, or community of history or psychology.[57]

The only qualification of the nationality that had to be protected is implied by the nature of the states on which the system was imposed. The allied powers took pains to explain that the mere existence of a minority nationality did not impose on the state an obligation to accept to adopt a system of guarantees of the rights of that minority. The obligation existed in a situation where historical and other circumstances suggested that that minority was likely to be oppressed. In the words of Woodrow Wilson, the allies were interested in guaranteeing against "the treatment which might in certain circumstances be meted out to minorities.[58] Thus, they thought it necessary to require the guarantees in the areas in which they feared that the minorities would be reduced to the status of the "oppressed" if the system of guarantees were not instituted.[59]

Under the league system, the rights that were to be guaranteed to the minorities fell into two categories. First, members of all nationalities, including minorities, were entitled to full rights of citizenship (and option), including rights of life, liberty, and religious freedom, and complete equality of all citizens, irrespective of nationality, with respect to civil, legal, and political rights. Second, members of minorities were guaranteed the right to the free use of their languages in a variety of situations, including before the courts and in their own charitable, educational, and religious and social institutions, which they had a right to organize and control at their own expense, and where they form a "considerable proportion of the population," with the aid of "an equitable share" of public funds. In addition, minority children were to be instructed in their own language in areas where they formed a considerable proportion of the population.[60]

It is clear from the above, that the minorities guarantee system was not designed merely to guard against possible discrimination directed toward a minority. It goes further than a mere assurance of nondiscrimination and attempts to provide for the minorities the opportunity to "preserve and develop their national culture and consciousness." In fact, to maintain the distinctive national characteristics and traditions of the minorities was the *raison d'etre* of the system, and it attempted to accomplish it by guaranteeing to the minorities a system of national-cultural autonomy.[61]

The new states were seriously opposed to the system of minority guarantees that were imposed on them, and accepted them with a great deal of reluctance and protest. Representatives of these states argued that the application of this system to them alone amounted to foreign intervention and an infringement on their sovereignty.[62] As important as this reason was, the most important objection of the new states was the fact that the rights to be granted under the system were those of national-cultural autonomy and would thus tend to perpetuate the minorities as a distinct element within those states. For their part, they were willing to grant to their minorities all of the rights of other citizens without discrimination. However, they were vehemently opposed to any system that would "impede the process of natural assimilation" of the minorities or encourage them to perpetuate their sense of separateness.[63] Prior to the war, many of the representatives of these new states, still in the position of subject nationalities, had been very instrumental in the development of the concept of cultural autonomy as an application of the principle of self-determination. Nevertheless, they were now committed to the idea that their states were national states, and their real intention was to subject the minorities to "painless assimilation," and create united nation-states.[64]

The League of Nations Mandates System

Before the end of the war, some allied statesmen had expressed the idea that the principle of self-determination was to be applied to all territorial questions, including the overseas territories.[65] However, when they began to consider these territories, they realized that none of the ways by which they had applied the principle of self-determination was suitable in this case. First, the delineation of territorial boundaries on the basis of ethnicity was quite inappropriate, because the problem of territorial boundaries was either nonexistent or quite peripheral.[66] Second, the concept of granting self-determination to peoples by recognizing their independence or granting them autonomy was unfeasible, because in the view of the allied powers, the inhabitants of these areas were incapable of governing themselves.[67] One way of resolving this problem, advocated by General Smuts and supported by many of the allied powers was the annexation, pure and simple, of these areas by the allies.[68] The position lost out to the one advocated by President Wilson that the dilemma did not absolve the allied powers from their responsibility and pledge to affect a general application of the principle of self-determination, and that another way just had to be found to dispose of these territories in accordance with the basic requirements of the principle of self-determination, that is, in accordance with the interests and desires of the people concerned. In the words of President Wilson:

> Some institutions must be found to carry out the ideas all had in mind, namely the development of the country for the benefit of those already in it, and for the advantage of those who will live there later. . . .[69]

The mandates system was born out of the attempt to find such an institution.

The mandates system derived its theoretical basis from the concepts of trusteeship and tutelage that for some time has been advocated in the literature of colonial administration.[70] These concepts implied that the rule over backward peoples should be viewed as a trust undertaken by an imperial power for the development of those people toward maturity and independence.[71]

It was essentially this principle that General Smuts presented to the peace conference as part of his plan for the application of the principle of self-determination. The Smuts Plan was the basis on which subsequent drafts of the mandates system were based. However, the credit for universalizing the principle and applying it to the former colonies of Germany must go to President Wilson. In his original plan, General Smuts had anticipated the application of the mandates principle to the peoples of territories that had been under the sovereignty of Russia, Austro-Hungary, and Turkey who could not administer themselves, and excluded the former colonies of Germany in Africa and the Pacific on grounds that the peoples in those territories were incapable of self-government. President Wilson decided to exclude Russian territory from the scope of the mandates system for the reason that its application to conditions in that area would be both undesirable and impracticable. Furthermore, the feeling developed among President Wilson's advisors that General Smuts' exclusion of territories in Africa and the Pacific was not only an attempt to provide a justification for territorial annexations planned by South Africa and other Commonwealth powers but was also inconsistent.[72] For how can a system designed for communities that were incapable of self-government be inapplicable to peoples because they are deemed incapable of self-government?

The final molding of the mandates principle into a system was far from uneventful. Several compromises had to be made between those who preferred outright annexation of the territories and those who wanted a full application of the mandates principle, as is evidenced by the creation of the three types of mandated territories and the distribution of the mandates.[73]

Article 22 of the League of Nations Covenant, which is the formal basis of the Mandates system, is a legal purist's nightmare, and unsurprisingly, it has attracted a variety of contradictory interpretations.[74] Also, there are many interesting questions about that document and the mandates system as a whole, such as, for instance, the sincerity of the allied powers' pledge to act in good faith as trustees of the peoples of the mandated territories. However, these are beyond the scope of this work, which is mainly concerned with investigating the meaning ascribed by the allied powers to the principle of self-determination. In order to do this, we have to attempt to establish the status of the units to which the system was to be applied and what its purpose was.

According to Article 22, the mandates system applies to some specified "colonies and territories ... which are inhabited by people not yet able to stand by themselves under the strenuous conditions of the modern world," and its purpose was to secure "the well-being and development of such peoples" by placing them under the tutelage of more "advanced nations" acting as mandatories on behalf of the League of Nations.

The significance of the mandates system is that its ultimate objective provides us with additional insight into the allied definition of self-determination. According to the text, this ultimate objective was to secure the "development" of peoples who were "not yet able to stand by themselves." The expression "not yet" is extremely significant, for it implies that the allied powers anticipated that at a later point in their development these peoples would be able to "stand by themselves." In this regard, it should be noted that the expression was a deliberate choice of the drafters, not the product of an accident in the construction.[75] Furthermore, the concept of tutelage indicates that the function of the mandates system was to lead these peoples to that point at which they would graduate from their wardship status and be mature enough to stand by themselves. That this was the logic of the sytem is indicated by Woodrow Wilson's assertion, in his Fourth Covenant draft of February 2, 1919, that each mandatory:

> ... shall adopt as the object of all tutelary functions discharged by it the development of that people, in as short a time as possible, into a political unit which can fully take charge of its own affairs, determine its own connections and choose its own policy.[76]

In fact, the concept of tutelage is illogical unless its success is defined in terms of the development or tutoring the ward toward a status of maturity and self-sufficiency. It can be said, therefore, that the logic as well as the intent of the mandate system was the development of the peoples to a point at which they would be capable of exercising their right of self-determination. As Quincy Wright puts it:

Article 22, however, seeks not so much to define a status as to guide an evolution. It attempts not merely to provide for the transfer of the territories and for the government of their inhabitants, but for the evolution in them of communities eventually capable of self-determination.[77]

What is not so clear, in the text of Article 22 as well as in the practice of the League of Nations, is the political form that was envisaged as the fulfillment of the right of self-determination. In general, the exercise of the right implies that the unit is to be self-governing. This general definition of self-determination seems to have been the one used by the league in this situation. For instance, the eighth session of the Permanent Mandates Commission accepted as being in "strict harmony with the letter and spirit of Article 22 of the covenant...,"[78] the idea that:

The mandate is a provisionary system designed to enable populations which, politically speaking, are still minors to educate themselves so as to arrive one day at full *self-government*.[79]

When it came down to the kind of self-government anticipated, some disagreement emerged. Article 22 of the League Covenant indicates that for some of these peoples—those in the A mandates—independent statehood was anticipated. In the case of the other types of mandates, some members of the Mandates Commission saw the end result of the system as creating self-governing societies culturally distinct and politically independent from the mandatory power[80] while others advocated a "slow, unforced assimilation of weak or inferior communities by strong or more highly developed communities."[81] From our standpoint, the difference between these two interpretations is insignificant. The important point is that whichever viewpoint is adopted, the only possible conclusion is that the people of a mandated territory were eventually supposed to develop the capacity to exercise their right of self-determination.[82]

If, as we have demonstrated above, the form that this exercise of self-determination was to take was either by the achievement of independence or by being incorporated on the basis of equality into the mandatory state, then it must be concluded that within the theory and practice of the mandates sytem, the allied powers were proceeding on the basis of the idea that *self-determination means the attainment of full self-*

government. As to the nature of the units that have a right of self-determination, the mandates system suggests two important attributes. First, it must be a group of persons within a specified territory, and second, it must be a group that was not self-governing at the time in question. These two criteria are not new. The mandates system's unique contribution to an understanding of the principle of self-determination is that it highlights the requirement of the capacity of the unit to exercise sovereignty in accordance to standards acceptable to the international community. As we have pointed out, the principle of self-determination was not applied to these territories at the outset, because the people that inhabited them were deemed unprepared to exercise their sovereign independence in ways satisfactory to the standards of the "civilized" states. The rationale for placing these territories under tutelage, rather than annexing them, was that the incapacity of these people to govern themselves did not extinguish their right to do so, for after undergoing a period of tutelage, they would develop this capacity and thus be able to activate and effectively exercise their right of self-determination. This construction raises two important questions, namely, (1) what body is competent to determine at what point in their development the people of a mandated territory should be considered mature enough to be qualified to exercise their right of self-determination; and (2) by what criteria is such a determination to be made?

According to the intent of the mandates system, people of the territory were supposed to be ready to emerge from the wardship status into maturity when they showed themselves as being capable of standing alone. The mandate system was not only a system of establishing the status of the peoples of the mandated territory but was also a system that contemplated an eventual and prescribed change in their status, so that, by establishing the mandates system, the League of Nations was stipulating, first, that there should be a period of tutelage and, second, that this tutelage should be terminated at the proper time. The league, however, did not specify the machinery for making the decision as to what the proper time would be. However, it seems clear that being the originator of the system, the league also had the competence to recognize at what point the aims of the system had been achieved and to change the status

91

of those peoples at the appropriate time. As Quincy Wright puts it, "Thus the League of Nations seems competent and alone competent to change the status of territory now under Article 22."[83]

The question of the criteria for determining this point is more complicated. According to the logic of the system, the point is reached when the people can stand by themselves. To say that a group of people will be allowed to stand by themselves when they are able to do so is not very helpful, for it does not indicate how one would recognize this capacity, or what phenomena would amount to valid evidence of this capacity. In fact, the concept of "standing by themselves" in international society may be viewed in terms of both its internal and external attributes. Article 22 provides no concrete indicators of either.

With regard to the internal attributes of the peoples of a mandated territory, the provisional recognition in Article 22, paragraph 4 of the communities in the A mandates as independent nations may provide some basis for inference. The independent nationhood specified in this article probably means internal self-government just short of full independence, because it was "subject to the rendering of administrative advice and assistance by a Mandatory until such time as they are able to stand alone."[84] The status of an independent nation may thus be seen as the final stage in the development of the mandates before full independence and self-determination. As the text indicates, the recognition of this final stage is based on the existence therein of a *community* that is politically and socially advanced.[85]

It would seem, therefore, that at least one evidence of the maturity of a mandated territory that would qualify it for internal self-government would be the existence of a well-organized, coherent community. The stipulation in Article 22, paragraph 4 of the covenant, that for A mandates, "The wishes of these communities must be a principal consideration in the selection of the Mandatory," suggests that according to the allies an important difference between these and the other types of mandates was that these could express a political consensus. This probably means that in this system one of the qualifications for internal self-government was that the community be organized enough to be able to express a political consensus, presumably through some representative process.

Once the peoples of a mandated territory achieve internal self-government, their final emergence into full participation in international affairs as an independent state depends on more qualifications, namely, the acquisition of political institutions, control over the population, a defined territory, and the capacity and willingness to meet international obligations.[86] In general, the accordance of recognition by one state to another is largely discretionary. However, in a situation in which the unit claiming statehood is emerging out of mandate status, the recognition of its independence by the majority of the states would probably depend on the institution that is responsible for the mandates system—the League of Nations.[87] Of course, the very fact that the community in question emerged from a mandate imposes an obligation on the league to recognize its independence. The system of mandates, as we have explained, is designed to develop a group of people from one status (mandated territory) to another (independent state), and it would be illogical to terminate the tutelary stage on the basis of the group's newfound capacity to stand alone while at the same time declining to inaugurate the beginning of its "standing alone" stage.

Because it is a system designated to prepare communities for the eventual exercise of their right of self-determination, the mandates system, by implication, provides an understanding of the principle of self-determination as it was understood by the allied powers. According to the foregoing analysis of the mandates system, it seems that the allied powers defined self-determination as self-government either by independence or in association with the mandatory power, and they defined the community that was deemed to have that right as a territorially based, coherent community that is non-self-governing.

Conclusion

The establishment of the territorial boundaries in Europe, the system of the protection of minorities, and the mandates system of the League of Nations were undoubtedly three of the most important aspects of the entire program of reconstruction that the allied powers had planned for the new era of international relations based on peace and justice. For a number of reasons, including the self-interest of the allied powers themselves, the principles were not always applied. However, to the extent that they were applied, their rationale and their actual operation suggest that they had one thing in common: they were designed to insure the removal of conscious and recognizable communities from foreign domination, restoring their destiny into their own hands, as far as was possible, within the framework of a stable international community.

The allied commitment to liberate such groups from servitude was based on their belief that it was both unjust and detrimental to international peace and security for one group of people to subjugate another group. Therefore, any subjugated group should become self-governing. In broad terms, this principle, that subjugated groups should be made self-governing, is what came to be known as the principle of self-determination. Thus, in asserting that they were going to apply this principle in the settlement of postwar problems, they meant that they were going to solve the problems in such a way that, as far as conceivable, no groups would be left in a position of subjugation. Therefore, the allied programs were designed to the following: establish state boundaries on lines of ethnicity, guarantee national-cultural autonomy, and tutor communities without making them subjects. These were all particular solutions to problems that had to be faced as part of the peace settlement in order to meet the requirements of the principle of self-determination.

It is generally said that the efforts of the allied powers to achieve the objectives of the principle by instituting these programs were not entirely successful. First, these programs did not always represent a consistent application of the principle of self-determination. The allied powers did not believe that the principle should be applied to the exclusion of all others, and sometimes they refused to apply it when it seemed that their own interests might be adversely affected.[88] Second, in some cases, the smooth application of the programs was hampered by obstructionist tactics of the parties involved, none of whom found the programs entirely satisfactory.[89] Third the success of the programs were sometimes inhibited by unclarified objectives and inconsistencies that were never completely resolved.[90] A general survey or evaluation of these programs is outside the scope of this work; however, what needs to be emphatically stated is that, whatever the problems encountered, these programs were important processes from which emerged the broad formulation of the principle of self-determination that was accepted by the allied powers as well as the new and the defeated states.[91]

According to this formulation, the principle of self-determination in general terms means that a group of subject peoples should become self-governing. In the application of this general principle to the different situations that had to be faced, it became clear that the formulation had to be made more specific. At the beginning, there was an attempt to define the term "nationality," which was then generally applied to the European groups demanding to be "liberated" from alien subjugation. The attempt to define "nationality" did not yield any fruitful results. It was discovered that it was not only impossible to find a general description that would fit all the groups that were generally called nationalities but also that the basis on which many of these groups identified themselves varied from common ethnicity to common culture or common religion.[92] Finally, in defining the group of people who should become self-governing according to the principle of self-determination, the term nationality was discarded. What emerged in its place was a political community, irrespective of its psychological or historical basis. For a group to which the principle of self-determination was to be applied, the crucial characteristic was that it be under the subjugation of an alien group.

The way in which the principle of self-determination was to be applied in a particular situation was deemed to depend on the nature of the groups involved. The allied powers were willing to recognize the total political independence of those subject communities in a compact territory that was physically separate or separable from the dominant community. Because most of these, however, were interspersed between dominant communities, it was decided that it would be better to "liberate" such communities without changing political boundaries and possibly unstabilizing the international system by creating a multitude of ministates. This "liberation" took the form of guaranteed equality and cultural autonomy of all the communities within the states. In areas where the communities were not fully developed, the people were not to be made subjects of any other groups, but they were to be put under tutelage until they had developed the necessary consciousness of community and the capacity for self-government.[93] In all these different cases, the common factor was that the principle of self-determination, based on allied utterances and, more important, their programs and policies, was defined thusly: a self-conscious community that was subject to an alien group should be permitted to become and to stay self-governing.

The principle of self-determination, thus defined, was considered by the allies as one of the most important bases of the new international order. To be sure, the allied powers never claimed that the subject communities had a right of self-determination under international law, except as it accrued from the international obligations of states created by international agreements, such as the Mandatory Agreements. However, they considered it an "imperative principle of political action," and it was considered so important that even with its difficulties it emerged, after the breakdown of the European political system, in the Atlantic Charter and, finally, in the U.N. Charter, perhaps the most universal and significant international instrument of our time.

CHAPTER V

SELF-DETERMINATION IN THE ERA OF DECOLONIZA-
TION:

U.N. CHARTER AND PRACTICE

At the end of World War II, the concept of self-determination was reintroduced into the international political arena as a component part of the allied program for the organization of a stable international order. From this standpoint, the parallel between the last stages of the two World Wars is quite striking. In much the same way as they had done in the first situation, the allied powers began to systematize and articulate their war aims and peace goals as soon as they began to realize that as victors the reorganization of the world would be theirs. As before, they were attempting to establish some principles that could underpin international peace and security by providing mechanisms for eliminating or solving conflicts. And just as they had done in the past, they tended to focus on attempting to find principles to cope with the particular conflicts that had led to the war they were fighting.

In the perception of the allied powers, issues involving the principle of self-determination were almost negligible as contributors to the war, and they did not seem to offer any particular difficulties in the future, and, therefore, the principle did not receive as prominent a place among Allied peace aims as it had at Versailles.[1]

In preparing their postwar plans, the attention of the allied powers, particularly Britain and the United States, was drawn to some territorial problems in eastern Europe that the war itself had created.[2] It was mainly in response to these territorial issues that they reactivated the principle of self-determination. Thus, the formulation of the principle that they chose to apply

97

to territorial disputes was the same as the one advocated earlier by Woodrow Wilson. This is evident in the text of the principles adopted by the allies, as well as in the subsequent comments of allied leaders.

The first statement of the allied principles was made when, in August 1941, Franklin D. Roosevelt and Winston Churchill signed the Atlantic Charter. In Articles 2 and 3 of this World War II equivalent of the Fourteen Points, the two leaders committed their countries to the principle of self-determination.

> Second, they desire to see no territorial changes that do not accord with the freely expressed wishes of the people concerned;
> Third, they respect the right of all peoples to choose the form of government under which they wish to live; and they wish to see sovereign rights and self-government restored to those who have been forcibly deprived of them . . .

In the above passage, there is an unmistakable echo of Wilson's pronouncements of the principle of self-determination.[3] This resemblance is not accidental. The cosignatories of the Atlantic Charter consciously modeled their principle on the Wilsonian concept of self-determination, which, as we have seen above, principally used plebiscites to settle territorial disputes. This conscious imitation of the Wilsonian concept and its application by plebiscite is illustrated in this memorandum from Roosevelt, written a few days after the signing of the Atlantic Charter:

> The self-determination of boundaries and forms of governments was the most substantial contribution made by the Versailles Treaty—i.e., the plebiscite method, which, on the whole was successful. This method can be extended in the case of certain populations and areas which have conducted century-old feuds. As an example, the people of Croatia should not be forced into a government with the Serbs, or with the Italians, or with the Hungarians, or compulsory independence by themselves, without an expression of their own views.[4]

From the time of the signing of the Atlantic Charter and its acceptance by the Declaration of the United Nations, the principle of self-determination was considered one of the principles of allied postwar policy. However, between 1941 and the signing of the U.N. Charter, allied conversations about the principle of self-determination seemed to be concerned less and less with the use of plebiscites in the settlement of territorial disputes and more and more with the liberation of colonial territories. In order to explain this developing conversion, it is necessary to sketch briefly what transpired between the Atlantic Charter and the U.N. Charter.

The Evolution of the New Allied "Policy" of Self-Determination

Just as Woodrow Wilson had been mainly responsible for the crystallization of the allied commitment to apply the principle of national self-determination to the subject nationalities, it was mainly President Roosevelt, Secretary of State Hull, and the U.S. government that led the allied powers into making a commitment to apply the principle to colonial peoples.

At the time of the signing of the Atlantic Charter, both Britain and the United States had colonial policies that were in general accord with the principle of trusteeship.[5] However, neither President Roosevelt nor Prime Minister Churchill saw the necessity to undertake a formal commitment, in an international instrument, to apply the principle of self-determination to their colonial territories. The formulation and administration of colonial policy was not considered an international matter, and there was no reason to make an exception in this case, because in their judgement colonial issues had no bearing on international peace and security.[6]

By the spring of 1942, however, the conviction was beginning to grow in the mind of President Roosevelt and in the Department of State that in view of the increasing strength of colonial nationalism the whole question of colonial administration might have ominous implications for international peace and order,[7] and, therefore, it would be necessary to enunciate U.S. policy on colonial territories clearly and formally. The formulation of such an official statement was not difficult. U.S. Official policy, as well as the general feeling of informed groups, had always upheld the view, going back to the American Revolution, that colonial peoples had a right to self-government and independence; that is to say, they had a right of self-determination. Therefore, the general feeling in the government at this time was as expressed by Under Secretary of State Welles, "The principles of the Atlantic Charter must be guaranteed to the world as a whole—in all oceans and in all continents."[8]

Official U.S. policy on colonial peoples, as it emerged after some discussion in the government, was expressed by Secretary Hull as a commitment " . . . to support the attainment of freedom by all peoples who, by their acts, show themselves worthy of it and ready for it."[9] As stated here, the U.S. government's policy toward colonial peoples is based on the principle of trusteeship. It upheld the right of colonial peoples to self-determination after they have been developed to the point of being "ready for it"; and it envisaged the creation of international machinery to act as trustee and supervise their development toward this goal.[10] It was immediately recognized that without the concurrence of the colonial powers, the U.S. declaration of policy would be totally ineffectual.[11] Thus, the intensive U.S. diplomatic offensive was initiated with the aim of securing a joint allied declaration of colonial policy along the lines of the principle of trusteeship as adopted by the United States.

From the summer of 1942 until the meeting of the San Francisco Conference, the U.S. government prepared several drafts that they intended to present to the allied powers to be used as a basis for a joint declaration on colonial policy.[12] The first preliminary draft, which was prepared in November 1942 by Secretary Hull, was entitled "The Atlantic Charter and National Independence." Its main purpose was to extend to colonial peoples the allied commitment to the principle of self-determination undertaken in Articles 2 and 3 of the Atlantic Charter. It argued that self-determination is applicable to *all peoples*, and, therefore, as outlined in the Atlantic Charter, it should properly be applicable not only to eastern European nationalities but also to *colonial peoples*. Therefore, they argued, the Atlantic Charter embodied a recognition of the right of colonial peoples to independence. In a second draft, "Declaration by the United Nations on National Independence,"[13] prepared by the Department of State in March 1943, the suggestion that the allied powers had already committed themselves to a policy of independence for the colonies was further elaborated. The draft stated that the Declaration of the United Nations incorporated the Atlantic Charter and thus pledged all signatories to the self-determination and continued independence of nations, to the restoration of the sovereignty of nations forcibly deprived of it, as well as to the achievement of independence to people aspiring to it. In pursuing this policy, the U.S. government asserted that because colonial peoples were "not yet ready" to exercise their right of self-determination did not abrogate their right of self-determination, it merely delayed the exercise of that right. In the meantime, by accepting the commitment to the principle, each colonial power undertook to base its colonial policy on its acceptance of the duty to develop the colonial peoples toward their eventual independence.

The various drafts prepared by the U.S. government contain the most systematic and lucid explanation of the logical connection between the concept of self-determination and the principle of trusteeship since the Smuts Plan. Simply stated, trusteeship is the motivating principle by which a group is prepared for political maturity, indicating that it has acquired the capacity to exercise its right of self-determination. In other words, trusteeship is *based on* the recognition of the right of self-determination; it is a method of making it operationally possible for a group to exercise its acknowledged right of self-determination by developing its capacity to do so.

The efforts of the U.S. government to secure a joint allied colonial policy based on the concept of self-determination and trusteeship proved to be extremely difficult and frustrating. One reason for this difficulty seems to have been the fact that unlike the United States most of the colonial powers still did not see the necessity for a joint declaration on what they considered an essentially domestic problem; and they disagreed with the U.S. contention that there was a relationship between colonial administration and international peace, either as a result of colonial rebellion or imperial rivalry.[14] The crucial reason for the difficulties, however, was the basic antagonisms of some allied powers to the implications of the trusteeship principle as advocated by the U.S. government.

Among the allied powers, the Soviet Union and China were not just willing to undertake such a commitment but wanted to go further and insist on the immediate granting of independence to colonial peoples.[15] On the other hand, the colonial powers were very resistant to the U.S. idea of trusteeship. The British and the Dutch, in particular, had a colonial policy that was generally based on a concept of trusteeship by which over-

101

seas territories were progressively being developed toward internal self-government or autonomy within a somewhat modified imperial framework.[16] But even for them, two features in the American proposal were unacceptable: the establishment of an international machinery to supervise colonial administration and, perhaps more crucial, the idea that the period of colonial wardship should end in total political independence of the colony. The British were particularly opposed to the idea of independence for the colonies. As Secretary Hull reports it, when he made the proposal to Anthony Eden at the first Quebec Conference in August 1943:

> " . . . the Foreign Secretary said that, to be perfectly frank, he had to say that he did not like our draft very much. He said it was the word 'independence' that troubled him, he had to think of the British Empire system, which was built on the basis of Dominion and colonial status."[17]

The British reaction was mild as compared to the attitude of the other colonial powers, particularly the French, who insisted that colonial policy and administration were the exclusive concern of each colonial power and entirely outside the purview of any international body.[18]

The problems caused by the intransigence of the colonial powers were exacerbated by conflicts that had begun to emerge within the U.S. government itself concerning the possible conflict between the requirements of U.S. security and defense interests and the application of the principle of self-determination in the Pacific Islands.[19] Finally, it was not until the U.S. government had retreated from its original position and removed from its trusteeship proposals the two elements that had been most disagreeable to the colonial powers, namely; international supervision and the requirement that the colonial territory be developed toward full political independence, that a tentative agreement was reached to incorporate the concept of trusteeship into the charter of the proposed U.N. organization.[20]

This agreement between the allied powers to provide for a system of trusteeship in the U.N. Charter came at the Yalta Conference in February of 1945. Apart from the change in the U.S. position on trusteeship, there were also some political factors that tended to increase the pressure on the allied powers to reach some agreement on including the principle of trusteeship in the charter. First, with the approach of the San Francisco Conference, the problems of working out a policy for the mandated territories and for disposing of colonial territories separated from the axis powers became more urgent. In thinking about these territories, the solution of trusteeship naturally presented itself, due to the precedent set by the League of Nations mandates system; and this solution could not be applied without at least raising the general question of colonial policy.[21] Second, with the developing intensity of colonial nationalism in countries such as Indonesia, there was an increasing realization that colonial issues were already matters of international concern. Furthermore, it was becoming clear to the colonial powers that the cost of not evolving principles that they could work with would probably mean having to cope with more radical and objectionable proposals from the new group of anticolonial states.[22]

Even with all this added incentive, the actual formulation of allied policy on the basis of the Yalta agreements still proved difficult. In fact, by the time the San Francisco Conference opened, the allied powers still had no common policy on the application of the principle of trusteeship to colonial areas. It was at the conference that they hastily put together the "Working Paper" that became the basis for incorporating the principle of trusteeship and, thus, the principle of self-determination into the U.N. Charter.[23]

On the basis of conversations held by the allied forces between the signing of the Atlantic Charter and the San Francisco Conference several conclusions can be made about the way in which the term "self-determination" was used. When the principle first appeared in the Atlantic Charter, it was presented in the form that we have described as the plebiscite theory. In the Wilsonian tradition of "let the people decide" this formulation was phrased as the right of people to choose the sovereignty under which they wished to live. As stated previously, it was in this sense that it was first enunciated in the Atlantic Charter to be applied to liberated Europe, and it was in this sense that it was later written into the Declaration on Liberated Europe.

This is the principle of the Atlantic Charter—the right of all peoples to choose the form of government under which they will live—the restoration of sovereign rights and self-government to those peoples who have been forcibly deprived of them by the aggressor nations. . . .[24]

Since 1941, however, the history of the concept of self-determination in allied preparations for the organization of peace and security was centered on its application to colonial territories in the form of the trusteeship principle. In this formulation, the principle of self-determination was resolved as a principle of national liberation that was reminiscent of the national equality theory. Thus, in the period prior to the San Francisco Conference, the concept of self-determination was used in both senses, with the allied powers showing a preference for one or the other. Britain, for instance, in preferring the plebiscite theory, claimed that the principle of self-determination was applicable to territorial settlement in Europe, but not to dependent countries.[25] While, on the other hand, the Soviet Union, interpreting self-determination on the basis of the *national* equality theory, wanted to see it applied immediately to the colonial territories, but could not see it applying to the border dispute between Poland and itself.[26] The United States was one of the very few states that defined self-determination to incorporate both applications.

Just prior to the San Francisco Conference, discussion of the principle of self-determination seemed to center on the trusteeship application, perhaps due to the fact that it was the most glaringly unfinished business. Therefore, it was mainly through the concept of trusteeship as presented in Chapters XI and XII that the principle was incorporated into the charter.[27] Thus, any attempt, such as this, to ascertain the meaning that the conference ascribed to the principle must start with an examination of those sections of the charter.

The U.N. Charter and the Meaning of Self-Determination

The text of Chapters XI and XII are fairly straightforward and do not require any detailed study to yield an indication of the meaning of the principle of self-determination as it applies to the groups that come under their scope. The U.N. trusteeship system, outlined in Chapter XII, was clearly meant to be a more up-to-date version of the League of Nations mandates system, especially in terms of providing for a more effective machinery for international supervision.[28] Like the mandates system, it was based on the principle of wardship by which a community is placed under tutelage until it has developed the capacity to exercise its right to self-determination. Logically, therefore, the trusteeship system was the obvious link with the prewar application of the principle of self-determination in the form of the mandates system.[29] However, the declaration of Chapter XI of the charter was no less a successor to the mandates system and the principle of trusteeship it represented.[30] In fact, the link between Chapter XI of the charter and the mandates system could not have been more direct. The draft declaration from which Chapter XI evolved, as presented by the British delegation, was largely a restatement and extension of Article 22 of the League of Nations Covenant.[31] Commenting on Chapter XI of the charter, Field Marshal Smuts, who had first introduced the trusteeship principle to the League of Nations, noted:

> The principle of trusteeship is now applied generally. It applies to all dependent peoples in all dependent territories. It covers all of them, and therefore, an extension has been given to the principle of very far-reaching and important character.[32]

Both Chapters XI and XII indicate that the signatories of the U.N. Charter recognized that the principle of self-determination should be applied to colonial peoples and that it was necessary to develop a system to supervise their development so that they can acquire the capacity for self-government. The objectives of both systems were the same; namely, to supervise the process by which these peoples are developed toward the required level of maturity and to make sure that at the end of the tutelage period the people are permitted to exercise their right of self-determination democratically.[33] The basic difference between the two systems has to do with two issues: the way in which the dependent peoples would eventually exercise the right of self-determination and the amount of control that the United Nations would have in this process. In the case of the colonial territories coming under Chapter XI, the administering power was to have unlimited discretion in the discharge of its responsibilities in administering the trust, and it was expected that the dependent peoples would exercise their right of self-determination by attaining a self-governing status short of total independence.[34] In the case of the U.N. trust territories, the organization established a mechanism for supervising the execution of the responsibilities of the administering power and declared that the people of the trust territory could exercise the right of self-determination by achieving "self-government or independence as may be appropriate to the particular circumstances of each territory and its peoples and the freely expressed wishes of the people concerned. . . ."

On the basis of Chapters XI and XII of the U.N. Charter, a tentative meaning may be ascribed to the principle of self-determination as it applies to colonial territories. According to such a definition, the right of self-determination means that colonial or dependent peoples have the right to eliminate their status by becoming self-governing or autonomous within the larger sovereignty of a transformed imperial relationship or by attaining a separate and sovereign statehood.

This derived meaning is properly termed tentative for several reasons. First, although after 1942, the allied powers discussed the application of the principle of self-determination merely in the form of trusteeship, they also attempted to apply it in connection with the European nations. In fact, the principle of trusteeship was considered a particular formula for the application of the principle of self-determination to a very specific set of circumstances, that is, in situations where the people with the right are considered as not having the capacity to exercise it. In Rooseveltian terms, "trusteeship [was] an intermediate step to self-government or independence for various colonial areas.[35] Evidence from the *proces verbaux* at the conference supports the conclusion that as it had been used in the other allied conversations the principle of trusteeship as it was written into the charter was meant to be a particular application of the principle of self-determination. This may seem surprising, for nowhere is the term "self-determination" actually used in Chapters XI and XII of the charter, nor is there any reference made in the charter to any relationship between Chapters XI and XII and Article 1, subparagraph a or 55, where the term is actually used. And yet there are at least three instances during the drafting of the charter when this connection is explicitly made. First, it was generally known that in initiating the insertion of the phrase "based on respect for the principle of equal rights and self-determination of peoples" into Article 1, paragraph 2 of the charter, the Soviet delegate was particularly interested in emphasizing the application of this principle to the same colonial territories that were subsequently put within the scope of Chapters XI and XII.[36] Second, while Article 76, (subparagraph b) was being drafted, the Soviet delegate had introduced an amendment to the effect that the purpose of the trusteeship system would be to develop the trust territories "toward self-government and *self-determination* with active participation of peoples of these territories, having the aim to expedite the achievement by them of full national independence."[37] His reason, he said, was to remove any doubt that the main aim of that chapter was the application of the principle of self-determination to those groups of territories in particular. The proposed amendment was withdrawn in the face of the opposition of the U.S. delegation and the insistence by Britain and France that it would cause more difficulties than it would resolve. Finally, it was decided that the insertion of the term would be redundant, because the wording of the article clearly reflected the principle of self-determination.[38] Third, it had been suggested that the concept of trusteeship should be written into the section on general purposes. This suggestion was dropped, because it was thought that the principle of trusteeship was a particular mode of applying the principle of self-determination, which was already mentioned in Article 1.[39]

If, as we have argued, the trusteeship principle, presented in Chapters XI and XII of the charter, is a particular application of a more general principle, then what is the meaning of the basic principle of self-determination? In its general form, the principle appears in Article 1, (paragraph 2). As an aid to ascertaining the meaning of the principle, however, that article is of little help, for it is simply a statement of the commitment of the U.N. members to respect "the principle of equal rights and self-determination of peoples. . . ." However, the meaning that the drafters of the charter intended may be suggested by the *proces verbaux*.

The record of the deliberation of the San Francisco Conference shows that there was some divergence of opinion concerning the meaning of self-determination. One of those definitions was the one advocated by the Soviet delegate. In explaining the reason for their amendment, he explained that the Soviet

Union attached great importance to the principles of equality and self-determination of *"nations,"* because they would draw the attention of *"the colonies and mandated territories,"* adding that it was important to see to it that *"dependent countries* are enabled as soon as possible to take the path of *national independence."*[40] According to this, the Soviet Union would define self-determination as the attainment of independence. To it, the group to which the right of self-determination is applied can be characterized interchangeably as "nations," "dependent countries," or "colonies and mandated territories." The fact that these terms are used interchangeably suggests that, for the Soviets, the necessary attribute is its status of being under alien subjugation and that anything beyond this characteristic, whether it is a nationality or a colony, is totally irrelevant. In short, the Soviet meaning of self-determination is that dependent communities have a right to be independent. As might be expected, the definition of the Soviet delegate is consistent with the original Bolshevik interpretation as expressed by Lenin and Satlin, which we termed the theory of national equality.[41] The explicit connection between equal rights and self-determination is from the Soviet standpoint extremely significant. It will be recalled that in the original Bolshevik formulation the right of self-determination derives from the sovereign equality of all nationalities.

The Belgian delegate, M. Rolin, proposed an alternative version of Article 1, (paragraph 2)[42] based on a somewhat different interpretation of the principle of self-determination. According to this proposal, the principle means the granting to "national groups which do not identify themselves with the population of a state . . . freedom of self-government within the sovereignty of member states. . . ." The Belgian delegate was particularly opposed to the Soviet claim that nationalities were endowed with sovereign equality and consequently the right of secession.

In rejecting the Belgian proposal, the committee commented, *inter alia*, that:

(3) The equality of states was dealt with and accepted under Chapter II, Principles, so that it was irrelevant here to the point at issue.

(4) That what is intended by paragraph 2 is to proclaim the equal rights of peoples as such, consequently their right to self-determination. Equality of rights, therefore, extends in the Charter to states, nations, and peoples.[43]

108

By this action, the committee upheld the Soviet claim of the "equal rights of peoples." On the other hand, the committee rejected the Soviet claim that the equal rights of peoples implies their right to secede, and supported the Belgian claim that the right of self-determination stops short of secession. The committee's position on this issue was stated in an earlier statement:

> Concerning the principle of self-determination, it was strongly emphasized on the one side that the principle corresponded closely to the will and desires of peoples everywhere and should be clearly enunciated in the Chapter; on the other side, it was stated that the principle conformed to the purposes of the Charter only in so far as it implied the right of self-government of peoples, and not the right of secession. . . .[44]

In its final report, the committee made the following comment:

> The Committee understands that the principle of equal rights of peoples and the right of self-determination are two complementary parts of one standard of conduct; . . .that an essential element of the principle in question is a free and genuine expression of the will of the people, which avoids cases of the alleged expression of the popular will, such as those used for their ends by Germany and Italy in later years.[45]

This reference to the interpretation of the principle of self-determination advocated by Germany and Italy is significant. It will be recalled that Germany and Italy advocated the principle of "one nation: one state," which we termed the theory of national determinism. In this statement, therefore, the committee explicitly rejected this. With respect to the other two interpretations represented in the Belgian (plebiscite principle) and Soviet (national equality) positions, the committee was somewhat undecided. In the final analysis, the committee endorsed sections of both interpretations, thus ending with a compromise that lends itself to divergent interpretations.

On the basis of the above discussion, it is clear that the principle of self-determination as it is preserved in the charter has within it an unresolved conflict between two general interpretations. However, to say that the meaning of the term is completely indeterminable would be an error. Certainly, the committee could not completely accept either of the two interpretations presented to it. However, by rejecting the German usage of the term, it clearly precluded the acceptability of that interpretation. Furthermore, a substantial area of agreement was achieved in the committee, based on some essential similarities in the two interpretations. Both the Soviet and the Belgian proposals described the groups to which the principle of self-determination was to be applied as groups that were separate from the state in which they politically exist. The Soviet proposal emphasized the fact that such a group was "dependent" or subjugated. The Belgian proposal stressed the fact that the group considers the state as alien. However, it is clear that the elements of dependency and alienness both exist in the two interpretations. It is difficult to conceive of a group as dependent unless it can be differentiated from the subjugating unit, and on the other hand, an alien group does not need to exercise the right of self-determination unless it is also in a subordinate position. Actually, the important operational difference between the two positions was the disagreement on whether or not the exercise of the right of self-determination goes beyond the attainment of self-government and includes secession. In denying that the right of self-determination included the right of secession, the committee seemed to reject the view that total independence is required in order to make a group self-determining. On the other hand, the committee's endorsement of a group's right to equality could conceivably be interpreted (and was so by the Soviet Union) as not precluding the attainment of independence. Thus, in saying that Article 1, (paragraph 2) of the charter contained an unresolved conflict, may be stating the case too strongly. It may be more accurate to call it an uneasy compromise. As we have seen, there was substantial agreement on the group to which the principle applied and the fact that the exercise of self-determination means the attainment of self-government. The only disagreement at San Francisco was the issue of total independence, and it was the main source of disagreement in the subsequent practice of the United Nations.

Taken together, Articles 1, 73, and 76 of the U.N. Charter give a reasonably clear idea of the meaning that the drafters agreed by consensus to give the principle of self-determination. In order to understand the meaning of the expression, "equal rights and self-determination of peoples," is to first attempt to ascertain what the framers of the charter meant by "peoples." On the basis of the preparation of that article, there is no doubt that there was general agreement that the term "peoples" was meant to refer to communities that live under (but do not share in) alien sovereignty.[46] The state or governmental apparatus that wields sovereignty over such peoples is owned and controlled by an alien people. That is to say, they are subjects or dependents, as opposed to citizens, of the state in which they live their political life. Beyond the attributes of alienness and dependency, Article 1, (paragraph 2) does not shed any more light on other attributes that such a people might have.

Articles 73 and 76 are more explicit in their description of the type of dependent territories that fall within the scope of the application of the trusteeship principle. A general description of these peoples is stated in Article 73 as "peoples who have not yet attained a full measure of self-government" and who live in territories governed by other peoples. It is important to note that the attributes described above were not intended to serve as a general definition of dependent peoples, but were merely a descriptive subcategory of dependent people.[47] For the purposes of Chapters XI and XII of the charter, this subcategory is made up of dependent peoples with certain special characteristics. The essential element that distinguishes dependent peoples of this type from other possible types was that their capacity to exercise their right of self-determination was not yet adequately developed, and therefore, they would be required to undergo a period of tutelage under the guidance of a state, at the end of which they would exercise the right.[48] Another characteristic of these dependent peoples is that they were all situated in territories geographically separated from the territory of the states administering them.[49]

There was also general agreement on an authoritative interpretation of the nature and extent of the right of self-determination that the "peoples" were to enjoy, both in the drafting of Article 1, (paragraph 2) and Articles 73 and 76, although none of the delegates were entirely happy with the agreement. The committee that drafted Article 1, (paragraph 2) decided that self-determination meant the right of self-government within existing states, specifically excluding the right of secession. In applying the principle of self-determination, it was agreed that after the people of the trust territory had completed their period of tutelage, they could exercise their right of self-determination by the attainment of self-government or independence, depending *inter alia* on the particular circumstances of each territory and the wishes of the people in it. The only way open to the colonial territories for exercising their right of self-determination, according to the text of the charter, was by the attainment of self-government. Independence was deliberately excluded from the text as a means of exercising the right of self-determination. However, the *proces verbaux* indicate that, in this case, a liberal reading of the text would give a misleading account of the interpretation that was actually adopted. In the committee, there were a number of states, including the Soviet Union, China, and Iraq, who would have preferred the text to Article 73 to state explicitly that the attainment of total independence was the only way of exercising the right of self-determination.[50] On the other hand, the colonial powers were vehemently against any interpretation of self-determination that would permit the colonies to secede. They insisted on the same position they had taken while drafting of Article 1, (paragraph 2), that self-determination meant the attainment of self-government short of secession and independence.[51]

The deadlock in the Committee was broken by a U.S.-supported compromise according to which the term "independence" would be excluded from the text with the understanding that self-government under certain circumstances includes the concept of total independence.[52] It was on the basis of this compromise interpretation that Article 73 was adopted.

On the basis of the text of the charter and the interpretations suggested by its drafters, the meaning of the principle of self-determination that emerges is not the most precise and sharply defined. On the whole, however, they do indicate agreement on some of the most crucial aspects of the principle. For instance, there was general agreement that the term "peoples" in Article 1, (paragraph 2) refers to groups that are distinct from and subordinate to the other people in a state. There was no serious attempt to achieve agreement on other attributes of such peoples, such as the basis of this distinctness or the minimum required size.[53] As shown above, the agreement emerged out of some difficult confrontations. The amount of bargaining and compromising on the interpretation of the term "self-determination," necessary for adopting the charter articles on the principle, were even more difficult. And the compromise that was finally settled upon did not fully put to rest the one serious disagreement on the independence issue. In such cases of unsatisfactory compromises, the parties accept because they cannot obtain general approval for their position, and they see the compromise as better than the opponents' position. Therefore, they accept the compromise as a *modus operandi* of some compelling force, and expect other parties to adhere to it in good faith. In accepting the compromise, however, such unsatisfied parties do not lose sight of their original claim. Thus, in later encounters, they attempt to obtain general acceptance of their original position, or, for that matter, new claims that seem to them to be called for. This phenomenon is an entirely normal part of the process by which international rules or standards of behavior are created. As part of the flow of international relations, claims are made that, if generally accepted, form the consensus on which old rules are modified or reinforced. Much of the subsequent activity of the United Nations in the area of decolonization may be seen as part of this process. At any one time, it should be possible to recognize the claims that are being made, as well as being able to identify the area of acceptable consensus.

U.N. Practice and the Definition
of Self-Determination

The very fact that the principle of self-determination was written into the U.N. Charter is evidence of the acknowledgment on the part of the states that issues involving the principle were already falling within the realm of international politics. Furthermore, it made the United Nations the arena within which the issues would be dealt with, and the U.N. Charter the reference point from which the claims based on the principle would be tested. In the diplomacy of self-determination, there were several substantive questions that had to be settled on a continuing basis. Most of these were questions on what interpretations of such concepts as dependent peoples could be considered valid. The test that was always applied was whether or not the interpretation was consistent with the meaning of the relevant powers of the charter. This, of course, immediately raised the question of whose interpretation should be considered authoritative for the purpose of U.N. action: the interpretation of individual states or that of the member states as a whole?[54] In terms of the interpretation of the charter in relation to the principle of self-determination, the solution to this problem began to emerge in the early 1950s.

At the beginning of the life of the United Nations, the majority of the states were willing to accept the right of each state to unilaterally define the principle of self-determination and act on the basis of that definition. Thus, in 1946, the General Assembly not only decided not to attempt to define the principle but it decided to accept without question the definitions of "dependent peoples" that eight states had adopted.[55] This practice of allowing states to unilaterally define the terms of the principle and the groups to which it applies caused conflicts that immediately became forcefully apparent. There was the obvious problem of trying to determine the rationality of a claim by an administering power that a territory that had originally been listed was no longer a non-self-governing territory.[56] This problem first became apparent when in 1947 Britain decided to drop Malta from her list of non-self-governing territories, and France decided to drop Guadaloupe, Guiana, Martinique, and Reunion from hers. There was also the problem of determining whether or not a claim that a certain territory is non-self-governing was valid.[57] The majority of the members of the United Nations decided that this situation was intolerable. As a result, a concentrated effort was mounted to assert the right of the General Assembly to make the final decision on the proper interpretation of non-self-governing peoples and other questions concerning the principle of self-determination. The process by which this right was established is outside the scope of the present discussion.[58] It is sufficient to note that in 1949 the General Assembly took the first step in asserting its responsibility to express its opinions on the validity of criteria used to make a determination on the non-self-governing status of a territory,[59] and thus started the trend that culminated in 1960, when the General Assembly on its own initiative declared that the Portuguese overseas possessions fell into the category of non-self-governing within the meaning of Article 73 (subparagraph e) of the charter.[60]

Having asserted its responsibility to express its opinions on the definition of non-self-governing territories, the General Assembly, in the same 1949 resolution, directed the Special Committee, "to examine the factors which should be taken into account in deciding whether any territory is or is not a territory whose people have not yet attained a full measure of self-government." This resolution was the beginning of a process of clarifications and refinements that culminated in the incorporation of the right of self-determination in the two Human Rights Conventions and the exhaustive definitions in Resolution 1541 (XV) (1960) of both the group entitled to the right and the ways in which the right may be exercised. Detailed accounts of the history of the work of the General Assembly and its subsidiary organs, such as the Human Rights Commission, the various Ad Hoc Committees, and the Committee of Twenty-four, have been more than adequately presented elsewhere.[61] All that will be necessary here is to sketch briefly the essential features of their efforts and to discuss the significance of their results as indicators of the definitions of the principle of self-determination that the majority of the states accepted.

The few significant advances to clarify and strengthen the legal nature of the principle were made in the General Assembly in 1952. In January of that year, the General Assembly initiated a two-pronged action through the Human Rights Commission[62] and an Ad Hoc Committee[63] it established to respectively incorporate the principle of self-determination in the Draft Convention on Human Rights and expand on the study of "factors" that the Special Committee had started in 1949. The reports of these committees started two simultaneous and complementary streams of activity resulting in the adoption by the General Assembly of two Human Rights Convenants in 1966 and the final clarification of the principle of self-determination by General Assembly resolution in 1960.

Refinement of the United Nations' Meaning
of Self-Determination

The process of clarification and interpretation of the principle of self-determination began with General Assembly Resolution 648 (VII), December 10, 1952, which provisionally approved the idea that a territory may attain a full measure of self-government by one of three ways, namely, "the attainment of independence," "the attainment of other separate systems of self-government," and "the free association of a territory with other component parts of the metropolitan or other country." By the same resolution, the General Assembly established a

115

second Ad Hoc Committee to continue the study of "factors" and to broaden the scope of its investigation by including:

(a) The possibility of defining the concept of a full measure of self-government for the purposes of Chapter XI of the Charter;
(b) The features guaranteeing the principle of the self-determination of peoples in relation to Chapter XI of the Charter;
(c) The manifestation of the freely expressed will of the peoples in relation to the determination of their national and international status for the purposes of Chapter XI of the Charter . . .

Obviously, what Resolution 648 (VII) attempts to do is to answer some of the questions concerning the principle of self-determination on which a consensus may be found and also to state as clearly as possible those questions that need to be answered. The approval of the list of factors indicates the judgment of the majority of members on the ways in which self-determination may be exercised. The three questions posed in the resolution are designed to elicit answers that will clarify the relationship that the charter hints at between the principle of trusteeship and the principle of self-determination. According to Chapter XI, the principle of trusteeship was supposed to be a way of applying the principle of self-determination to "peoples who had not yet attained a full measure of self-government." Such people, known as non-self-governing or dependent peoples, were placed under tutelage. This was a way of guaranteeing their eventual exercise of the right of self-determination, for under this system: (1) their administering authority was obligated to develop their capacity for self-government; and (2) after developing this capacity, these people would freely decide whether to be independent or self-governing within a larger state. Bearing this in mind, the three questions can easily be translated into the following. From the standpoint of the purposes of the trusteeship principle as enunciated in Chapter XI of the charter:

(1) What is the definition of non-self-governing people;
(2) What administering policy will be required to develop these peoples so as to guarantee their eventual exercise of the right of self-determination; and
(3) When deciding which option they should take (independence or self-government) in the exercise of self-determination, what procedures may be considered indicative of an accurate representation of the freely expressed will of the people.

Subsequent resolutions of the General Assembly may be considered attempts to answer these questions, to the extent that enough consensus could be found to sustain the conclusions.

A few days after the adoption of Resolution 648 (VII), the General Assembly adopted another resolution based on the report of the Human Rights Commission, wherein they endorsed the incorporation of the right of self-determination into the draft of the Human Rights Conventions. In addition, the General Assembly recommended that members "uphold the principles of self-determination of peoples and nations" and that members administering non-self-governing territories recognize and promote the right of the peoples of trust territories to self-determination. Furthermore, the administering powers were to prepare them for the exercise of the right by developing their capacity for self-government. Finally, the right of self-determination should be exercised according to the freely expressed wishes of the people through plebiscites or other recognized democratic means, preferably under the auspices of the United Nations.[64]

The incorporation of the principle of self-determination into what was designed to be a legally binding treaty was, of course, an important step in the establishment of self-determination as a binding rule of international law.[65] Our concern in this essay, however, is not in proving the legal nature of the principle. What we are concerned with is attempting to establish what the term means as indicated by the practice of the majority of the states. From this standpoint, the fact to be noted is that the way in which the principle was inserted in the draft convenants amounts to a definition of the term. Thus, in the covenant, the right of self-determination is defined as the "right freely to determine their political, economic, social and cultural status . . . including the permanent sovereignty over their natural wealth and resources."

From the standpoint of the insight it gives into the meaning afforded the principle of self-determination by the General Assembly, the first part of Resolution 637 A(VII) is truly remarkable. First, this resolution is the first explicit statement of the fact, hinted at in the proceedings at San Francisco, that the groups that are mentioned under Chapters XI and XII of the charter are a subcategory of "peoples and nations" that have a right to self-determination.[66] Second, the recommendations of

117

the resolution, almost as if by design, provide answers to the questions that Resolution 648 (VII) had posed for the second Ad Hoc Committee just a few days before. After asserting that the non-self-governing and trust territories had a right of self-determination, it went on to note, in accordance to its obligation to respect this right, that the administering power's responsibility was to facilitate the exercise of this right in such a way that the people are able to choose self-government or independence by plebiscite or other democratic procedure; and that in preparation for this eventual exercise, it will continue to be the administering power's responsibility "to *prepare them* for complete self-government or independence."

The Ad Hoc Committee's response to the same questions, as presented in their report to the eighth session of the General Assembly,[67] was almost identical to that of the Human Rights Commission. The report lists among the features guaranteeing the principle of self-determination of peoples, in relation to Chapter XI of the charter, their political development in the use of representative government, with the procedural individual rights necessary for such performance, and their ability, at the time of exercising the right of self-determination, to choose its status by a free, uncoerced, and effective decision. By such a decision, the non-self-governing peoples could choose one of the three situations outlined in the list of factors that was also prescribed in the report of the second Ad Hoc Committee. This list of factors, which was essentially a refinement of the list originally prescribed in 1952, was approved by the General Assembly in Resolution 742(VIII), which also noted that out of the three ways the achievement of self-government was primarily through the attainment of independence.

By the end of 1953, the General Assembly had made some operational definitions with increasingly larger majorities indicating that they shared in a collective definition of many aspects of the principle of self-determination, with particular reference to its application to groups being administered according to the principle of trusteeship. In particular, there had evolved in the practice of the General Assembly reasonably clear meanings for such things as: (1) the kind of preparation deemed necessary to enable non-self-governing people to develop the capacity to exercise its right of self-determination; (2) what procedures were satisfactory for ascertaining the will of the

118

people; and (3) in what ways they could become fully self-governing. The development of these operational meanings had been made possible by a consensus among a large percentage of the members of the United Nations. However, no new consensus had developed on which a generally formulated, or newly evolved, definition of dependent peoples could be based. The only generally accepted description of dependent people was the one implied by the assembly's acceptance of the original list of non-self-governing territories preserved by administering powers. However, as we have pointed out, this was merely a list of territories that could fit in that category, not an exhaustive statement on the essential characteristics or a definition of a dependent territory that could if necessary be applied to a new situation.

Since the first session of the General Assembly, some states, particularly Belgium and France, have attempted to expand the application of Chapter XI of the charter so that more territories may be brought into the category of non-self-governing. There have been efforts in the General Assembly to initiate a systematic study of a possible definition of "people of non-self-governing territories"[68] All of these attempts were unsuccessful. It was not until 1959 that the General Assembly was prompted by the refusal of Spain and Portugal to submit information on their overseas possessions, in accordance with Article 73, (subparagraph e) to create a Special Committee of Six to study the issue.[69] On the basis of the report of this committee, the General Assembly adopted Resolution 1541(XV), which is to this date the most comprehensive statement on both (1) the criteria for identifying a dependent territory and (2) at what point such a territory can be said to have exercised its right of self-determination.[70] The most relevant sections of the list of principles annexed to the resolution are presented below:

Principle IV

Prima facie there is an obligation to transmit information in respect of a territory which is geographically separate and is distinct ethnically and/or culturally from the country administering it.

Principle V

Once it has been established that such a *prima facie* case of geographical and ethnical or cultural distinctness of a territory exists, other elements may then be brought into consideration. These additional elements may be, *inter alia*, of an administrative, political, juridical, economic or historical na-

119

ture. If they affect the relationship between the metropolitan State and the territory concerned in a manner which arbitrarily places the latter in a posibion or status of subordination, they support the presumption that there is an obligation to transmit information under article 73(e) of the Charter.

Principle VI

A Non-Self-Governing Territory can be said to have reached a full measure of self-government by:

(a) Emergence as a sovereign independent Satte;
(b) Free association with an independent State; or
(c) Integration with an independent State.

On the day before the Fifteenth General Assembly adopted Resolution 1541(XV), it had adopted Resolution 1514(XV), known as the Declaration on the Granting of Independence to Colonial Countries and Peoples. A cursory glance at the two resolutions leads immediately to the conclusion that they represent fundamentally different approaches to the application of the principle of self-determination to colonial territories. In terms of their indication of the consensus that has emerged in the United Nations on the definition of the principle of self-determination, their fundamental differences on two issues are particularly relevant: namely, (1) the call for the immediate transfer of power to colonial peoples; and (2) the attainment of full independence as the only way of exercising the right to self-determination.

As indicated above, Resolution 1514(XV) recognizes, that provided it is based on the free choice of the dependent peoples themselves, the right of self-determination would have been satisfied by their emergence as a sovereign independent state, their free association with an independent state, or their integration with an independent state. Furthermore, Resolution 1541(XV) was based on the acceptance of the idea that Article 73 of the charter will continue to be operative. The resolution states in its third operative paragraph that the approved principles "should be applied (in the future) . . . to determine whether or not an obligation exists to transmit information under Article 73(e) of the Charter." The call here is not for immediate transfer of power. It is the establishment of criteria for identifying non-self-governing territories so that they can be put under the regime of the general principle of trusteeship in preparation for and pending their eventual exercise of their right of self-determination. Worded differently, this idea of wardship separates two concepts: the existence of the right of self-determination and the conditions under which it may be exercised. So that while asserting the right of colonial peoples to self-determination, the principle of trusteeship also asserts that the right may be exercised only when the group has acquired the capacity to do so.[71]

This condition, implied in the concept of trusteeship, was singled out for attack in Resolution 1514(XV) with the statement that "inadequacy of political, economic, social, or educational preparedness should never serve as a pretext for delaying independence." In addition, the declaration states that "continued existence of colonialism, . . .impedes the social, cultural and economic development of dependent peoples. . . ." Taken together, these statements are an emphatic repudiation of the whole idea of trusteeship. The logic of Resolution 1514(XV) is that not only is colonial administration incapable of realizing the claim of the trusteeship concept to develop the people, but that it actually does the opposite. This was the theoretical basis of the demand for the immediate transfer of power to the colonial peoples.

The insistence on independence "without any conditions or reservations" is also based on the rejection of the concept of trusteeship, and the unwillingness of the majority of the states to, as it were, consent to the fruits of assimilationist policies implemented under the guise of the trusteeship principle. There was a general suspicion on the part of the most ardent supporters of decolonization that the choice of a dependent people for any stakes other than independence was not genuine but rather the result of colonial machinations.

Due to its dramatic impact and the innumerable references made to it in subsequent U.N. resolutions, the Declaration on the Granting of Independence to Colonial Countries and Peoples has received so much publicity that for many commentators it "has become the standard by which the Assembly judges all colonial matters and represents a crucial extension of the United Nations role in the decolonization process."[72] On the basis of the practice of the United Nations, however, it seems that this judgment is not warranted. When Resolution 1514(XV) is taken together with the continuing stream of U.N. action, it becomes readily apparent that the declaration's effect on the General Assembly's definition of the right of self-determination and its various aspects has been much more peripheral than was first thought. On the other hand, Resolution 1541(XV) seems to be more consistent with the practice of the United Nations from its inception, and it continues to represent the basic principles underlying U.N. actions since 1960.

The very first instance in which the Genearl Assembly dealt with the disposition of colonial territory was with the Italian colonies in North Africa. This case illustrates three different ways in which the General Assembly applied the right of self-determination: independence (for Lybia), trusteeship (for Somalia), and federation as an autonomous unit (for Eritrea).[73] In its supervision of the exercise of self-determination by the trust territories, the General Assembly has shown the same willingness to permit the people of the trust territories to choose between alternative modes of exercising their right of self-determination. Thus, the peoples of the trust territory of Togo were given a choice between integration into an independent Ghana or continued trusteeship pending future determination of status.[74] And the peoples of the trust territory of British Cameroun were given a choice of either union with Nigeria or intergration with Cameroun.[75]

In the decolonization of non-self-governing territories under Chapter XI of the charter, the basic activity of the General Assembly has been to verify and legitimize the termination of dependent status. Starting from 1953, the General Assembly accepted the status of Puerto Rico as a commonwealth in association with the United States as satisfactory evidence of the exercise of the people of Puerto Rico of their right of self-determination[76] The exercise of the right of self-determination by the people of Netherland Antilles and Surinam by free association was also accepted by the General Assembly[77] as were the exercise of self-determination by Greenland,[78] and Hawaii and Alaska,[79] As Philip M. Allen has noted:

> In all these cases, the United Nations was not involved directly. The General Assembly, therefore, restricted to expressing its opinion on the new status of former non-self-governing territories, on the basis of documentation and explanations presented by the administering powers as evidence that the people had freely exercised their right of self-determination[80]

In spite of the Declaration on the Granting of Independence to Countries and Peoples, the definition of the principle of self-determination as spelled out in Resolution 1541(XV) continues to be the basis of the decolonization activity of the General Assembly with regard to both the Portuguese overseas possessions[81] and Rhodesia.[82] In both cases, the resolution did not call for immediate independence to these territories, as would have been consistent with the declaration. Instead, they insisted on the responsibility of the administering powers—Portugal and Great Britain, respectively—to bring these territories under the regime of Article 73, (subparagraph e) of the charter and to adopt formally their responsibilities to prepare those peoples for the eventual exercise of self-determination, in accordance with the principle of trusteeship.

Again, in actions regarding the termination of dependency, even with the more radical tone of the Committee of Twenty-four, the General Assembly has accepted the dependent people's free choice of alternative modes of attaining complete self-government.[83] With the shifting of the focus of the General Assembly's decolonization activities to Oceania, in the past few years, the realization of the problems of creating a multiplicity of ministates has brought the question of the modes of exercising self-determination to the fore.[84] In dealing with these cases, there has been renewed emphasis in the General Assembly on the necessity to give more favorable consideration to the other modes of exercising self-determination, short of independence, on the basis of the free choice of the people of the territory. Thus, the trust territories of Nauru and Western Samoa were both given the choice, which culminated in independence for Nauru and the association of Western Samoa with New Zealand.[85] The acceptance by the General Assembly of the validity of the exercise of self-determination by the people of Cook Island to associate with New Zealand is consistent with their general approach.[86] Thus, while the General Assembly continues in its general resolutions to affirm "the inalienable right of the people to self-determination and independence" in its consideration of individual cases there appears to be an increasing awareness that total independence may not be the best alternative for many small territories.[87] The sum total of all the evidence suggests that Resolution 1541(XV) represents the principles on which the practice of United Nations decolonization is based.

The nature and effect of General Assembly resolutions has been the subject of several important studies in the past few years. In particular, questions have been raised with reference to their legal significance, quasi-judicial role, and usefulness as evidence of customary international law.[88] Interesting and important as these questions are, it is essential to note that the focus of our discussion here is limited to the use of General Assembly resolutions as evidence of state practice. In short, as the votes of the members amount to state practice as understood in the context of law-creating processes?

Each state that voted in favor of Resolution 1541(XV) in effect made a formal declaration that it accepts the definitions implied in it. However, as in the case of other formal acts of state, one official action is ordinarily not enough to justify a conclusion that the state always acts that same way. States have on occasion behaved in ways inconsistent with their usual practice; therefore, the fact that a state may have voted in favor of a particular resolution does not make that vote consistent with its usual practice.[89] However, if a state voted in favor of Resolution 1541(XV), as well as all previous, similar resolutions, then it should be concluded that, for that particular state, support of the statement in Resolution 1541(XV) is a matter of longstanding official policy and practice.

As we have demonstrated above, the meaning that the Genearl Assembly has ascribed to the principle of self-determination since 1949 has been consistently the same. To be sure, this basic contention has been constantly undergoing a process of refinement and clarification, for it seems inevitable that the concept, which is the basis of so much activity, should become progressively, more explicitly and clearly defined. Resolution 1541(XV) represents the last clear statement in this continual process. In this regard, it is significant that Resolution 1541(XV) is consciously based on Resolution 742(VIII), the last previous statement of the same principles. The resolutions that preceded Resolution 1541(XV) were adopted by large majorities. The states that made up these majorities and the bulk of the new membership of the United Nations were responsible for the large majority with which Resolution 1541(XV) was adopted.[90] Therefore, the adoption of that resolution did not only indicate that a large majority supported the meaning of self-determination implied by it but also that their vote was entirely in line with long standing and continuing practice. Furthermore, the decolonization activities of the General Assembly in the past ten years, which have also been endorsed by over-whelming majorities, have been based on the meaning of Resolution 1541(XV).[91]

Conclusion

The way in which the allied powers anticipated using the principle of self-determination in the post-World War II international order has undergone some dramatic changes. The principle was reintroduced into the international political arena by the allied powers, most of whom were also the leading colonial powers. As they had in the aftermath of World War I, they had expected to use it at their discretion and in conjunction with other principles to solve problems on an ad hoc basis in the interest of themselves and of international peace and security. What happened was beyond their expectations. A large group of states emerged from colonial status and were admitted into the United Nations. Having just come out of colonial subjugation and convinced that that status, together with the racial and cultural discrimination that seemed to go with it, was detrimental to humanity, they concentrated their efforts on eliminating colonialism from the face of the earth. The international political alignment provided them with enthusiastic allies. They have been a crucial factor in the almost complete success of eliminating the then current type of colonialism.[92] These new states were also largely responsible for the focus that was given the principle of self-determination at the expense of other ways in which it had been applied in an earlier period.

As we have seen, the groups foremost in the minds of the parties to the Atlantic Charter were national groups in eastern Europe, and the way they had thought of applying it was in the plebiscitary way suggested by President Wilson. We have seen that as the postwar problems began to present themselves and the problem of dealing with overseas territorial possessions began to loom larger the discussion of the application of the principle of self-determination was shifted into that area.

As the date of the San Francisco Conference approached, allied discussions on the principle of self-determination were concentrated on its application to the colonial territories in the form of the principle of trusteeship. At San Francisco, they made what they considered to be minimal commitments to abide by the principle of trusteeship in their colonial policies and settled back almost complacently to what they anticipated would be a new and perhaps rather sophisticated period of imperial administration. Throughout this period, however—and this is important—the allied powers did not cease to think of the principle of self-determination as also applicable to the other problem—territorial settlement and restoration of sovereignty in eastern Europe.

As the United Nations got underway, the principle of self-determination was applied almost exclusively to colonial and trust territories. The principle came to be thought about mainly in that way; and as a consequence, it was defined principally in terms of its usage in connection with the emancipation of colonial territories. On the basis of the charter and the practice of the United Nations, it may be said that self-determination was defined as the attainment of self-government and equality (with other peoples) in conformity with the freely expressed wishes of the peoples involved. Implied in this self-government is the right to freely determine the economic, social, and cultural policies of the peoples. The three ways by which this self-government can be achieved are total independence, integration, or association on the basis of equality. In order to invoke this right, the peoples must be a territorially based, organized community and must be under alien subjugation. The right is, therefore, an inherent right, the exercise of which may be activated under conditions of deprivation of sovereignty due to alien overrule. Although the right is inherent in the group, it cannot be exercised unless the group has the capacity to do so. In the absence of this capacity, however, the right does not lapse; the exercise of the right is merely deferred, and in the meantime, the international community takes upon itself the responsibility of a trustee of the group, preparing it systematically until it acquires the capacity for self-rule and is thus able to exercise the right.

To conclude from this definition that the right of self-determination was only allowed to colonial territories,[93] would be a serious misperception. The following conclusion by Benjamin Rivlin seems more appropriate:

Certainly, the pure concept of self-determination is not applicable exclusively to colonial territories, but it does not exclude them. Instead of being viewed as a "distortion," the preoccupation with self-determination in the United Nations should be viewed as a warning of a maladjustment that requires attention and action.[94]

The preoccupation of the United Nations with self-determination as applied to colonial territories is the result of a political situation that changed after World War II. The way in which international society responds to such principles as self-determination is conditioned in an important way by who is making the claim. It will be recalled that in the final stages of World War I the groups that were agitating for self-determination and independence were the European nationalities. They were making the claims. Therefore, the question of self-determination was posed as "national self-determination." The answers that the allied powers sought to provide came, at least initially, in relation to "national self-determination." The application of the principle of self-determination in the mandates system came as something of an afterthought. After World War II, it was not the European nationalities that were in revolt, it was the overseas colonies. It was they who were making the claim. Thus, the answers have been provided in relation to colonial peoples—self-determination of peoples.[95]

Even in spite of the concentration on decolonization, the meaning of self-determination according to a reading of the charter and the *travaux preparatoires* clearly indicates that the pure meaning of the right takes in the special application to colonial territories, and is also applicable to other subjugated groups. To that extent, the Belgian Thesis is entirely logical and consistent with the charter definition of self-determination as well as the way the principle had been applied during the interwar period. As Kenneth Robinson notes:

> The discussions of these issues have certainly emphasized the arbitrary and illogical basis on which certain territories of a small number of Western European powers (and the United States) have been singled out as "non-self-governing territories",...However, it is not then obvious that there is any clear distinction between the political status of the people of some "colonial" dependencies and, for example, those of the "native reserves" of South Africa, or in the hinterland of Liberia....[96]

As logical as the Belgian Thesis is, it has, as we have seen, been almost totally irrelevant, except as a constant irritant. The simple reason is that it is *politically* irrelevant. In developing rules of operation and legitimacy, the international community responds to political claims with political counterclaims, or protest, or acquiescence. The community of states does not respond to logical statements or deductions. Therefore, until there are groups with access to the international political arena making these claims, either for themselves or for groups to which they are seriously committed, the Belgian Thesis will continue to get almost no attention.

As we have already seen, the U.N. Charter sufficiently indicates that the categories of groups who may invoke the right of self-determination are more than is encompassed in Chapters XI and XII. Various General Assembly resolutions on self-determination have been framed in such a way as to indicate that "the right exists in a wider category of countries and territories.[97] Furthermore, the General Assembly has shown that when a claim of the right of self-determination has been made it has been able to recognize the issue and make the appropriate response. Thus, during the Hungarian Crisis of 1956, the General Assembly adopted Resolutions 1004(ES-II) and 1005(ES-II), upholding the right of the Hungarian people to self-determination and calling on the Soviet Union to take steps to respect that right. It is clear from the above, that according to the U.N. Charter, self-determination is a claimable right of all subject communities. However, due to a set of political circumstances, the only groups who have been able to press their claims have been the colonial territories. For this reason, the practice of the United Nations has been limited to these groups. The extent to which other subject groups will be able to press their claims to the right, as allowed under the charter, remains to be seen.

CHAPTER VI

SELF-DETERMINATION IN THE ERA OF DECOLONIZA-
TION:

GENERAL INTERNATIONAL PRACTICE

It has been aptly stated that because state practice exists both within the United Nations as well as in general diplomatic activity, the quest for its evidence should not be limited to the activities within the organization.[1] Therefore, to base our conclusions on the decolonization activities of the United Nations alone could be misleading. This danger is particularly present because the actual substantive role played by the United Nations in the decolonization of the great majority of colonies has been small. It is true, of course, that the United Nations, "has been very much involved in the business of decolonization . . . " but it has done this mainly by being "a kind of international funnel into which . . . the politics of decolonization has been notably concentrated . . . "[2] The direct action of the General Assembly increased dramatically after the establishment of the Committee of Twenty-four. However, by that time, most of the largest colonies were either completely independent or clearly on their way to becoming independent. The fact is, however, that before 1960 the major processes of decolonization were carried on outside the United Nations, with the exception of direct action in the early special cases of Palestine and the Italian colonies. The major contribution of the organization was in sustaining a climate of opinion favorable to decolonization and giving the new states its blessing by accepting them speedily as members.[3]

Self-Determination and Colonial Practice

The practice of colonial powers merits particular attention because during the era of decolonization they were the targets against which the claims of self-determination advanced. Therefore, their responses to these claims should be important, as evidence of both the definition of the scope and content of the principle as well as the element of acquiescence which has ripened it into a right under international law.

Great Britain:

Ever since the loss of the thirteen American colonies, the policy of developing colonies to eventual self-government has been the hallmark of British colonial procedure. Beginning with Durham's Report in 1839 to the Statute of Westminster in 1931, they developed a series of well-defined constitutional stages through which the control exercised over the colony was increasingly diminished until it became totally self-governing. This process (crown colony, representative government, responsible government, dominion status) was the vehicle through which Canada, Australia and South Africa became independent Dominions:

> " . . .autonomous communities within the British Empire, equal in status, in no way subordinate one to another in any aspect of their domestic or external affairs, though united by a common allegiance to the Crown, and freely associated as members of the British Commonwealth of Nations."[4]

By the time World War II began, the idea of developing colonial peoples as they increased capacity for eventual self-government within the British Empire was a well recognized British policy. As expressed in 1938 by Malcom MacDonald, then Secretary of State for the Colonies:

> "It may take generations, or even centuries, for the peoples in some parts of the Colonial Empire to achieve self-government. But it is a major part of our policy, even among the most backward peoples of Africa, to teach them and to encourage them always to be able to stand a little more on their own feet."[5]

Later, MacDonald's successor, Colonel Oliver Stanley, expressed this theory of tutelage and trusteeship even more explicitly:

> "We are pledged to guide Colonial people along the road to self-government within the framework of the British Empire."[6]

With a few refinements, this was the same constitutional process that the British colonies of Asia, Africa and the Caribbean went through to gain their independence. It was not always without political difficulties. Frequently, the British government and the colonial peoples disagreed on the speed with which devolution of power should take place, and in some cases, such as Kenya, there was bloody confrontation. But, whatever difficulties were encountered, it was a constitutional process which was supposed to end in self-government with the actual form that self-government would take being determined by the free choice of the people. Thus, some of the colonies eventually became dominions, republics, and associated states within the Commonwealth,[7] while some left it after attaining independence.

All these different post-colonial conditions were clearly understood to be manifestations of self-determination, as is illustrated by the following statement of British policy on the independence of Sudan:

> "Her Majesty's Government is glad to know that the Sudan has for some time been and is now moving rapidly in the direction of self-government. In their view this progress can and should continue on the lines already laid down. Her Majesty's Government will, therefore, give the Governor-General their full support for steps he has taken to bring the Sudanese rapidly to the stage of self-government as a prelude to *Self-Determination*."[8]

What this practice clearly demonstrates is that the progress of a colony toward self-government has taken the form of a *constitutional* devolution of authority. Therefore, the principle of self-determination, defined as the right of colonial peoples to self-government, is one that has legal standing in British constitutional law as well as the constitutional law of the ex-colonies. Consequently, it is evidential of British practice relating to international law.[9]

France:

The official ideological justification of French colonialism was that, by virtue of its superior culture, the French have a mission to civilize their colonial subjects. General Catroux, himself an ex-colonial governor, stated that French colonial policy was:

" . . . based on the conviction that the low level of political, economic and social development of the indigenous populations when they came under French control made them incapable of advancing or of managing their own affairs without a long period of political apprenticeship, and experience in the techniques and principles of good administration. . . .It was also assumed that the indigenous leaders, who would later provide the nucleus of a government, should be shaped by the mold of French culture because of its indisputable superiority and universality."[10]

Thus France was the advocate *par excellence* of the idea of tutelage and trusteeship. Unlike the British, however, the French repudiated the notion that this tutelage should end with independence for their colonial wards, and, as late as 1944, French colonial policy rejected the possibility of self-government for its colonies. As stated at the Brazzaville conference of colonial administrators:

"The aims of the work of civilization accomplished by France in its colonies exclude all idea of autonomy, all possibility of evolution outside of the French bloc of [sic] the Empire; the eventual establishment, even in the distant future, of self-government is to be dismissed."[11]

On the basis of this policy, the French government fashioned the constitution of the Fourth Republic in 1946, placing the colonies firmly within one "indivisible" French Union. In its preamble, the Constitution states:

" . . . France proposes to guide the peoples for whom she has assumed responsibility toward freedom to govern themselves and democratically to manage their own affairs."

However, this was to be achieved, not by making them independent of France, but by transforming them from subjects into citizens of France.[12] This arrangement proved to be untenable in the face of nationalist developments in the colonies. Starting with the *loi-cadre* of 1956, there ensued a series of constitutional reforms which transformed the colonies, first into "autonomous republics" in the French community, and finally into fully independent states in a "commonwealth *a la francaise*."[13]

By 1958, France had abandoned the legal fiction of the indivisibility of the republic, and recognized the right of colonial peoples to choose total independence as their right of self-determination. But it did so reluctantly, always using a variety of inducements in attempts to influence the colonial people to choose autonomy rather than independence. France's determination not to permit the right of self-determination to break up the empire was evident in the vindictiveness with which it withdrew from Guinea after the latter had voted for total independence in the 1958 referendum.[14] Later, France was so determined to force Algerians to retain the existing status of overseas department instead of independence, that it took eight years of bitter fighting to make the French government concede that:

" . . . the solution of the independence of Algeria in cooperation: with France is the one which corresponds to this situation."[15]

Netherlands, Spain, Belgium:

The colonial practice of these states shows, more or less, the same principles of trusteeship as we have seen in the case of the major colonial powers. Early in the twentieth century the Netherlands developed the "Ethical Policy," in which they affirmed the principle of developing native societies in the East Indies toward self-government.[16]

On becoming a member of the United Nations, Spain declared that her overseas possessions were "overseas provinces" of a unitary Spanish state. By 1961, however, Spain had accepted the U.N. General Assembly's designation of its possessions as non-self-governing territories, and declared its intention to abide by the principle as defined by the United Nations.[17] As a result, Equatorial Guinea became independent in 1968.

As early as 1946, Belgium accepted the designation of the Congo as a non-self-governing territory, and the application of the principle of trusteeship under international supervision outlined in Article 73, subparagraph e of the U.N. Charter.[18] However, like France, the plans that Belgium had for the Congo did not include independence. King Baodouin stated in 1955 that the Belgian government was committed to establishing in the Congo a eurafrican society integrally linked with Belgium which, " . . . will ensure the perpetuity of a genuine Belgo-

Congolese community guaranteeing to all, Black and White, the share due them in the government of their country."[19] Again, like France, Belgium was forced by circumstances to change this policy, and it granted independence to the Congo in 1960.

In the United Nations, Belgium has consistently argued that the application of the principle to only colonial territories is unfair. According to the Belgian Thesis, there are many groups of peoples to whom the principle of self-determination should be applied within the territorial boundaries of member states, whose relations with the states concerned was essentially the same as that between European countries and their overseas territories. The Belgian argument was as follows:

> "A number of states were administering within their own frontiers territories which were not governed by the ordinary law; territories with well defined limits, inhabited by homogeneous peoples differing from the rest of the population in race, language and culture. Those populations were disenfranchised; they took no part in the national life; they did not enjoy self-government in any sense of the word. . . .He could not see how anyone could claim that states administering such territories were not what the Charter called states which have or assume responsibilities for the administration of territories, whose peoples have not yet attained a full measure of self-government."[20]

This thesis was not so much a repudiation of the U.N. definition of self-determination as it was an attempt to enlarge the size of the group to which it should be applied.

United States of America:

The U.S. government takes the position that the United States became independent by invoking the right of self-determination and so concludes:

> "We surely cannot deny to any nation that right whereon our own is founded—that everyone may govern itself according to whatever form it pleases and change these forms at its own will."[21]

But the United States has also advocated the principle of trusteeship—that dependent peoples should exercise their right when they have been developed to the point at which they have the capacity to exercise it. Only those, "who, by their acts, show themselves worthy of it and ready for it,"[22] should be permitted to exercise their right of self-determination. This, and other political considerations, caused the United States to be equivocal in its support of colonial peoples seeking independence.[23] But, in its own colonial practice, the United States recognised the principle and, unlike the European powers, has always recognized the right of its colonial peoples to choose freely among many modes of self-determination, including independence. Thus, U.S. colonial territories became self-governing by merger with the United States (Hawaii and Alaska), by association (Puerto Rico) and by full independence (the Philippines). In the United Nations, the United States, like Belgium, has tried to widen the scope of the application of the principle to include the Soviet satellite countries, but with no success. Speaking to the Sixteenth General Assembly, President Kennedy claimed:

"the tide of self-determination has not reached the Communist Empire, where a population far larger than the officially termed 'dependent' lives under governments installed by foreign troops instead of free institutions."[24]

Portugal:

Portugal's colonial policy was based on an ideology similar to France's *"mission civilizatrice"*. An explicit expression of this ideology in the Native Statute of 1954 is as follows:

"The State shall endeavour by every means to improve, both materially and morally, the living conditions of the indigenous inhabitants . . . and to educate them . . . by transforming their primitive usages and customs, directing their activities into useful channels, and actively integrating them into the community. . . ."[25]

Characteristically, Portugal asserted that the only way to accomplish this mission was by assimilating them into Portuguese citizenship. The idea of eventual independence for the colonies was ruled out, because Portugal was not a colonial power, but "is and has always been, a unitary State, regardless of the relative geographic situation of its various possessions."[26] Thus, Portugal's colonial policy was characterized by the theory that natives could become *assimilado* after successfully meeting the qualifications established by the Portuguese.[27]

Faced with the anti-colonialist onslaught, Portugal took refuge in another constitutional fiction. In 1961 it transformed all the subjects into citizens by law, and argued that the overseas territories were truly independent, because Portugal's laws applied equally to all people of the Portuguese state, and, "as integral parts of the nation, all our extra-european provinces have always shared in the independence of the nation."[28] This subterfuge did not save Portugal from the fierce disapprobation of the General Assembly which believed that the law was at variance with the actual status of the Portuguese subjects in Africa. However, Portugal continued to maintain this position until July 17th, 1974, when after a costly colonial war and the demise of the Caetano dictatorship, the new government, under President Spinola, adopted a constitution recognizing "the right of self-determination and independence for all overseas territories under its administration."[29]

Republic of South Africa:

Although it is not a colonial power in the classic sense of having overseas colonies, the Republic of South Africa is generally considered a "prototype of a colonial power."[30] This is due to the fact that it rules its non-white population and the native population of Namibia[31] through a policy of " . . . deliberate subordination of the vast majority of the people to an inferior status."[32] Thus, it is considered by the United Nations as a state administering territory inhabited by non-self-governing peoples, which is carrying on a policy "based on the assumption that African peoples of South Africa, who constitute a great majority of the population, are colonial subjects of the White nation and its Government."[33] Viewed from this perspective, the South African policy of *apartheid* or "separate development" may be considered its colonial policy, and therefore, evidential of the Republic's attitude to the principle of self-determination.

Since the official enactment of the policy of separate development in the early 1950s, the South African government has made no secret of the fact that its main purpose was to keep the Black people of South Africa in a state of perpetual subjugation. The following statement made by Prime Minister Verwoerd in 1963 is only one example of a constantly reiterated theme:

"Reduced to its simplest form the problem is nothing else than this: we want

136

to keep South Africa White. . . .'Keeping it White' can only mean one thing, namely, White domination, not 'leadership', not 'guidance', but 'control', 'supremacy'. If we are agreed that it is the desire of the people that the White man should be able to continue to protect himself by retaining White domination . . . we say that it can be achieved by separate development."[34]

This policy of separate development has been severely attacked in the United Nations as an infringement on the right of self-determination of the African peoples of the Republic and Namibia. Since its inception, the United Nations has waged a constant battle of trying to remove Namibia from the exclusive jurisdiction of the republic by a large number of resolutions and legal moves,[35] while at the same time, by a series of sanctions and embargoes, attempting to force an abandonment of the policy of *apartheid*.Having failed in all these attempts, the U.N. General Assembly adopted a resolution affirming that "the people of South-West Africa have the inalienable right to self-determination, freedom and independence in accordance with the charter of the United Nations." This terminated the Republic's mandate over the territory, making it the direct responsibility of the United Nations.[36] So far, the Republic of South Africa has virtually ignored this and subsequent resolutions of the General Assembly and the Security Council and refused to allow any interference in that area. However, it has moved to assuage some of the international disapprobation by introducing policies that have a semblance of being consistent with the principle of self-determination. For instance, it has declared the intention of preparing the Bantustans for eventual independence, with the Transkei leading the way in 1976. Also, in Namibia, it is willing to consider a variety of alternatives including the independence of the territory as a unitary state if the majority of the population desired it.[37] The latest repressive activities of the government and its refusal to allow a U.N. presence in the area raise some serious questions about the sincerity of these declarations.

What the 'colonial' practice of South Africa indicates is that its definition of self-determination as the right of subject peoples to self-government and independence is the same as the definition of the principle in U.N. and general international practice. Where it differs from the other members of the international community is that it has consistently refused to respect that right with regard to dependent peoples under its administration. From the beginning South Africa has admitted that the African peoples in the Republic of South Africa and Namibia are non-self-governing. But it has also blatantly stated that it had no intention of granting them self-government, and it has rejected the right of the United Nations to regulate or supervise its policies. Recently South Africa instituted a plan of autonomous Bantustans with the declared prospect of eventual independence. However, these were not introduced as a result of the expressed wish of the people affected, but imposed by a government as a means of continued subjugation.[38] Bearing in mind its declared aim of using the policy of separate development to maintain white domination, this latest plan of Bantustan independence is an attempt to create a constitutional subterfuge behind which it can take refuge while continuing to deny the African peoples the right of self-determination.

The Anti-Colonial States and Self-Determination

In the era of decolonization, the states which have been making and backing claims of the right of self-determination have been the states newly emerged from colonialism and their allies. Before the mid-1950s, when these states began to make their appearances in the United Nations, the undisputed champion and leader of the anti-colonial group was the Soviet Union.[39] Because they consistently advocated the right of self-determination of oppressed nationalities and colonial peoples as far back as the early Bolshevik days,[40] and because of their position as one of the superpowers in the United Nations, an examination of Soviet practice is important for establishing the accepted meaning of the principle in international law.

The Soviet Union:

Self-determination is one of the central principles of the multi-national federal structure of the Soviet Union. Its first constitutional act, the November 1917 Declaration of the Rights of the Peoples of Russia, affirmed the principle of equal sovereignty and free self-determination, including the right of secession of all the nationalities.[41] It was on the basis of this and other declarations that many of the component parts of the Russian empire, such as the Ukraine, first seceded, gained their independence, and finally concluded a federal agreement with the Russian soviet.[42] Subsequently, the principle, including the right of secession, was written into the 1923 and 1936 Soviet Constitutions. It has also been introduced in the form of plebiscites to determine the disposition of disputed territories, as in the Soviet-Finland Treaty of 1918 with regard to the province of Pechanga.[43] Further, the principle is evident in early Soviet treaty practice. For instance, Article IV of the Turko-Soviet treaty of March, 1921, states:

"The Contracting Parties, establishing the national movement for the liberation of the eastern peoples and the struggle of the workers of Russia for a new social order, solemnly recognize the right of the nations to freedom and independence, also their right to choose a form of government according to their own wishes."[44]

Consistent with the Bolshevik definition of the principle as the right of oppressed peoples to secession, the Soviet Union always insisted, during the decolonization era, that the self-determination of colonial peoples can be achieved only through complete independence. As we have already seen, the Soviet delegate to the San Francisco conference, Vyacheslav Molotov, defined self-determination as the attainment of national independence. In line with this definition, the Soviets have always maintained that the status of Puerto Rico as a commonwealth "associated" with the United States is merely a trick to obscure its actual colonial status.[45] In 1960, the Soviet Union presented a draft resolution demanding immediate independence for all colonial peoples. The resolution was rejected in favor of Resolution 1514(XV).[46]

In addition to the demands for immediate independence, the Soviets have also claimed that the principle includes the right to initiate armed struggle against colonial powers. Therefore, all Communist parties should "consider it their duty to support the sacred struggle of the oppressed people and their just anti-imperialist wars of liberation."[47]

Although the Soviet position on self-determination is acceptable to many members of the Afro-Asian group, it is more extreme than the group as a whole has been willing to accept. This is revealed in the process through which they achieved independence, as well as their practice in and out of the United Nations. With the exception of Algeria and the Portuguese colonies, all the colonial territories have gained their independence through negotiations with colonial powers. As these negotiations show, they have been willing to accept (a) constitutional evolution to self-government, and (b) a definition of self-government as autonomy, association or independence. Furthermore, as they emerged from colonial status and took a speedy decolonization by total independence. These principles became the basis of the decolonization offensive of the Afro-Asian states in the United Nations. The renewed efforts of these states to push for recognition of the relationship between self-determination and human rights and the explicit statement of the right of dependent peoples to self-determination were felt in the General Assembly during the examination of the Draft of the Human Rights Covenants. Five years later, the effect of the Bandung Communique was still potent. Parts of Resolution 1514(XV), especially its first operative paragraph, are *verbatim* reproductions of the sections of the Bandung Communique.

The Belgrade Declaration of Non-Aligned Nations of September 1961 represents another step in the ongoing struggle for the liberation of dependent peoples. It explicitly reaffirms Resolution 1514(XV) of the U.N. Charter and reiterated all the important principles therein, including (1) a "demand" for the immediate termination of colonial occupation; (2) the restoration of the territorial integrity and full independence of dependent peoples; and (3) a reaffirmation of their conviction that "all nations have the right to unity, self-determination and independence . . . "

Two new principles of some importance to the Afro-Asian definition of self-determination are introduced in the Belgrade Declaration. Article 9 of the declaration states:

"The participating countries declare solemnly the absolute respect of the rights of ethnic or religious minorities to be protected in particular against crimes of genocide or any other violation of their fundamental human rights.

The importance of this article lies in its tacit recognition of group rights (as opposed to individual rights) that could potentially presage the future establishment of international undertakings for group protection, on somewhat the same lines of autonomy as in the League of Nations increasingly active role in formulating resolutions, on the whole, the claims they have made have been consistent with the way they achieved self-government. On the basis of this practice it may be concluded that this anti-colonialist group has acquiesced in the concept of trusteeship, and the principle of self-determination as defined to include the notion of apprenticeship before the right can be exercised. Ocassionally there have been tendencies in this group to make more extreme demands but, on the whole, these tendencies have not prevailed.

The Afro-Asian organizational focus for eliminating colonialism was first revealed at the Bandung Conference of April, 1955, when they laid the foundation for concerted action in the United Nations on the issues of self-determination, human rights, and colonial independence. The fight against colonialism was the keynote of the Bandung Conference, as it was to be in subsequent meetings of the group. With regard to this issue, the final communique indicated the following agreed-upon principles:

1) full support for "the right of peoples and nations to self-determination" as set forth in the charter and resolutions of the United Nations;
2) affirmation that the exercise of the right of self-determination is the "prerequisite of the full employment of all fundamental Human Rights and especially the eradication of racial discrimination";
3) affirmation "that colonialism in all its manifestations is an evil which *should especially be brought to an end*";
4) affirmation that the subjection of peoples to alien subjugation is a denial of fundamental human rights and contrary to the U.N. Charter;
5) committment to support "the cause of freedom and *independence* for all" dependent peoples.

Of particular interest are the principles that establish a direct relationship between self-determination and human rights and the committment to minority treaties. Article 14 of the Belgrade Declaration is important because of what it indicates about the Afro-Asian position on the validity of the use of force to achieve independence. It states the following:

> The participating countries express their determination that no intimidation, interference or intervention should be brought to bear in the exercise of the right of self-determination of peoples, including their right to pursue constructive and independent policies for the attainment and preservation of their sovereignty.

Some of the delegates wanted the conference to go on record as endorsing the concept of national liberation wars as legitimate self-defence against the "permanent aggression" of colonial domination. However, most of the delegates found it impossible to accept this view of "just wars" and therefore the conference adopted the compromise wording of "the right to pursue constructive and independent policies. . . ."[48]

The issue of defining national liberation by the use of force as legitimate self-defense was not merely academic. On August 1, 1961, exactly one month before the Belgrade Conference was to begin, Dahomey had "liberated" the adjacent Portuguese enclave of Sao Joao Batista, and three months after the conference, on December 19, 1961, India "liberated" Goa. In both cases Portugal charged aggression, and as was expected the two states, particularly India, justified their actions as self-defense against Potuguese "permanent aggression."[49] Since the Goa incident, the concept of self-defense against permanent aggression as a justification for the use of force in the exercise of the right of self-determination has been gaining adherents among the Afro-Asian states. In 1962, a conference of Afro-Asian jurists meeting at Conakry made the following statement:

> All struggles undertaken by the peoples for their full national independence or for the restitution of their territories or occupied parts thereof, including armed struggle, are entirely legal.[50]

This tendency is graphically illustrated in the Organization of African Unity Charter, and the conferences of the African states. The Addis Ababa Conference of 1963, at which the OAU Charter was adopted, was dominated by the twin themes of *total independence* and *unity* of all African peoples. In particular, all the delegates were unanimously convinced of the "imperious and urgent necessity of co-ordinating and intensifying their efforts to accelerate the unconditional attainment of national independence by all African territories still under foreign domination." So important was this principle considered that it was specifically written into Article 2 of the OAU Charter as one of the purposes of the organization. It also made the central point in a special resolution on decolonization which explicitly and emphatically commits the African states fully to supporting and financing fighters to carry on a full scale war of liberation against the white supremacist states of southern Africa.[51]

Without exception, the Afro-Asian states have resisted any attempts to apply the principle as defined to groups within their territorial boundaries. Since 1960, Somalia has been claiming the right to unify all Somalias including those in Kenya, Ethiopia and French Somaliland into one state. This claim has received practically no support from the African states whose position is reflected in the following 1964 OAU resolution which:

(1) solemnly reaffirms strict respect by all Member states of the organization for the principles laid down in paragraph 3 of Article 3 of the charter of the OAU (respect for the territorial integrity and the independent existence of states).
(2) solemnly declares that all Member states pledge themselves to respect the borders existing on their achievement of national independence.[52]

On the basis of these principles, the claims of Katanga and Biafra to the right of self-determination were overwhelmingly rejected by the Afro-Asian states.[53] The case of Biafra is particularly instructive because even Somalia, which had previously claimed the same right, rejected Biafra's claim and argued that "the international community on its part should refrain from any action detrimental to the peace, unity and territorial integrity of Nigeria."[54] Confronted by monumental problems of nation building in the face of real or potential secessionist movements, the new Afro-Asian states have drawn considerable attention to themselves by their emphatic insistence on maintaining their territorial integrity and asserting that the principle does not apply to sections of a state that wish to secede:

The principle of self-determination has relevance where FOREIGN DOMINATION is the issue. It has no relevance where the issue is territorial disintegration by dissident citizens."[55]

The same fear of national disintegration explains why the secession of Bangladesh had so few supporters. Apart from the

Soviet-bloc states, only Sweden, Chile, Madagascar and India gave it strong support, while most of the Afro-Asian states took a position similar to the one presented below:

> If we wish to speak of self-determination in our respective states, we will be surprised to see the over-all number of states grow by four or by ten because of various internal problems, and our organization which has 131 members to-day might have more than 600 members tomorrow, as a result of this splitting of states. . . .Pakistan is a sovereign state which is free to settle its matters as it wishes. Our duty is to assist it to maintain its national unity within the framework of respect for the principles contained in the Universal Declaration of Human Rights. . . ."[56]

Thus, it was not by the general recognition of its right to self-determination that Bangladesh won its independence, but by its own might and that of its ally India.

Conclusion.

On the basis of the state practice described above, the conclusion can be drawn that there has emerged a general consensus on the meaning of the principle which is shared by practically all the members of the international community. The colonial powers have adopted and implemented, with varying degrees of reluctance, policies that are generally acceptable to the United Nations and the anti-colonial states with regard to the definition of a dependent territory, the obligation of trusteeship, and the ways in which a colony may exercise the right of self-determination. Their policies have been consistent with their voting records in the United Nations, and in spite of numerous hesitations and abstentions they have shared fully in the anti-colonial consensus which has emerged. After an extensive study of voting records, Edward Rowe's findings to this effect seem surprising. He notes:

> This general finding conflicts somewhat with one of the observations commonly made by writers on the United Nations and colonialism—i.e. that the decline in moderation among the anti-colonial states produces a general reaction among the colonial powers uniting them behind pro-colonial positions. . . .On the contrary, during the last few sessions at least, the increasingly extreme character of the anti-colonial proposals put forward have been accompanied by the colonial powers moving closer to the anti-colonial majority."[57]

What Rowe's findings seem to indicate is that not only has a consensus emerged in the United Nations with regard to the meaning and application of the principle of self-determination but also, that this consensus is not an unstable compromise caused by hopeless impasse, but rather represents the increasing acceptance of all the protagonists in the decolonization issue. Even the Republic of South Africa shares this definition although it refuses to abide by it.

It is certainly true that different groups of states have on occasion attempted to gain general acceptance for an expanded definition of self-determination. For instance, many of the anticolonial states have shown a preference for a definition meaning total independence, and these states seem to have scored a major psychological victory in the adoption of Resolution 1514(XV). However, as we have seen, vis-à-vis world politics they have had to retreat from that position. Resolutions that they have subsequently introduced and voted for have not advocated total and immediate independence for the remaining colonial territories as indicated in Resolution 1514(XV). On the contrary, their voting behavior suggests that they are willing to retain the concept of trusteeship, and insist on adequate preparation of non-self-governing peoples before eventual self-government.[58] Furthermore, they have been willing to accept integration, or association, as satisfactory modes of exercising the right of self-determination.

Other states have also tried to expand the meaning of self-determination but with little success. Some states have asserted that the principle should be applied to dependent peoples *within* the territorial boundaries of other states that they wish to embarass; for instance, the United States wanted the principle applied to the Soviet sattelites.[59] Such demands have been rebuffed consistently. There seems to be a general understanding that once the door is opened to applying the principle to minorities or "backward peoples" within their territories, practically no state would be able to escape the disapprobation of the international community.[60] As a result, there has been a tacit understanding that no really serious effort will be made to expand the scope of the principle beyond its application to colonial peoples.[61] This "conspiracy" against dependent groups within national territories was in effect even before the advent of the Afro-Asian states into the international community, but once in, they have embraced it with great tenacity.

After 1960, the claim that the right of self-determination could be exercised by using force against an intransigent colonial power, on grounds of self-defense against "permanent aggression," has been gaining favor among the anti-colonial coalition. The claim was rejected. However, the failure of Portugal to get its allies to support its claim of aggression against India in the Goa incident shows that there may be a trend toward its acceptance. As Inis Claude notes:

> " . . . the doctrine that India invoked in the Goa case has not been universally accepted, but the United Nations is moving steadily in that general direction. The collective legitimization of anti-colonialism has been very nearly completed in the United Nations, and almost any anti-colonial tactic can be expected to escape censure, if not to gain the endorsement of the organization."[62]

The recognition and support that the United Nations has given to the national liberation movements in Angola, Mozambique and Guinea-Bissau, and the granting of observer status to the Palestine Liberation Organization at the General Assembly bear out the truth in Claude's statement.

The practice of the states has been significant not only in the development of the meaning of self-determination, but also in providing evidence of the ripening of the principle into an international legal right. Before World War II, it was written into many treaties, and although legally effective, it was not generally recognized as a right under international law. In the immediate aftermath of the war the principle was applied by the colonial powers with varying degrees of conscientiousness. However, it was applied as a policy, emanating from the enlightenment of the colonial powers, not as a duty created by a corresponding right of the subject peoples. During the era of decolonization the principle matured into a right. The charter and practice of the United Nations, and general international practice provided the *opinio juris sive necessitatis* which developed self-determination into a principle of international law. This development did not take place without a struggle. Initially, the colonial powers insisted that questions concerning their colonies were exclusively within their domestic jurisdiction, and they attempted to bring these matters within the scope of Article 2, (7) of the U.N. Charter. Eventually all, with the exception of the Republic of South Africa, came to accept the fact that the right of self-determination of subject peoples is a matter of legitimate international concern.[63]

Britain, the Netherlands and the United States were the first to concede the legitimacy of the U.N. role in the supervision of decolonization. France, Belgium and Portugal were more intransigent at the outset. For instance, in 1953 Belgium resigned from the Special Committee because it felt that the committee was "progressively assimilating the system of non-self-governing territories to the international trusteeship system" and thus encroaching on matters within the domestic jurisdiction of the colonial powers.[64] As we have already noted, Portugal did not concede until 1974.[65] However, all colonial powers accepted the authority of the United Nations, even if on some specific issues they doubted the wisdom of its resolutions. Today, there is no doubt that self-determination, as defined in U.N. and general international practice, is a principle of international law which yields a right to self-government that can be claimed legitimately by *bona fide* dependent peoples.

The era of decolonization is almost over. However, this does not signal the demise of the principle or the disappearance of groups that are convinced of the legitimacy of their claim to that right. As we have seen, many groups of people throughout the world are now claiming the right of self-determination, and there is every indication that their numbers will increase. Given the nature of the new states in particular, a reactivation of claims based on the right of self-determination will not come from "salt-water" colonial dependencies, nor are the older states completely immune. Although it cannot be predicted with absolute certainty what groups will be agitating for equality, it may not be too courageous to predict that the form in which the issue will be raised might tend to resemble its manifestations in Europe during the inter-war period. That alone is reason enough to clarify the meaning that the international community has agreed to give the principle in such a way as to benefit from the entire span of practice and, hopefully, to escape the pitfalls of excessive historical parochialism.

147

CHAPTER VII

SELF-DETERMINATION REEXAMINED

Self-Determination in International Law

The principle of self-determination has been the basis of a great mass of international practice, which is obvious from the trouble it has caused and the hope it has generated. It was probably on the lips of the student whose bullet at Sarajevo provoked Austria into the actions that plunged Europe into World War I. Even before the war was over, self-determination was presented by Woodrow Wilson and Lenin as the principle upon which would be built a new world of justice and peace. Barely fifteen years later, the principle was used by Hitler to justify one of the most blatant acts of aggression ever seen, only to become later the basis of what has been described, as one of the most important issues of the United Nations.[1] The evidence of the past seventy years suggests that the principle of self-determination has not only been invoked in connection with these and other instances of extreme international upheaval but that it has also been used to justify a wide range of national policies and a numerous variety of claims on the international level.

In the past few years, there has been a debate among publicists concerning the legal nature of the principle of self-determination. As compared to the totality of the literature on the subject, this debate is quite young. Prior to World War II, there was a general consensus among writers that there was no right of self-determination, and therefore, the writing on the principle, insofar as it related to international law, was confined largely to *de lege ferenda* propositions. Therefore, that this debate started at all was in itself testimony to the fact that the principle had been in enough international usage to make the question relevant. While the debate went on, the international community, with characteristic disregard for writers, has provided massive evidence that suggests that the principle has indeed ripened into a rule of international law. First, the League of Nations Committee of Jurists, while denying that the principle had standing in international law, noted that it had been incorporated into some international treaties. After that came the entire doplomatic practice of the interwar period, including the recognition of the successor states, the League of Nations' mandates system, and the minorities protection system. Then, the Atlantic Charter, the U.N. Declaration of Liberated Europe, and, finally, the U.N. Charter and the cumulative effects of the General Assembly resolutions and declarations; the two Human Rights Conventions, the OAU Charter, the Pacific Charter, the Bandung Communiques, and the Belgrade Declaration. Faced with this massive evidence, those publicists who have given this question any attention seem to agree that the states, by a number of means, have accorded the principle of self-determination the status of a rule of international law,[2] or that they are very much on the way to doing so.[3]

While asserting that the principle of self-determination has become a legal norm, however, some writers feel compelled to say that "It is true that the concept of self-determination is subject to considerable doubt as regards its scope and subject."[4] As they rightly point out, the question of the legal nature of the principle of self-determination is separate from the question of its scope and content.[5] Indeed, there are many principles of international law, such as the principle of nonintervention, the right of self-defense, and others, that are formulated in general terms so that their particular manifestation would vary in accordance with the situation to which they are applied. The principle of self-determination seems to be of this nature.[6] Thus, it is not unique, and the problem of defining it is essentially the same as is usually and routinely encountered in any attempt to define any principle of international law with varied situational application.[7] The real difficulty seems to have been caused by the publicists themselves, as we suggested earlier. Perhaps due to the traditional association between the concept of self-determination and the powerful concepts of popular sovereignty, nationalism, and socialism, most writers who have given any attention to the problem have shown a curiously un-shakable tendency to define the principle as a derivative of the political or ideological principle from which they think it *ought* to be derived, without paying much attention to the practice of states (who, after all, are the ones with the capacity to effec-tively accept or reject such definitions). Furthermore, when some writers have observed state practice, they have done so for the purpose of demonstrating that that practice is inconsis-tent with their doctrinally derived formulations and are, there-fore, erroneous![8]

As a consequence of this type of analysis, there has developed a formidable gap between the definition of self-determination as it might be suggested by international practice and the de-finition upon which writers have insisted. The seriousness of this doctrinal gap is illustrated by the fact that a work pub-lished in 1968 advanced a definition of the principle of self-determination that is the same as the one that had been advo-cated in the early twenties as a derivative of the theory of popular sovereignty, and that had been subsequently discre-dited due to its inability to explain in terms of its theoretical framework the basis on which the international community de-termines the unit or group that may legitimately claim the right of self-determination.[9]

What we have attempted to do in this work is to bridge this doctrinal gap by seeing if international practice, which has been described in the foregoing chapters, will yield answers to the questions that the publicists have correctly identified as those that will have to be answered in order to arrive at a de-finition of the principle. What we are saying is that writers have performed an invaluable service in delineating categories, such as "recipient unit," into which we must fit our mass of data. Where they made their error was in attempting to answer their questions from a theoretically derived, *a priori* definition of such groups as "nationality" or "peoples," instead of ascer-taining those groups that have successfully claimed the right of self-determination and then attempting to describe their es-sence.

Any attempt to define the nature of a group is based on the capacity to separate the essential from the irrelevant or inci-dental qualities and the tendency to put individual units into a category on the basis of those essential characteristics which they have in common. By posing the question, "What is the nature of the unit recipient of the right of self-determination?" publicists provided us with a relevant categoric focus or checklist of group characteristics. What we need to do, then, is to ascertain, on the basis of international diplomatic practice, those characteristics which were sufficient to qualify the group for the application of the right of self-determination. Then we must determine whether, while operating under widely different historical and social circumstances and exhibiting a massive array of different qualities, the essential characteristics which qualified each group for the right was the same in all groups. At that point we shall be able to make a general statement on the essential nature or characteristics of groups accorded the right of self-determination in the international community. Apart from the recipient unit, publicists provided us with a number of other questions which have to be answered.

In sum, the following is a list of questions which most writers felt should be answered in order to define the concept of self-determination:

1) The nature of the beneficiary—internal composition and size;
2) The nature of the right of self-determination—specific rights of the Beneficiary; conditions indicative of the satisfactory exercise of the rights of the Beneficiary, and specific obligations to the Beneficiary;
3) The nature of the obligatee—internal composition and size;
4) Sources of the rights and obligations.

Bearing these questions in mind, we shall now analyze the international practice of self-determination. As we shall see, although some are important from the standpoint of the orderly legal mind, they have been considered irrelevant by the international community in its development of the practice.

Summary of International Practice of Self-Determination

In the post World War I period there were four situations in which the policies of the allied powers had some relevance to the principle of self-determination. These were, the recognition of the successor states of eastern Europe, and the establishment of the boundaries, the system for the protection of the minorities, and the League of Nations' mandates system. As we have seen, one of the factors which conditioned the policy of the allied powers in relation to the new states was the feeling that their secession from the eastern european empires was entirely legitimate.[10] Furthermore, due to the geographical conditions in the empires, the secession of the new states invariably posed the problem of deciding the proper territorial limits. Thus, one of the most important problems which the peace conference had to cope with was the establishment of territorial boundaries. In settling this problem, the allied powers did not always apply the principle of self-determination, for in some areas, they had interests that would have conflicted with its application. However, in many areas, they applied what they believed to be the principle of self-determination. In such situations, what they attempted to do was to draw the territorial boundaries to coincide with nationality. The theory behind this was that by putting border populations in the same state as people of the same nationality they would not be in a "subject" or "oppressed" position, and that by removing this status of subjugation, the principle of self-determination would be satisfied.

The minorities protection system was necessitated by the fact that not all such nationalities could be "liberated," but instead were placed within the jurisdictional limits of a state controlled by members of that same nationality. In such situations, the allied powers felt that the requirements of the principle of self-determination could be met by eliminating their "subject" status without changing territorial boundaries, that is, by guaranteeing their self-government or autonomy.[11] There were still other groups that were not deemed politically organized enough to be objects of the application of the principle of self-determination. To such groups, the mandates system was applied to a variety of groups. All these groups had one charaction of the principle of self-determination, but guaranteeing future application by providing for their evolution into viable political communities capable of self-government under the tutelage of an assigned mandatory power.[12]

In all these instances, the principle of self-determination was applied to a vareity of groups. All these groups had one characteristic in common: none of them was self-governing. They were considered as "subject" to or "oppressed" by an alien group. The differences between the groups required that the principle of self-determination be applied in different ways. In all these different ways, however, the purpose was to eradicate the "subject" or "oppressed" status of the group and permit it to be self-governing. Thus, as applied by the allied powers, the principle of self-determination was defined as a policy of removing a community from alien subjugation and making it self-governing.

In many ways, the formulation of the principle of self-determination after World War II was more explicit than it had been during the interwar period. In the U.N. Charter, the connection between self-determination and the equality of groups was made more explicit, and the use of the term "Peoples" suggested that the groups that could exercise the right were not to be limited to those that had historically been characterized as "nationalities." Furthermore, in the practice of the United Nations, and a series of international instruments that followed, in the policies of the colonial powers, and in the anticolonial efforts of the Third World countries and their Soviet bloc allies, it became more and more clear that the application of self-determination was supposed to mean the "correction of the status of subordination to alien rule."[13] In actual practice, however, the application of self-determination was limited virtually to only one type of situation. Almost without exception, the only issues in which the right of self-determination was successfully invoked were in the attempts of European overseas colonial peoples to become independent: hence, the expression "self-determination during the era of decolonization."

Analyzing the nature of the right of self-determination in this period has sometimes led to excessive focusing on the application of the principle to the process of decolonization, thus rendering the essential similarity between its application in this situation and in other situations, such as that of the minorities protection system of the League of Nations, somewhat difficult to grasp. From another analytical standpoint, however, this focus on decolonization has been a fortuitous development, for it has clearly brought out the very important fact that the purpose of invoking the right of self-determination is to justify the liberation of a community from foreign subjugation. The great benefit of this is that it clearly sets the issue of self-determination apart from such issues as border disputes and secessions that are only peripherally connected to the principle of self-determination, but that have, nevertheless, confused much of the research into its meaning.[14]

In the first of the two general periods under consideration, the principle of self-determination was applied by the allied powers, even though it was not a rule of law. This fact strongly supports the contention that the definition of the principle is independent of its legal nature. More important is the fact that, in international practice of the principle as a political policy and later as a principle of international law, there has been so much similarity in the specific rules used that there can be traced between them a developmental continuity and unity that transcends either period. The principle of self-determination may in this sense be seen as including more specific rules that can be applied to different situations.[15] It is this meaning of the principle that we are interested in acquiring by attempting to answer the questions posed by the theorists, by reference to both the maintenance of flexibility in the law in such a way that it may be applied *mutatis mutandis* to colonial peoples, minorities, occupied countries, and other types of subjugation that, perhaps yet unimagined, might plague the international community at a future date.[16] Such a development may be forthcoming as the international community faces a future of changing political exigencies. For the present, our concern is the definition of the principle of self-determination, *lex lata*.

The Principle of Self-Determination Defined

In attempting to define the scope and content of the principle of self-determination, it is important to draw attention to the teleological dimension. This is equally true whether self-determination is just a principle or a legal right. A policy is a deliberate program of action that is designed to achieve a certain purpose. A legal right, in this case, gives rise to certain procedural rights by which the holder is supposed to realize certain goals. In either case, a clear delineation of the purpose of the principle or the right should indicate the nature of that principle or right.

A study of international practice involving the principle of self-determination indicates that in all the different circumstances of its application the purpose in each case was to remove a community from the political domination of another group and permit it to gain control of its own destiny. In this sense, the principle of self-determination is essentially connected to a policy that is designed to remedy or eradicate a deprivation. Thus, while in theory the principle may be applied to all communities, it would be meaningless or redundant to apply it to a community that is not laboring under this kind of deprivation. In other words, the application of the principle of self-determination to a community that is already self-governing would be meaningless. Thus, the principle of self-determination is one that may be properly invoked only on condition of subjugation of that group; in much the same sense, under international law, although every state has the right of self-defense, it may be properly invoked only if under attack.

Bearing in mind, then, the fact that the principle of self-determination becomes relevant to a situation only when subjugation is an issue, we are now in a position to attempt a definition of the principle and the rights and obligations it may give rise to, by responding to the categories suggested by the publicists on the basis of data taken from international practice.

The Beneficiary

Definition:

> The beneficiary of the right of self-determination is a self-conscious *politically coherent* community that is under the political subjugation of another community.

Comment:

In the aftermath of World War I, there were attempts to define the beneficiary in terms of, "nationality." As we have seen, three general types of definition of nationality were advanced.[17] It was at this point that questions of minimum size and internal composition became important as determinants of whether or not a particular nationality qualified for the application of the principle. All these definitions were found inadequate in some important sense. Slowly, the realization grew that nationality was neither based on objective characteristics nor on political will, as had been argued by writers, but on a subjective self-identity that was created by each group on the basis of a wide variety of attributes: religion, ethnic, linguistic, cultural, racial or (in the case of colonies) common political history.[18] At this point, the attempt at a sociological definition of beneficiary was discarded[19] What was important was to find out those groups whose qualifications seemed acceptable to the states.[20]

International practice:

As far as state practice is concerned, the only attributes of any real importance to a community that may invoke the right of self-determination are *political coherence* and *subject status*. The other two categories introduced by the writers, namely, the internal composition of the community or its size, have received very little attention.

Subjugation:

This is probably the most important characteristic required to validate a claim to the right of self-determination. In the past, the groups that have successfully claimed the right have been characterized as "subject nationalities," "oppressed nationalities," or "dependent peoples" and "non-self-governing peoples." Their status was essentially defined in terms of a relationship with a separate, alien, or foreign group by which they were ruled. Although this relationship could be manifested in a variety of historically determined situations, it was this relationship of subjugation that was considered crucial, as the wording of Resolution 1541(XV), paragraphs iv and v indicates. This was the plight of the nationalities that the allied powers set out to "liberate" in World War I. This was the plight of the colonial territories that were "liberated" during the U.N. decolonization era.[21] It must be noted in this connection that the claims of certain groups to the right of self-determination have not been generally accepted precisely on grounds that they are not under subjection.[22]

The establishment of the personality of a community as a subject group has usually taken the form of ascertaining the constitutional relationship between the subject community and ruling group. Some of these relationships were those that the minority treaties were supposed to eliminate. The list of "factors" adopted by the General Assembly in Resolution 1541(XV) represents an attempt to provide a more definitive and comprehensive criteria for establishing the status of a subjugated community.[23]

Political coherence:

The requirement that the group that claims the right of self-determination be politically coherent is contained in the definition itself. In order to make decisions about itself, a group has to be a political entity. Without a political process, decision-making is impossible. In fact, it would seem that a group would be unable to make the decision to claim the right of self-determination unless it were politically organized and coherent.

In theory, the existence of a politically coherent community has not been deemed to be dependent on a common territory. This was the basis of the theories of self-determination in the form of extraterritorial cultural autonomy that were advocated by the Austrian Socialists during World War I.[24] The allies also accepted the contention that it was possible to have politically coherent communities that were dispersed among an alien population. This attitude shows up grudgingly in the minority treaties, in which some of the rights that were guaranteed to the minorities were clearly rights that required effective action on the part of agencies representing those minorities. As we have shown above, however, the recognition of group rights under the system of minority guarantees was an uneasy problem for the allies.[25] The more usual pattern in international practice is to associate political coherence with territorially based communities. This tendency was pushed to the limit in the charter of the United Nations, in which communities are described as "peoples of non-self-governing territories."

In international practice, certain communities have been recognized as inchoate political communities. These were the communities that were placed under the League of Nations' mandates system and the United Nations' trusteeship system, as well as those described in Chapter XI of the U.N. Charter as "peoples of non-self-governing territories" that were to be administered under the general principle of trusteeship. Euphemistically referred to as "communities *not yet* able to stand on their feet," they were generally considered to be on their way to political coherence under colonial tutelage. A few other communities in Europe were accorded the same status under the theory that their interaction within the same territorial boundaries would, over a period of time, generate political coherence.[26]

According to international practice, the right of self-determination for such inchoate political communities under subjugation did not lapse. However, their exercise of the right was deferred until the completion of their development into a fully coherent political community. In many ways, this was an important step in the development of international society, for it led to the establishment of an agent of protection entrusted with the task of guaranteeing the eventual exercise by such communities of their right of self-determination.

Internal Composition:

Beyond the requirement of political coherence, the international community has paid very little attention to the internal composition of the community concerned. In particular, the claim that the right of self-determination meant the creation of homogeneous nation-states has been most emphatically rejected. Germany's claim before World War II for the creation of a German state of all German-speaking people was generally deplored. A much later claim by Somalia to create a state of "Greater Somalia" made up of all people that are ethnically Somali has been emphatically rejected by her African neighbors.

In the meantime, all the entities that have achieved their independence under the claim of the right of self-determination and have been recognized as such have been ethnically and culturally heterogeneous. The successor states of the eastern European empires were *"instant nations."* The newly independent states of Asia and Africa are notorious as "plural societies." Furthermore, the international community has indicated in the interwar period that the exercise of the right of self-determination did not require secession and total independence, but could be achieved by autonomy within a larger political structure on the basis of equality among all communities. The decision by the states in the General Assembly, indicated in Resolution 1541(XV), that self-determination may be achieved not only by independence but also by integration or association on a basis of equality is further proof of this.

Size:

The concern by the international community for the size of groups claiming the right of self-determination is not directly related to the right itself, but to the problem of the possibility of creating a multiplicity of ministates and the problems their vulnerability might generate for the international community.[27] While such concern exists, the flexibility afforded by the fact that there are other modes of exercising the right of self-determination short of complete independence has tended to alleviate the concern. In general, size has not been used by the international community as a criterion for deciding the validity of a group's claim of the right of self-determination.

The Right of Self-Determination

Definition:

> *The right of self-determination is the right of all communities to equality and full self-government.*

Comment:

At the beginning of the interwar period, widespread expectation that the allied powers would be implementing the principle of self-determination led to speculation among publicists that the application of the principle would invariably lead to untold chaos in the international system. This appraisal of the situation was based on the fact that they defined self-determination as the separation of a group from a state and the formation by that group of a separate state. According to this definition, which is linked with the *national determinism doctrine*, self-determination invariably meant the act of secession.[28]

As the situation developed, some writers began to reject the definition of self-determination in terms of secession as impraticable and attempted to define it on the basis of another doctrine. They argued that popular sovereignty in appropriate doctrine. Therefore, for these writers, self-determination was defined in terms of the plebiscite doctrine, according to which the principle of self-determination was the same as the principle of democratic government applied to questions of transfer of sovereignty. That is to say, whenever the cession of a territory was being considered, the people in that area were to be consulted by plebiscite, and their wishes were to be given decisive effect.[29] In both definitions mentioned above, *the principle of self-determination was defined as an act* that was undertaken by the group. In one case, it was supposed to be an act of secession. In the other, it was supposed to be an act of deciding by plebiscite the sovereignty to which they wish to belong, or as the contemporary advocates of the doctrine still assert, "self-determination is the process by which a people determine their own sovereignty status"[30]

In spite of the fact that these two doctrinal definitions are still being advocated, the evidence of international practice indicates that there is no inherent relationship between the principle of self-determination and the general problem of territorial settlement either by plebiscite or by secession. As opposed to the act of secession and the act of chosing a sovereignty, *self-determination is not an act or a process*. During the interwar period, it was a principle that could be applied in order that a group may achieve a condition of equality, and in the decolonization era, it has become a right by which a group may attain equality and full self-government. Insofar as the right of self-determination is connected to plebiscite or secession, it is the right on the basis of which those actions may be validated or justified.

International Practice:

Conditions Indicative of the Exercise of the Right

The relationship between the right of equality and the right of self-determination, which is explicitly stated in Article 1, paragraph 2 of the U.N. Charter, may be expressed as *par in parem non habet imperium*. In this sense, the right of self-determination represents the application of the principle of sovereign equality to communities. As a right, the principle of self-determination asserts that all communities are equal, and therefore, each community has the right to govern itself without interference. Thus, self-determination means the right of a community to full self-government.

As the practice of states has indicated, the full self-government called for by the right of self-determination may be realized in a number of ways. During the interwar period, the allied powers attempted to apply the principle of self-determination in such a way that the group in question may reach one of these conditions: *independence, autonomy* within a larger political unit, or *cultural autonomy* (by "minority protection"). In the decolonization era, three conditions were also delineated as ways by which the groups in question might attain self-government: *independence, integration* into another state, or *association* with another state on the basis of equality. The similarity between these two sets of modes is striking. The really significant difference, though, may be attributed to the fact that while in one case the principle of self-determination was a political principle later on it was deemed to have become a right. This difference is manifested in the fact that during the interwar years the allied powers applied the principle in such a way that the group would achieve one of these conditions. The choice as to which condition was more appropriate belonged to the allied powers, and they decided on the basis of what they thought would be more suitable to the group in question, without disturbing international peace.[31] In the decolonization era, however, with the recognition of the right of self-determination, (as opposed to the principle), the decision as to which condition of self-government would be appropriate was decided by the group itself.

Secession:

Because, according to the right of self-determination, one of the three ways by which a group may attain self-government is by independence, it means that the exercise of the right may entail the act of secession. However, to assert on this basis that the right of self-determination simply means the right to secede would be erroneous. In fact, what the right of self-determination does, is to distinguish between legitimate and illegitimate secessions. In other words, the international community seems to be saying that an act of secession is valid *if* it is based on a legitimate claim of the right of self-determination. And the legitimacy of the claim depends on the ability of the group to meet the qualifications of a beneficiary of the right of self-determination, that is, it must be under the subjugation of another community. Thus, the allied recognition of the independence of Czechoslovakia and Yugoslavia during the final years of World War I was partly motivated by the allied conviction that their secession from the Austro-Hungarian empire was legitimate on grounds of their claim of self-determination. In the decolonization era, an important reason

162

why the attempted secessions of Katanga and "Biafra" received little international support was that their claims to being "subjugated" and therefore entitled to the right of self-determination were deemed unacceptable. The analogy with the right of self-defense may again prove instructive. The use of force by a state is an act. It may be considered legitimate if the state committed that act under certain conditions that the international community is prepared to recognize as justifying a claim of self-defense. However, the same act may be considered illegitimate if those conditions do not exist. The relationship between the *right* of self-determination and the *act* of secession is of the same nature.

The International Plebiscite:

In spite of the scanty use of the international plebiscite, the definition of the principle of self-determination in terms of the plebiscite is more widespread. It should be pointed out, however, that international practice does not support this view. As we have seen, the right of self-determination may be exercised by the attainment of three conditions. The relevance of the plebiscite is only that it has been recommended as the most impartial and clear method by which the choice of the community can be ascertained. It must be made absolutely clear that *the use of the plebiscite is not in itself the exercise of the right of self-determination. It is merely a method for determining which mode of exercising the right is chosen by the community.*

In support of their definition of self-determination as the application of the plebiscite to territorial boundaries, they point to the fact that the allied powers employed the principle in European territorial settlements after World War I. While the assertion that the principle of self-determination was applied is correct their analysis of its application is incorrect. As we have explained above, the way in which the allied powers attempted to apply the principle of self-determination was to draw the territorial boundaries to coincide with nationality boundaries in order to avoid, as far as possible, the continued existence of alien "subject" nationalities within the new territorial boundaries. In this respect, it will be recalled that while at the outset the allied powers decided to use the plebiscite to determine the nationality of border populations to determine in which state they should be put, they ultimately discarded that in favor of using other evidence of nationality, and used plebiscites only when the other evidence was considered indeterminate.[32]

Again, it must be said that there is no connection between the principle of self-determination and the general problem of territorial settlement. In relation to the principle of self-determination, the problem of territorial settlement is raised only under very special circumstances. If a community decides to exercise the right of self-determination by the attainment of integration or by association with another state, the question of territorial settlement is not even raised. The question becomes relevant only if the community chooses to become independent by seceding. Even in such a situation, the question of territorial boundaries is not necessarily raised. As the decolonization era amply demonstrates, the secession of the colony from the metropolitan power never raised the issue of territorial settlement, because the two territories were not contiguous. Even in situations where the territory of the seceding community is contiguous to that of the mother territory, the question of territorial settlement is not necessarily raised if the separation is to be done on established lines, such as provincial or state boundaries.[33] In fact, the only time the issue of territorial settlement is raised occurs when there is some disagreement as to what the boundaries should be between the seceding community and the mother state. This rather special case was the situation that prevailed after World War I. It is instructive to recall that the boundaries that were successfully claimed by the new states were invariably not based on the plebiscite but were justified on historical grounds.[34] Furthermore, in the cases discussed above, a plebiscite would have determined only the boundary between the two communities, not the issue of self-determination, which would already have been successfully claimed. In the light of the foregoing discussion, it must be said that to assert that the right of self-determination means the right of a group to choose the sovereignty under which it shall live is simply incorrect.

Specific Rights of the Beneficiary

Definition:

The principle of self-determination gives rise to two types of subsidiary rights under international law:

1. The right to recognition, and
2. The rights of dependent peoples, which may be subdivided into
a) the liberty to take steps to achieve full self-government without hindrance,
b) the right to interim protection,
c) the right of permanent sovereignty over their natural wealth and resources.

Comment:

One of the important differences between the two periods under consideration has been in the development of an obligation on the part of the international community to recognize sub-state groups, as well as in the clarification of the rights that these groups acquired as a result of such recognition. In the interwar period, as we have seen, the allied powers as well as the general community of European states developed reasonable, workable and coherent criteria of identifying the category of entities known as "subject nationalities" or "minorities."[35] The fact that such groups could be identified, however, did not mean that they could be afforded recognition, which is considered a discretionary act by which a state admits or declares that it considers a certain political unit as having the rights and duties that flow from statehood.[36] The concept of recognition becomes relevant to governments in situations where the succession of a government is in doubt. Recognition may also be applied to substate groups under very proscribed circumstances, if they are categorized as belligerents or insurgents. Even in such cases, such recognition ran the risk of being premature, according to generally accepted criteria, and thus being condemned as a denial of the sovereignty of the state in question.[37] Beyond these cases, there was no basis in international law for affording recognition to substate groups, except on the basis of a treaty.[38]

In the past few years, international practice, particularly in the United Nations, indicates that this situation has changed somewhat. Thus, it may now be correct to assert that there exists in contemporary international law the concept of affording recognition to a community as "dependent people" having the rights and capacity that flow therefrom,[39] and also that such recognition is no longer purely discretionary but has become a right to which "dependent peoples" are entitled.

International Practice:
The Right to be Recognized

The minority protection treaties were an example of international instruments by which substate groups were identified for the purpose of making them third-party beneficiaries of the agreement. To this extent, the identification of the groups involved would certainly have been consistent with the norms of the period. But even in that situation, as we have seen, the allied powers were not entirely comfortable with the concept of group rights. Thus, while it was clear that some of the rights that were to be guaranteed under the terms of the treaty could not have been effectively exercised without collective group action, the instruments are constructed in such a way that the rights appear to be rights of individuals.[40]

The same hesitation to recognize substate groups as having certain rights is evident in allied policy toward the subject nationalities. For instance, it is clear that the recognition that various allied powers accorded to the Czech National Committee was motivated in part by their belief that the struggle of the Czech "national liberation movement" against the Austro-Hungarian empire was entirely legitimate. It must be noted, however, that the allied powers were extremely careful to base their several acts of recognition not on the legitimacy of the nationalist movement but on the fact that the movement led by the Czech National Committee had acquired the attributes of statehood, as demonstrated in their participation in the war.[41]

The establishment of the mandated territories represents the first major breakthrough in the international recognition of political units other than states with international personality. As we have seen, the mandated territories were third-party beneficiaries of the agreements between the League of Nations and the mandatory powers. In this sense, they were not much different from the minorities. What was really significant about the people in the mandated territories was that unlike the minorities they were not nationals of the mandatory powers. It was not entirely clear whether or not the inhabitants of the C mandates were expected to become citizens of the mandatory power administering their territory. It was quite clear, however, that communities in the A mandates were expected to become independent. In all cases, the intent and logic of the mandates system seemed to suggest that these groups were to be permitted "to stand on their own feet." Thus, their status may be described as "prestate," as opposed to "substate"; they were, as it were, states-in-preparation. Fully developed, they would be independent states, or incorporated into independent states. As such, they were entitled, according to the terms of the agreement, not only to protection but also to the right to be developed toward the point at which they would be able to stand on their own feet.[42]

As revolutionary as the system was, the international personality of the units established under it was quite severely limited. They acquired no capacity to bring claims on the basis of their rights under the agreement, and even the Permanent Mandates Commission, which was the agent entrusted to guarantee their rights, had no direct access to the facts of their existence.[43] The really significant point, in relation to later developments, was the fact that although these units acquired rights to protection and to eventual self-determination these rights flowed out of the agreements and, therefore, did not as such represent a general recognition of such groups as entities with rights under international law.

The creation of rights for such prestate units under the mandates system turned out to be a very significant factor in the subsequent development of the general acceptance by the states of the rights of groups based on their status as dependent peoples. Thus, it may now be said that there exists in international law a category of entities called "dependent peoples," which, while not having the personality of states, nevertheless have a certain international personality with the capacity to bring international claims to maintain their rights.[44] Thus, on being accorded recognition as "peoples of a dependent territory," a group immediately acquires these rights.

The development of a category of entities known as "dependent peoples" has occurred mainly in the practice of the U.N. General Assembly. The main feature of this development has been that the General Assembly has been able to assert that it alone has the right to determine what groups belong in the category of non-self-governing and at what point they should be considered as having emerged from that status.[45]

In the determination of the status of groups, the General Assembly applied certain criteria, or guidelines, and afforded "recognition" to a group on the basis of its qualification.

The "recognition" that was afforded to a group as a "dependent peoples" in the practice of the United Nations differs from recognition as it is traditionally applied to states. Unlike traditional recognition, the "recognition" of dependent peoples is not discretionary, for, in asserting its competence to be the final determinant of the status of these groups, the United Nations took the identification of these units out of the discretionary control of the administering states (as well as the claimant groups). Thus, the identification of a group as "dependent people" by any state is considered as having no effect in international law unless it is endorsed by the United Nations.

As a corollary of the right of the United Nations to determine the status of such groups by "recognition," the groups also acquire the right to have their claim examined by the United Nations that they have the attributes of a "dependent people" amounts to "recognition" of the groups.

Such "recognition" classifies the group as a "non-self-governing people" and thus formally asserts that the group has certain rights under international law as a result of its recognized status. In this sense, this form of recognition is constitutive. It is important to note, however, that in this case *only the recognition* of the status of the groups by the General Assembly is constitutive. Individual acts of recognition by states cannot establish an international personality for groups. In conclusion, the practice of the U.N. General Assembly indicates that groups have a right to be examined for the purpose of being accorded recognition as non-self-governing peoples. On the basis of being accorded such recognition, they acquire an international personality as well as procedural standing for the purpose of bringing claims to maintain those rights.

As the United Nations developed the organizational machinery to supervise and activate the process of decolonization, the access that such groups have had to these machineries in the way of rights of petition and appearance before United Nations bodies has tremendously increased the general acceptance and routinization of the personality of such groups as legitimate substate groups in international practice. This is evident in the General Assembly Resolution 3089D (XXVIII) which recognized "that the people of Palestine are entitled to equal rights and self-determination," and the reception accorded Yasir Arafat of the Palestine Liberation Organization (PLO) at the 29th Session of the General Assembly.

In the practice of the United Nations, self-determination is the basic right that has been claimed for dependent peoples. In order to be able to exercise their right of self-determination by attaining full self-government, these groups enjoy subsidiary rights involving: (1) the right to self-liberation; and (2) the right to interim protection and development. This is indicated in a General Assembly resolution that stated *inter alia* that the General Assembly:

> . . . 1. Reaffirms the right of the populations of the African territories under Portuguese domination to self-determination and independence and recognizes the legitimacy of their struggle to achieve the rights laid down in the U.N. Charter, the Universal Declaration of Human Rights and the Declaration on the Granting of Independence to Colonial Countries and Peoples.

The accordance of official recognition to entities in the category of liberation movements has received some recognition in general state practice. This development, spearheaded by Soviet theorists, has found expression in the general practice of non-aligned states who have accorded delegate or observer status to the representatives of such movements at a variety of conferences, including the Bandung Conference of 1955, The Addis Ababa Conference of 1963, and the "First Tricontinental Conference" of 1966.

The Right of Self-Liberation

The first right that develops out of being accorded the *bona fide* status of dependent peoples is the right to take steps toward the achievement of full self-government without hindrance. Again, the major difference between pre-United Nations and post-United Nations practice is the transformation into an international legal right of what had been asserted, at least since the American Revolution, as the *political* right of revolution. In the practice of the colonial powers, this right has meant the right of the group to negotiate the timing and conditions of their attainment of full self-government, including the mode of

169

all self-government that the groups would choose and the conditions under which the choice would be made. This practice has been in full accord with the rules established in the United Nations Practice for Trust Territories and has received the legitimacy of various general and specific U.N. resolutions endorsing as appropriate the cessation of information in accordance with Article 73, (subparagraph e) of the charter.

Cases in which negotiations of this nature had broken down due to the intransigence of colonial powers have raised the question of the right of the dependent group to use force in attempting to achieve full self-government. Although the paucity of such cases does not at this point yield a clear statement of the rights involved, it seems that many of the states, particularly the Soviet bloc members and the Afro-Asian states, have accepted as valid the contention that such groups have the right to use force against intransigent colonial governments in self-defense. Although the doctrinal formulation of this right of self-defense on the basis of the concept of "permanent aggression" may be difficult to sustain in view of the U.N. Charter, it could be argued that the use of repressive measures against colonial nationalists amounts to aggression under the charter and a violation of the Universal Declaration of Human Rights. In some cases, the General Assembly has taken such a position.[46] Whether these rights will finally be inserted into the general corpus of international law under the concepts of self-defense or some form of self-help must await future development.

The Right to Interim Protection

Perhaps one of the most important developments in international society has been the recognition of group personality, which has occurred mainly under the auspices of U.N. decolonization efforts. The beginnings of this recognition, as we have shown, can be seen in the minority protection treaties. However, the uneasiness with that concept was not resolved until the connection between human rights and group rights was finally established, when the right of self-determination was incorporated into the Human Rights Conventions. With the realization that in some cases the deprivation of individual rights is based on the fact of the membership of that individual in a group,[47] it was finally recognized that in such cases there could not be effective protection without admitting the concept of protection for the entire group. Thus, the essential similarity between the status of "oppressed minorities" and colonial peoples was formally recognized.

Under the power of this logic, the principle of trusteeship was introduced in a situation in which the international community withheld the exercise of the right to a group on grounds of incomplete development. The result was the establishment of an agent of protection, under the aegis of the international community, entrusted by treaty with protection of the groups' inchoate rights and supervision of their eventual realization. Of necessity, this produced community organization of machinery, establishment of standards, and rules of procedures that asserted themselves against the jurisdiction of the states, with far-reaching prospects for increasing the community's capacity to make decisions affecting all aspects of national life.

The Right of "Permanent Sovereignty over Natural Wealth and Resources."

This concept is perhaps the most controversial aspect of the principle of self-determination. Although this right of 'economic self-determination'[48] is firmly established in the Human Rights Covenants, it has been very difficult to achieve general concensus on the precise nature of the rights which it generates. The reason for this difficulty stems from the fears of the capital-exporting countries that the right of permanent sovereignty over natural wealth and resources might be regarded as an endorsement of the right of states to expropriate foreign property without the generally recognized remedy of compensation.

If, as the article reads, this right of permanent sovereignty should be exercised without prejudice to obligations arising out of international economic cooperation, based upon the principle of mutual benefit, and international law, then clearly any interpretation of that right to confiscate foreign property without compensation cannot be allowed; for it is recognized in both treaty and customary international law, that a state's right to acquire property within its own jurisdiction goes hand in hand with the internationally recognized obligation to pay adequate, prompt and effective compensation.[49] Furthermore, there is no evidence in the *travaux preparatoires* or any consistent international practice before or after the adoption of the Human Rights Covenants to support such an interpretation.

What then is the meaning of the right of permanent sovereignty over natural wealth and resources? The most reasonable line of interpretation follows from the realization that the recipients of the right are not states but *dependent peoples*. This is not only clearly stated in the covenant, it is also consistent with the meaning of the principle of self-determination of which this right is a part. It is also clearly indicated in the *travaux preparatoires*, in which examples of the beneficiaries cited by the draft supporters were all dependent peoples, such as a tribe in Tanganyika being deprived of their ancestral lands, and the population of the Island of Nauru.[50]

In accordance with the U.N. practice of decolonization, these dependent peoples would be under the tutelage of administering powers who would be obliged to prepare them to develop the capacity for the eventual exercise of their right of self-determination. Seen in this context, the only possible interpretation of the statement that ". . . in no case may a people be deprived of its own means of subsistence" is that while in their status of dependent peoples, they have a right to have their resources safeguarded against exploitation by the administering power. However, because dependent peoples do not possess the ability to exercise this right, its enforcement can take place only after the people concerned have acquired the necessary capacity by attaining self-government. Thus, the particular right of permanent sovereignty is the right of a newly independent country to enforce the retroactive right of its people to protect their natural wealth against exploitation. The right is definitely not a blanket endorsement of expropriation without compensation. It is the right of the newly independent country to review concession and development agreements made on the peoples' behalf during the period of dependency, and to eradicate any deprivations where it can be shown that their right to economic self-determination had been violated by the policies of the administering power. The expectation is that in such cases, although the previous violation of the peoples right to economic self-determination is not enough to completely negate the rights of foreign property owners, it would tend to cause a deviation from the usual standards of compensation. The extent of

172

reduction of compensation is a matter to be settled by negotiations or arbitral tribunals.

Specific Obligations:
1. All states have an obligation to refrain from acts leading to the subjugation of other peoples;
2. All states have an obligation to refrain from taking any actions in opposition to attempts by any subject peoples to exercise its right of self-determination;
3. The United Nations has the obligation to recognize and protect the rights of subject peoples;
4. States which are directly responsible for the administration of subject peoples have an obligation to prepare them for self-government or independence.

Comment:
Because the substantive right of self-determination is formulated as a liberty, the obligations that arise do not in the final analysis call for any action. What is called for, is a general prohibition against the subjugation of a group. In other words, any act or policy of subjugation would constitute an infringement on the right and any such infringement would be unlawful under international law.

The prohibition is quite clear in terms of future acts of colonization, occupation or maintenance of sovereignty over non-self-governing peoples. All such acts will be considered illegal and therefore, justification for that community to take actions which may be classified under the concept of self-help, including actions in self-defense if necessary in order to restore its sovereignty. In this connection, any action taken by the initiator of the illegal act to inhibit the self-help efforts of the victim would also be illegal.

International Practice:
International practice provides ample support for taking action in self-defense against aggression, or in taking various kinds of action in self-preservation and self-help. Admittedly, there is some controversy about the admissibility of such pleas of self-help in the light of the U.N. Charter,[51] and some debate about the exact meaning and scope of Article 51 of the U.N. Charter which admits to "the inherent right of individual and collective self-defense."[52] It is clearly beyond the scope of this

173

work to enter that field. The point that is being made here is that whatever the international community accepts as valid in that realm is applicable to the prohibition against colonialism. In the past, relations of superordinancy and subordinancy between distinct groups have been initiated by conquest. Presumably this will continue to be the case. Therefore, at the beginning of the drama of conquest the prospective victim, being sovereign at that point, may invoke their pleas as a sovereign state. Thus, it seems that for the present and the future, "subjugation, which is the taking of possession of territory . . . cannot be regarded as a legal method of acquisition of title to territory,"[53] primarily due to the prohibition of the threat or use of force in Article 2, (paragraph 4) of the charter, but also due to the prohibition against inhibition of the attempts of the victim to restore itself to its sovereign status.

The more interesting and more controversial aspect of this prohibition concerns its application to subject peoples who were subjugated in historical times when conquest was an acceptable method of acquiring title to territory, and when the principle of self-determination had no legal standing. Another situation of similar complexity is the application of the prohibition to areas where, due to reasons obscured in history, the process of state building led to the incorporation of distinct subject peoples within the states' territorial limits. Therefore, what are the specific obligations which the states have to peoples who are already subject to alien jurisdiction?

As we have seen, since self-determination achieved legal standing the practice of the international community concerning this situation has been limited to the colonial situation. The regime of the Minority Protection Treaties indicate what allied policy was, and what the minority states had to grudgingly accept. It still remains true, however, that those treaty obligations were applied in a relatively small area, and even in this area they were inconsistently applied. The mandates system provides a legal system of an essentially remedial character that was further developed into a generalized trusteeship principle in the U.N. system. Although this system has operated for a relatively short period of time, it seems to provide interesting speculative prospects for the development of a general theory of trusteeship that could be applied in plural societies.[54]

What seems to have happened, schematically, was that under the regimes of Chapters XI and XII of the charter, the colonial powers decided that:

a) these peoples were still under their sovereignty;
b) their subject status would be eliminated within the framework of that sovereignty and in accordance with their capacity;
c) the sovereign will undertake to protect their rights and develop their capacity for self-government.

What is really interesting is the similarity of this program to the Minority Protection System. In both cases, eventual self-determination was provided for within the sovereignty of the state and in accordance with their capacity (for the minorities, in veiw of dispersal, they were only capable of self-government on the level of local cultural autonomy and equality; for the colonies, their lack of familiarity with modern institutions necessitated their development over time). In both cases, the states pledged to protect their rights and develop their capacities. (The minority states were not sure if they wanted to fully develop their sense of cultural separateness, or to assimilate the minorities; the colonial powers were not keen on having the colonies become self-governing by secession.)

A doctrinal statement of this development, to be purely speculative, might be framed as an assertion that—bearing in mind the acceptability of the three modes of attaining full self-government and the fact that secession is not a necessary concomitant of self-determination—the pledge of the Colonial Powers to aid dependent peoples to achieve full self-government effectively destroys any allegation of illegal action on their part with respect to the right of self-determination. This, of course, is all too clear in the current practice of the United Nations. Speculatively, this practice can logically be extended to future cases. In this way self-determination can be applied to claimant groups already within established territorial boundaries, especially in the new Afro-Asian states, as well as in Europe and the Americas, given the understandable reluctance of the international community to encourage secessions. The Belgian thesis has already suggested that those dependent peoples should be permitted to exercise their right of self-determination.

The generalization of this concept of "trust" has necessitated the creation of an agent of protection, whose functions may easily be expanded to cover the guarantor of interim protection afforded such dependent peoples and their development towards full self-government.

As we witnessed in 1974 the reluctance of Portugal to transform its dependent peoples into prospective self-governing peoples under the trusteeship principle of Chapter XI led to a direct attack on the validity of its title to these territories. The attack was based on the contention that the initial occupation of its African territories constituted aggression and, therefore, a breach of the right of self-determination. Portugal was also considered guilty of the second prohibition—against performing acts to inhibit the attempt of a community to attain full self-government. It seems to me that it might also be suggested that Portugal's claim or original title to those territories was invalid due to its incapacity to meet the requirements and standards of the presently prevailing international legal system, as required by the principle of intertemporal law.[55]

Obligatees

Definition:

1. The 'active' obligatee regarding the right of a people to self-determination is the state which wields sovereign power over that people.
2. The right of a people to self-determination necessitates the creation of an International Agency of Protection, the responsibility of which is to protect the interim rights of dependent peoples and supervise their development towards full self-government.

Comment:

Since the right of self-determination calls for a general obligation on all states to desist from subjugating other peoples, it does not necessarily call for a specific obligatee. In this sense, self-determination and subjugation simply take their place with such pairs as self-defense and aggression among the "rights and duties" of states.

However, the existence of a dependent or subject peoples under the right of self-determination calls for an 'active' obligatee. This obligatee is the perpetrator of the act of subjugation. Specifically, its obligation is to restore the subjugated community to full self-government in a manner consistent with the norms of international society. The relationship between this obligatee and the beneficiary, which often lacks the capacity to remedy its situation, is such that "the protection of beneficiary rights and interests requires the interpolation of an Agent of Protection."[56]

International Practice:

Throughout both periods of the application of the principle, whether as a principle of policy or as a right, the unit that has been singled out as bearing primary responsibility for the restoration of the subject community to self-government has been the state which wields sovereignty over it.

During the inter-war period, when there was no recognized right of self-determination, the state wielding sovereignty over subject nationalities or colonial peoples was under no *international* obligation to restore those communities to self-government. As indicated by the International Committee of Jurists in the Aaland Islands dispute, the entire issue was at the discretion of the state concerned. The cases in which this obligation was undertaken were the minority treaties and declarations, and in the mandates system. The important point to note is that in both cases the obligatee was the state administering or wielding sovereign authority over the subject peoples in question.

During the era of decolonization, the obligation of the United Nations as an international agency for the protection of subject peoples became an established fact. By the time of the establishment of the Committee of Twenty-four, the responsibility of the United Nations stated in chapters of the U.N. Charter had been transformed into a formidable machinery which had successfully supervised the transformation of some seventy dependent entities into independent member states of the United Nations.

The work of the U.N. machinery has been in the development and enforcement of an internationally recognized definition of dependent peoples who could legitimately claim the right of self-determination, and to see that their interim rights and the development of their capacities towards the eventual exercise of their right of self-determination are guaranteed. A major aspect of this work has been the efforts of the United Nations to get the obligatees—the administering powers—to honor their obligation to prepare the peoples of the dependent territories under their control for self-government.

Size and Internal Composition:

As in the case of the beneficiary, the international practice indicates that size and composition of the ruling state as a factor in determining the validity of the claim of the subject group to the right of self-determination has received very little attention, except perhaps by writers.[57] In both the inter-war period and the decolonization period, neither the ratio of population between the ruling state and the subject community, nor the relative territorial size of the ruling state, as compared to that of the subject group,[58] seem to have been given much consideration in the application of the principle or the acknowledgment of the right of self-determination.

Sources of Rights and Obligations

The existence of the right of self-determination in international law now seems to be generally accepted. Not only can we point to massive international practice of some longevity and consistency, but we can also cite within this practice, from the minority treaties to the decolonization efforts in and out of the United Nations, strong evidence of the necessary *opinio juris* that has ripened the practice into a right of self-determination. As we have seen, the important aspect of the principle is that it yields a right to self-government that a community may legitimately claim, if it meets certain criteria; and this further entitled that community to certain interim rights including the right to protection and development, the right to petition, and access to an Agent of Protection.[59]

The development of this category of substate entities with international personality and capacity has occurred mainly in the practice of treaties, international conventions and declarations. Insofar as the principle of self-determination can be said to yield a right in customary international law, it has essentially been a spillover or generalization from treaty law.[60] In some cases, such as the Polish nationality treaty declarations, or the U.N. Declaration on the Granting of Independence to Colonial Countries and Peoples, the rights of such groups have their source in obligatory declarations, the legal force of which is generally recognized in international law.[61] In other cases, such as the mandates and trusteeship agreements, and in the U.N. Charter, these groups acquire their rights as third party beneficiaries.[62] Again the legal standing of such rights and responsibilities is well established.[63] For instance, in 1962 the International Court of Justice determined that the instrument establishing the mandates was "... an instrument having the character of a treaty or convention and embodying international engagements for the mandatory as defined by the council and accepted by the mandatory."[64]

The creation of third party beneficiary rights necessarily creates obligations for an obligatee and for a guarantor or agency for the protection of the beneficiary rights. In fact, the obligatee creates the beneficiary rights by undertaking obligations towards the beneficiary; and the relationship between these two is such that the protection of the rights of the beneficiary requires the interpolation of a guarantor.[65] Therefore, the treaties from which the beneficiaries derive their rights are of the character of "treaties concluded within organizations,"[66] that is, treaties which are organizationally linked to an implementing organ endowed with the obligation to guarantee the rights of beneficiaries. Within the regimes established by such treaties, the government of the obligatee is supposed to be exercised as a *trust* that enables it to achieve a specific purpose and for which it is *accountable*. For instance, this relationship is evident in the mandates system of the League of Nations, "the most comprehensive demonstration of the fundamental role of *trust* in international law."[67] The same principle of *trust* underlies the system of minority treaties and the U.N. trusteeship system; and indeed, all regimes set up for the recognition and protection of the rights of substate groups, whether they be colonies, minorities, or any other type of subject or dependent peoples. This principle of trusteeship, using the term in a generic sense, applied in all cases of contractual or declaratory instruments that provide protection for subject peoples is, under international law, the source of the rights of the beneficiaries as well as the source of the obligations of the obligatee and the agency of protection.

CHAPTER VIII

SELF-DETERMINATION AND WORLD ORDER

The emergence of self-determination as a matter of international concern has been a relatively recent development, and its ripening from a principle of international public policy into a principle of international law even more so. What we have done in this study is to analyze the nature of the principle by bringing to bear on the available international practice contemporary techniques of international legal analysis, and to describe as clearly as possible the scope and content of the principle.

Doctrine and Law of Self-Determination

In ascertaining the international legal definition of the principle of self-determination, we found the writings of publicists to be helpful, for they raised important questions that gave us insight into the categories under which we could classify our findings. For instance, it is largely through the conceptual aid of publicists that we were able to evolve the category of "recipient unit", under which we placed all groups whose claim to the right of self-determination has been accepted by the international community. We then established that in spite of wide situational, geographical and historical differences, these groups shared the crucial characteristic of *subject status,* so we concluded that in order to have its claim to the right of self-determination accepted in international law the claimant group has to be "oppressed," "dependent," or "subject" according to internationally accepted standards.

In spite of this useful function, publicists have also created some difficulties due to the persistance with which they have advocated doctrinal or theoretical definitions of self-determination that could not be reconciled with the mass of data provided by state practice. These difficulties were caused by the normative connotations of the principle and the powerful tendency of political thinkers to associate it with such highly valued concepts as liberty and equality, which led most political thinkers to define self-determination as the expression of the principles of liberty or equality, depending on which of the two principles they were willing to accord the higher normative value. Thus, for those thinkers who place a high value on liberty, self-determination calls for policies which maximize the liberty or freedom of people. That is to say, the principle of self-determination is the same as the principle of popular government. Conversely, for those political thinkers who consider *equality* as the supreme political value, self-determination calls for policies which enhance equality; for them, the principle of self-determination is tantamount to the principle of egalitarianism. Essentially, these thinkers were considering the principle in terms of national rather than international political organization.

At the turn of the century when self-determination became a matter of international concern, these thinkers began to direct their attention to an examination of the implications of the application of the principle on the international level. In this new venture, the political analysts merely extended their normative definitions of self-determination to the international situation. As a result, the advocates of the principle of popular government argued that the meaning of self-determination in international politics was merely the application of the principle of popular consent to international situations, such as territorial settlement. Hence, their definition of self-determination in terms of the *plebiscite theory*. Similarly, the advocates of the egalitarian principle defined in terms of the application of the principle of equality to international situations; hence, the *national equality theory*. In a sense, these normative definitions of self-determination are satisfying, especially as they relate to national political organization. Whatever logical problems they entail, these doctrines point to the fact that in the final analysis assertions of the right of self-determination are assertions of human rights against tyranny either by totalitarian governments or alien oppressors. But, it is important to note that however normatively satisfying these doctrines may be, they cannot be confused with the definition of the principle in international law. That can only be established, as we have done here, by an examination of international practice and the establishment of the necessary *opinio juris*.

Law and Politics of Self-Determination

In an important sense, the establishment of the principle of self-determination in international law was a consequence of political factors—specifically, the politics of hetero-ethnic rule and its potential effects on international politics, of which it has always been an important issue. Traditionally, this issue was settled politically; there was no recognition of a legal right of self-determination either in national or in international law. Groups believing they had the right to self-determination revolted and usually had to fight for their independence or autonomy. If they were successful, they achieved independent status and were accorded recognition on the basis of the usual criteria of effective control of a defined territory and population.[1] Hence, the issue of self-determination was always associated with violent conflict.[2] This internal conflict, which characterized issues of self-determination, always had the potential of spilling over into international conflict and, in some cases, actually spilled over with dangerous international consequences.[3] Not until the first decade of the twentieth century did it become starkly obvious that internal conflict associated with demands for self-determination could spill over into dangerous international armed conflict. This increased danger was itself due to two new developments of serious consequence to international politics. First, the increase in European nationalism caused a great increase in the frequency and intransigence with which various peoples were pushing demands for self-determination, and the result of this was increased frequency of vicious and uncompromising nationalist clashes. Second, the new modern and total warfare that had been ushered in by a combination of new techniques of nationalist mobilization and new weaponry was of such magnitude that, when the spill over of nationalist clashes did occur, its result was a particularly catastrophic general war which shook the peace and security of the entire world.

From the aftermath of World War I to the present, the states,

183

realizing this new and dangerous threat, moved toward a progressive adoption of international obligations. One of Woodrow Wilson's basic goals at the Peace Conference was the accommodation of the national aspirations of nations ". . . without introducing new or perpetuating old elements of discord and antagonism that would be likely in time to break the peace of Europe and consequently of the world."[4] In the same vein, the minority treaties were justified in terms of guaranteeing the peace, and the mandates were thought of as a way of forestalling colonial rivalry that would likely lead to war. And during the decolonization era, one of the basic purposes of the Declaration on Non-Self-Governing Peoples and the trusteeship system, as expressed in Articles 73, (subparagraph c) and 76, (subparagraph b) has been the furthering of international peace and security.

The ripening of the principle into international law has been one of systematic erosion of the exclusive domain of individual states over their colonies and minorities.[5] The states, it must be noted, have not given in without a struggle. But, considering the tenacity with which they always guarded their sovereignty, their willingness to come as far as they have in relinquishing their exclusive control over matters formerly considered within their domestic jurisdiction is testimony of the seriousness with which they have viewed the potential explosiveness of situations involving the principle of self-determination. It is true, of course, that many advocates of the right have been motivated by a desire to see justice done. However, it cannot be denied that their compelling reason has been their realization that some amount of international control was infinitely better than the possible dangers which will inevitably ensue from the uncompromising conflict between a demand for independence and the state's insistence on its right to maintain the integrity of its sovereignty.

Self-determination and International Organization

The effect of the development of the right of self-determination on international organization has been very dramatic indeed. As we have shown, the principle gives rise to beneficiary rights that must be guaranteed by an agent of protection. As the right has evolved, this agency has developed also in function and capacity, beginning with the modest Plebiscite Commission to the United Nations and its powerful Committee of Twenty-four. As an agent of protection, the United Nations does not merely protect peoples of the dependent territories against present abuses, it also guarantees their right to self-government and supervises their development toward that goal. Another significant point is that this decolonization activity of the United Nations represents an increase of the domain of the community of states as 'a whole, at the expense of individual states, in the determination of the composition and membership of the international community. This activity has gone as far as to create status where none might have existed, as in the case of the Trust Territory of Micronesia.[6]

The function of protection is only one of many performed by international organizations such as the United Nations with regard to the principle of self-determination. The role of the United Nations as the institutional arena for claims and counter claims of the principle has already been noted.[7] In addition, it has provided mediational facilities for compromise, and failing that, a ready made face-saving device for some of the states forced to decolonize.

The effect of the principle on general international law is more difficult to assess. However, several new directions seem to be suggested. For instance, by virtue of the right of self-determination, it is generally agreed that colonies have acquired some standing in international law and some capacity to take obligations under it.[8] There is the possibility that this situation might be generalized to cover all substate groups considered oppressed by international standards.

The international practice on self-determination promises to provide some interesting theoretical comments on the debates concerning recognition. In terms of the contemporary definition of self-determination, it could be arqued that there exists an obligation on the part of the institution to recognize the group for the purpose of protection. It may also be argued that this type of institutional recognition is constitutive in the sense that it activates rights and obligations. The practice of the United Nations suggests that, for the present, such institutional recognition has no legal effect with regard to states who dissented from the majority decision to recognize. However in such situations the institutional recognition has tended to increase the political pressure on the dissenting state to accord recognition. How this situation will develop in the future is not clear.

Self-determination and International Peace and Security.

Whatever the contribution of the principle has been to the development of international organization and international law, the overriding question that must be asked has to do with its role in fostering international peace and security. Has it had a salutary effect on peace and security as the statesmen expected, or has it led to anarchy and a threat to world peace as some writers have suggested.[9] The facts suggest that, on balance, the application of the right of self-determination in international relations contributed to international peace and security. During the interwar years, the general acceptance of the validity of the principle was an important factor in stabilizing the areas of Eastern Europe, by making the nationalities in that area less disposed to challenge the territorial settlements. And later, the impact on international peace of the successful application of a recognized right of self-determination is clearly manifested in the fact that the United Nations has presided over the peaceful decolonization of over seventy territories, the most massive display of peaceful change in modern history.

The successful application of the principle is due to its effect on the *political* behavior of the claimants of the right, and the response of the states to the claims. In this process, the United Nations has been able to establish by concensus what actions may be considered legitimate. Furthermore, it has made these behavioral standards established by collective legitimization so highly visible and explicit that states have been forced, even if unwillingly, to address themselves to these standards. In addition, the activity in the United Nations has made support for or antagonism against certain actions so explicit as to diminish the chances that a state might overestimate the amount of international support it has and therefore adopt or maintain an intransigent attitude. For instance, there is no doubt that the reluctant change in French policy, from total rejection of decolonization in 1944 to its acceptance in 1958, is due at least in part to the overwhelming support of the international community as a whole for the right of self-determination.

From the standpoint of international peace and security the excellent record of the application of the right has been marred by two problems. One has been the problem of non-compliance. A certain amount of non-compliance is to be expected. There are no laws which achieve total compliance. In this case the problem is not serious for the amount of compliance is almost total. With the latest implied defection of Portugal from the so-called White Redoubt, the states that have refused to comply with the accepted interpretation of the right of self-determination have been reduced to two—the *Republic of South Africa* and Rhodesia. It must be noted, however, that this does not detract from the gravity of the problem. A serious threat to international peace could come from only one conflict. And it is precisely these two cases which present the most crucial challenge to international peace and security. The issue of self-determination in that area is infused with a particularly poisonous racial element which, if ignited, could lead to a conflagration that could destroy the entire international system as we now know it.[10]

The second problem is the fact that as it is now defined, the scope and content of the principle of self-determination is too narrow to be useful in consideration of new demands that are being made. Although the charter of the United Nations and subsequent declarations state clearly that the right of self-determination belongs to all oppressed peoples, in practice it has been restricted to colonial and trust territories. As a result of this narrow and parochial application, the employment of the principle to ethnic minorities has been rendered impossible. This represents a serious *lacuna* in the regulation of the relations between the various groups in multi-ethnic societies and the guarantee of the rights of minorities. In that respect, we are back to settling issues involving self-determination by force of arms, as was the case in both Bangladesh and Biafra. These two cases provide us with a grim warning of what the future may have in store for international peace and security. They are not only examples of the new demands for self-determination that are likely to be advanced by ethnic minorities on a widespread basis, they are also examples of the sheer savagery with which these demands will be fought.

Self-determination and World Order

If the international community is going to be able to deal with issues of self-determination in a way that will achieve justice, peace, and security, then we must develop a principle of self-determination on the basis of three realities. First, we can be sure that even after the era of decolonization the right of self-determination will continue to be claimed by groups which consider themselves "oppressed." These groups may be ethnic minorities, or they may be a new type of substate group as yet unfamiliar to us. It is certain, however, that when groups feel that they are laboring under alien subjugation or oppression they will seek to be liberated. Second, in dealing with such situations, a legal principle of self-determination will be impotent if it does not have the support of states accepting a definition of recipient units of the right that is broad enough to include these new groups. Third, so far as the right of self-determination includes the right of secession, the states will resist the notion of self-determination for internal minorities.

In order to cope with these three realities, what is required is to avoid the built-in rigidity that seems to afflict all legal formulations and attempt to define and redefine the principle so that it will interface with political reality. In particular, the right should be made to apply effectively to all subject peoples, whether they be colonies, ethnic minorities, or religious minorities. How can we implement such an expanded definition of self-determination? By following the logical thrust of the development of the principle, and by emphasizing the logical relationship between human rights and self-determination.

When one takes the long view, it is readily apparent that the principle has been applied to many diverse groups, including minorities and mandated territories. In fact, the first self-conscious attempt to apply the principle internationally was when it was applied to national minorities. Therefore, there is no logical reason to deny ethnic minorities and other new claimants the right of exercising it. This position is supported by the logical relationship between human rights and self-determination. In spite of the fact that this relationship is clearly spelled out in the Human Rights Conventions and in the U.N. Declaration on the Granting of Independence to Colonial Countries and Peoples, the states have been reluctant to accept any international control over issues of human rights within their own territories. And yet the two rights are indissolubly linked to each other. For while some types of deprivation of individual rights have no relevance to group membership, other types of deprivations, such as racial or religious or ethnic discrimination are based on the fact that an individual is born into and is attached to a certain group. As Lador-Lederer eloquently suggests

". . . when a million or so of inarticulate children in Nazi camps had *'ope legis'* been done to death because of their having been born to Jewish parents, such death was not a capital punishment imposed upon an articulate crime; it was a fatality resulting from group community. Nothing, not even the innocence of children, gave them the opportunity to opt out from genocide."[11]

Whether the group in question is territorially based, separate from the state or dispersed within it, the subjugation of a group based on its distinctiveness seems to be the condition that must qualify that group for a remedy. For while homogeneous society does not preclude the violation of human rights, the subjugation of one community by another involves *ab definitio*, a violation of human rights. Once this relationship is generally understood and accepted, it would be possible to develop state practice along the lines of the legal doctrine of *trust* in all matters of hetero-ethnic rule including colonies, minorities, mandates, trust territories, indigenous populations, and scattered communities.[12]

Of course, no amount of doctrinal neatness will induce the states, who are after all the creators of international law, to adopt this suggested line and broaden the current practice of the right of self-determination; especially while secession continues to be subsumed under that right. Even if only in principle, they cannot legitimately be expected to endorse their own dismemberment. A possible solution to this problem is the progressive development of the principle along lines emphasizing autonomy or association on the basis of equality and deemphasizing independence. With the concern over the plight of ministates, this already seems to have some appeal in the United Nations. It may be that with the development of more sophisticated insight in the factors controling political unification, it may be possible to strengthen this tendency. Under such circumstances the states may be expected to adopt a more favorable attitude toward the broadening of the principle of self-determination.

In spite of the dangers of speculation, we can be sure that as international society evolves, new ramifications of old problems may emerge. It is possible that the definition of "oppressed" may change with evolving international practice, just as the meaning of "armed attack" under Article 51 of the U.N. Charter has become problematic due to the new technology of weaponry. Similarly, concepts of national sovereignty may also change in view of the diminishing defensibility of states in the face of the new weapons. Indeed, even the groups making demands for self-determination may change and their demands may assume other substantive forms.

As these demands become relevant in the international arena as they inevitably will, the requirements of peace and security would again necessitate more and more international action. Hopefully, such action will focus on the essential relationship between the principle of self-determination and human rights, and assert the essential nature of the right of self-determination as a right that justifies the remedying of a deprivation by restoring self-government. With this focus, it should be possible for the law governing the right to be applied with consistency under any new set of political circumstances. Perhaps as a response to such consistency the impulses toward peaceful change may be enhanced.

NOTES

Notes to Chapter I

1 On May 30, 1967, the Eastern Region of Nigeria declared that it had seceded from the Federation of Nigeria and formed an independent state with the name of *"Biafra"* thus precipitating the civil war. In the minds of many private and public persons, what the "Biafrans" were fighting for was their right of self-determination. For instance, United States Congressman, Donald Lukens stated that, "It is time for the United States to issue an official statement in support of Biafra's moral right to be heard *in her struggle for self-determination." Readers Digest*, May 1969, p. 77. [Italics are mine]

2 For instance, at the 22nd Session of the U.N. General Assembly, 20 out of 46 substantive agenda items dealt with issues involving the principle of self-determination (by far the largest on any single issue), and 89 our of 100 speakers in general debate referred to the principle as crucial to international security.

3 For a sample of Arab claims, see *U. N. Documents* A/BUR/PV. 29, pp. 4-10 and *U. N. Documents*, A/BUR/PV.70, P. 312. For an Israeli statement see *U. N. Documents*, A/BUR/PV.55, pp. 31-32.

4 See A. G. Mezerik, ed. "Vietnam and the United Nations, 1967," *International Review Service Publication*, Vol. XIII, NO. 95 (1967) for contradictory claims by the United States and the Viet Cong.

5 See Mohammed A. Shukri, *The Concept of Self-Determination in the United Nations* (Damascus: Al Jadidah Press, 1965), p. 9ff., for examples of some claims based on the right of self-determination.

6 Clyde Eagleton, "Excesses of Self-Determination," *Foreign Affairs*, Vol. XXXI, No. 14 (July 1953), p. 604.

7 Robert Lansing, "Self-Determination: A Discussion of a Phrase," *Saturday Evening Post* (New York: May 1921), p. 16. See also, Frank A. Golder, "Will the Unrestricted Self-Determination of all National Groups Bring World Peace and Order?" *Journal of International Relations* (Worcester, Mass.: January 1920), Vol. 10, p. 283; Henri Lambert, "National Self-Determination," *The North American Review* (New York: April 1918), Vol. 207, p. 547.

8 Henri Lambert, Loc. Cit.

9 Alfred Cobban, *National Self-Determination* (London: Oxford University Press, 1945), p. 21.

10 Erich Hula, "National Self-Determination Reconsidered," *Social Research*, Vol. 10, No. 1 (1943), p. 5.

11 See Clifford Geertz, "The Integrative Revolution: Primordial Sentiments and Civil Politics in the New States," *Old Societies and New States* New York: The Free Press of Glencoe, 1963), p. 109; Myron Weiner, "Political Integration and Political Development," *The Annals of the American Academy of Political*

191

and Social Science, Vol. 358 (March, 1965), p. 52.

12 As Ali Mazrui puts it in his stimulating essay, "Violent Contiguity and the Politics of Retribalization in Africa," *Journal of International Affairs,* Vol. XXIII, No. 1 (1969), p. 104; "Some of the more fundamental causes of violence within each border are due to elements of disintegration. Prominent among the centripetal forces is the phenomenon of retribalization in African countries. A further sense of national identity had begun to grow under the impact of a shared anti-colonialism and the old ambition to create a joint citizenship in freedom. On attainment of independence, the sense of nationhood has sometimes emerged as a little too fragile, so ethnic flames which have begun to subside have flared up again. The great African anti-models of tragic ethnic resurgence are the Congo and Nigeria, *yet these might be no more than extravagant manifestations of more widespread tendencies."* Italics are mine.

13 "If the past and present are instructive, it can be expected that cultural and political consciousness will spread with increased communications and the ethnic hodgepodges that are Asia and Africa will produce a host of new demands for the redrawing of political borders." Walker Connor, "Self-Determination: The New Phase," *World Politics,* Vol. 20 (1967), p. 46.

14 Such a list might include the following countries: Burma, the Sudan, Guyana, Iraq, Rwanda, Uganda, Canada, Switzerland, Belgium, Yugoslavia, India, and Cyprus, to name just a few. See Walker Connor, *op. cit.,* pp. 30ff.

15 Although the present Vietnam war has obscured their struggle, some of these tribesmen have organized a full fledged nationalist movement called FULRO (Front Unis pour la Liberation des Races Oppresses).

16 See *New York Times,* October 30, 1966.

17 Walker Connor, *op. cit.,* p. 43.

18 George Codding, Jr., *The Federal Government of Switzerland* (Boston, 1961), p. 154, *et passim.*

19 Quoted by Richard Pipes, "The Forces of Nationalism," *Problems of Communism,* Vol. XIII (January-February 1964), p. 4.

20 "No multi-national structure has been immune to this surge of nationalism. Authoritarian and democratic, Communist and non-Communist societies have been similarly affected." Walker Connor, *op. cit.,* p. 53.

21 On June 28, 1956, Foreign Minister of West Germany, Dr. Heinrich von Brentano made the following statement in the Bundestag: "The Federal Government maintains unchanged its determinate position with regard to the eastern boundaries. . . .In conformity with the declared will of the entire German nation, it has time and again called attention to the fact that Germany continues to exist within the boundaries of 1937, and that unilateral decisions made during the years following the complete breakdown of Germany are not recognized by the German people. The right to their homeland and to self-determination are inalienable prerequisites for settling the fate of men and people living in exile and bondage." Quoted in Carroll B. Reece, *Peace Through Law: A Basis for an East-West Settlement in Europe* (New Cannan, Conn.: The Long House, Inc., 1965), p. 62.

22 See K. Deutsch and L. J. Edinger. "Foreign Policy of the German Federal Republic," in Roy C. Macridis, ed., *Foreign Policy in World Politics* (Englewood Cliffs, N.J.: Prentice-Hall, 1967), pp. 143-147.

23 Rupert Emerson, *From Empire to Nation* (Boston: Beacon Press, 1960), p. 295.

24 Alfred Cobban, *National Self-Determination* (Oxford University Press, 1945), p. 3. See also, Arnold J. Toynbee, "Self-Determination," *Quarterly Review* (London), Vol. 243, (April 1925), p. 328.

25 "Self-Determination," *Quarterly Review* (London), Vol. 243, (April 1925), p. 327.

26 Arnold J. Toynbee, *op. cit.,* p. 323. See also, Raymond L. Buell, *International Relations*, Rev. ed., (New York: Henry Holt & Co., 1929), pp. 33-34; Clyde Eagleton, "Self-Determination in the United Nations," *AJIL*, Vol 47 (1953), p. 92; Rupert Emerson, *op. cit.,* p. 331; Frank A. Golder, *op. cit.,* pp. 282-283; Erno Wittman, *Past and Future of the Right of National Self-Determination* (Amsterdam: Van Holkema & Warendorf, 1919), p. 116. Of the extremely few cases in which secession has been achieved without recourse to violent revolution, prior to World War I, the best known are the secession of West Virginia from Virginia in August, 1861; and that of Norway from Sweden in June, 1904. As Johannes Mattern points out in his *The Employment of the Plebiscite in the Determination of Sovereignty* (Baltimore: Johns Hopkins University Press, 1921), pp. 112-124, these two situations are the exceptions which prove the rule.

27 See, for instance, Raymond Buell, *op. cit.,* pp. 29 and 45-46; Robert Lansing, op. cit., pp. 8-11; Philip M. Brown, "Self-Determination in Central Europe," AJIL, Vol. 14 (1920), p. 239; Henri Lambert, *op. cit.*, pp. 541-545.

28 Clyde Eagleton, *op. cit.*, p. 595.

29 See James Barros, *The Aaland Islands Question: Its Settlement by the League of Nations* (New Haven: Yale University Press, 1968), pp. 288-291.

30 Mohammed Aziz Shukri, *op. cit.*, p. 7; Benjamin Rivlin, *Self-Determination and Dependent Areas*, 501 International Conciliation (1955), p. 199-200.

31 Rupert Emerson, *op. cit.*, p. 297.

32 For instance, according to the author, Arthur M. Brazier, *Black Self-Determination: The Story of the Woodlawn Organization* (Grand Rapids, Michigan: William B. Eerdmans Publishing Co., 1969), is " . . . an insider's report on a controversial self-help organization. . . .[which] offers guidelines to future inner-city programs."

33 Arnold J. Toynbee, *op. cit.*, p. 317.

34 "In the current temper of world opinion no one can in principle oppose what has come to be the almost self-evident right of peoples to dispose of their own destinies, . . ." Rupert Emerson, *loc. cir.* See also Benjamin Rivlin, *op. cit.*, p. 204.

35 See, for instance, J. G. Starke, *An Introduction to International Law*, 4th ed. (London: Butterworth & Co., Ltd., 1958), p. 102; also Clyde Eagleton, *op. cit.*, p. 595; Rupert Emerson, *op. cit.*, p. 297; Benjamin Rivlin, *op. cit.*, p. 199-200; Mohammed Shukri, *op. cit.*, p. 7.

36 See, for example, B. V. A. Roling, *International Law in an Expanded World*, (Amsterdam: Djambatan N.V., 1960), p. 78.

37 Sir Hersch Lauterpacht, *International Law and Human Rights* (New York: Frederick A. Praeger, Inc., 1950), pp. 148-49.

38 Georg Schwarzenberger, *The Inductive Approach to International Law* (Dobbs Ferry, N.Y.: Oceana, 1964), p. 76. See also Obed Y. Asamoah, *The Legal Significance of the Declarations of the General Assembly of the United Nations* (The Hague: Nijhoff, 1966), p. 181.

39 Clyde Eagleton, "The Excesses of Self-Determination," p. 593 asserts that "The textbooks of international law do not recognize any legal right of self-determination nor do they know any standards for determining which groups are entitled to independence, . . ."

40 *Ibid.*, p. 595.

41 Consensus on the part of international lawyers to the effect that international law is created by state practice is of long standing. In 1914 E. T. Holland wrote in his "Letters to 'The Times' upon War and Neutrality" (1914), p. 105, that he considered it a sign of ignorance of the nature of international law to be "under the impression that it has been concocted by 'bookworms,' 'jurists,' 'professors,' or other 'theorists,' instead of, in fact, mainly by statesmen, diplomatists, prize-courts, generals and admirals." Descamps is reputed to have made the following statement during a meeting of the League of Nations Advisory Committee of Jurists in 1920: "Doctrine and jurisprudence do not create law, but they assist in determining rules which exist. A judge should make use of both jurisprudence and doctrine, but they should serve only to clarify." In Karol Wolfke, *Custom in Present International Law* (Wroclaw, 1964), p. 117. See also Torsten Gihl, *op. cit.*, p. 74; "Neither the doctrines embodied in the writings of authorities of international law nor juridical decisions are sources in the formal sense of the rules of law, they are only sources of knowledge concerning the law, and they do not in themselves give rise to international law." Perhaps the most picturesque comment ever made on this subject is the one made by the English High Court of Admiralty in 1778 and quoted by Judge Jessup in his *Transnational Law* (New Haven: Yale University Press, 1956), p. 11: "A pedantic man in his closet dictates the law of nations; everybody quotes, and nobody minds him." For views similar to those expressed above, see Hersch Lauterpacht, *The Development of International Law by the International Court, Rev. Ed.* (London: Stevens, 1958), pp. 23-25; Clive Parry, *The Sources and Evidences of International Law* (New York: Oceana Publications, 1965), p. 105; Charles Rousseau, *Principes Generaux du Droit International Public* (Paris: Pedone, 1944), pp. 816-820; Georg Schwarzenberger, *International Law, Volume I: International Law as Applied by International Courts and Tribunals. Third Edition* (London: Stevens, 1957), pp. 26-27; Max Sorensen, *Les Sources du Droit International* (Copenhagen: Munksgaard, 1946), pp. 177-190.

42 See, for instance, Arnold J. Toynbee, "Self-Determination," *Quarterly Review* (London), Vo. 243, April 1925, p. 319ff.

43 "In fact, the concepts of *people* and of *nation,* in the sense here intended will always remain vague and scientifically ungraspable concepts, . . ." Florent Peeters, *op. cit.*, p. 177. See also Rupert Emerson, *op. cit.*, p. 90, "No one has succeeded in devising a definition which is watertight in the sense that, without opening up a number of leaky 'ifs' and 'buts' it enumerates the constituent elements of the nations we know. . . ."

44 Quincy Wright, "Recognition and Self-Determination," *Proceedings of the American Society of International Law*, 48th Annual Mtg., (April 1954), p. 32.

45 Georg Schwarzenberger, *op. cit.*, pp. 18-19.

46 Hans Kelsen, *The Law of the United Nations* (New York: Frederick A. Praeger, 1950), pp. 52-53. See also, P. N. Drost, *Human Rights as Legal Rights* (Leyden: Sijthoff, 1951), pp. 28-31.

47 See Chapter III, pp. 8ff., *infra.*

48 *UNCIO Documents*, Vol. 6, Doc. No. 723 I/I/A19, p. 704.

49 See, for instance, Clyde Eagleton, *op. cit., in toto.*

50 Georg Schwarzenberger, *op. cit.,* p. 8.

51 "It is also clear that the international lawyer is entitled to make proposals *de lege ferenda* for new law. But that is a political task. Further such proposals must start from the law actually in force; politics of law necessarily presupposes a theory and science of law." Josef Kunz, "The Changing Science of International Law," *AJIL,* Vol. 56 (1962), p. 499; See also Georg Schwarzenberger, *op. cit.,* p. 51.

52 The inevitable role of unilateral national claims in the development of customary international law is brilliantly described in the following passage in which Professor McDougal describes the formation of the international law of the sea as " . . . a process of continuous interaction, of continuous demand and response, in which the decision-makers of particular nation states unilaterally put forward claims of the most diverse and conflicting character to the use of the world's seas and in which other decision-makers, external to the demanding State and including both national and international officials, weigh and appraise these conflicting claims in terms of the interests of the world community and of the rival claimants, and ultimately accept or reject them." Myres S. McDougal, "The Hydrogen Bomb Tests and International Law of the Sea," *AJIL,* Vol. 49 (1955), pp. 357-358. Similar views are expressed by I. C. MacGibbon, "Customary International Law and Acquiescence," *BYIL,* Vol. XXXIII (1957), p. 115; Morton A. Kaplan and Nicholas deB. Katzenbach, *The Political Foundations of International Law* (New York: John Wiley & Sons, Inc., 1961), pp. 21-23; Karol Wolfke, *Custom in Present International Law,* p. 65; Percy Corbett, *Law in Diplomacy* (Princeton, N.J.: Princeton University Press, 1959), pp. 271-278; Grigory I. Tunkin, *Droit International Public: Problems Theoretiques* (Paris: Pedone, 1965), p. 170.

53 "On the plane of legal analysis, the international lawyer is only concerned with the evidence for any asserted principle of international law. If the evidence exists, the principlemust be stated in full scope, whether, *de lege ferenda,* it is considered beneficial or otherwise. If evidence is lacking, the alleged principle must be shown to be spurious and then rejected. Aggressive descriptions are no proof of the non-existence of a legal principle, and laudatory epithets no substitute for evidence." Georg Schwarzenberger, *op. cit.,* p. 84.

54 Myres S. McDougal, *op. cit.,* p. 358.

55 See Chapter III, p. 102-104, n. 46.

56 See Chapter II, n. 61, *infra.*

57 See Chapter II, n. 73, *infra.*

58 See Johannes Mattern, *The Employment of the Plebiscite in the Determination of Sovereignty* (Baltimore: John Hopkins University Press, 1921), pp. 76-79; J. Carlton Hayes, *Essays on Nationalism* (New York: Russell & Russell, 1966), pp. 44-49.

59 Johannes Mattern, *op. cit.,* p. 77.

60 Sarah Wambaugh, *Plebiscites Since the World War* (Washington: Carnegie Endowment for International Peace, 1933), p. 28.

61 See Chapter II, n. 84, *infra.*

62 Harold S. Johnson, *Self-Determination within the Community of Nations* (Leyden: Sijthoff, 1967), p. 10.

63 *Ibid.,* p. 9.

64 Mohammed A. Shukri, *op. cit.,* p. 5.

65 *Loc. Cit.*

66 *Ibid.*, p. 132.

67 Josef Stalin, *Marxism and National and Colonial Questions*, p. 19.

68 C. A. Macartney, *op. cit.*, p. 197.

69 See Chapter III, p. 99.

70 See n. 48, *supra*.

71 See Chapter III, n. 91, *infra*.

72 See Chapter III, n. 64, *infra*.

73 See Chapter III, pp. 40-41, *infra*.

74 See Chapter I, pp. 3-4.

75 " . . . the process of formation of a custom is entirely natural—one might say, assimilating itself with the very current of international life with which it changes and develops." Karol Wolfke, *op. cit.*, p. 67. See also Grigori Tunkin's statement, "Les normes coutimières de droit international naissent de la pratique des relations entre Etats, de leurs actes de politque étrangere. Il est naturel, pour autant que la diplomatie occupe une place capitale dans leur action de politique exterieure, que ces normes s'elaborent pour une grande part au cours de l'activité diplomatique." *Droit International Public*, p. 170.

76 Georg Schwarzenberger, *op. cit.*, p. 93. A similar idea expressed by Karol Wolfke, "While the object of ascertaining customary rules is to determine their content and range of validity at a certain period, the formation of custom, like international relations themselves, is a continuous process. Neither the formation of custom nor even the most authoritative ascertainment of a customary rule completely interrupts the incessant evolution of custom. Even codification of a customary rule does not halt this evolution by accumulated practice. It is precisely this continuous evolution of customary international law which compels us to a frequent ascertaining of customary rules, or at least to checking whether they still correspond to the actual international reality." *Op. cit.*, p. 61. See also Myres S. McDougal, *op. cit.*, p. 358.

77 Torsten Gihl, *op. cit.*, p. 73.

78 Michel Virally, "The Sources of International Law," in Max Sorensen, *ed., Manual of Public International Law* (New York: St. Martin's Press, 1968), p. 143. Even within this broad area of agreement there is a body of opinion almost universally accepted which holds that only customary international law is international law in the proper sense, conventions being not really a source of law but only a source of specific obligations *inter partes*. Torsten Gihl expresses the essence of this argument: "In relation to international custom, treaties are a secondary source of law, existing so to speak on a different plane from custom. Their relation to custom is that of *lex specialis, quae derogat legi generali*. If, as has been maintained here, only custom can be regarded as international law in the proper sense, the expression 'general international law' is a pleonasm. It ought to be sufficient to describe international custom simply as 'international law,' or conversely to allow 'international law' to mean 'international custom.' " *Op. cit.*, pp. 71-72. For the representatives of this school of thought, the validity of treaties is itself based on a rule of customary international law, and, therefore, treaties are only "secondary" sources of rules of law, on a level inferior to custom as a source of law. "That a treaty is a law creating fact, that by a treaty obligations and rights are established, or, in other terms, that a treaty has binding force, is due to a rule of customary international law which is actually expressed in the formula *pacta sunt servanda*. This rule is the

reason for the validity of treaties, and hence the 'source' of all laws created by treaties, the so-called conventional international law is inferior to the customary international law." Hans Kelsen, *Principles of International Law*, Second Edition by Robert W. Tucker (New York: Holt, Rinehard, and Winston, Inc., 1966), p. 466. See also, Josef Kunz, *The Changing Law of Nations* (Columbus: Ohio State University Press, 1968), p. 348; Sir Gerald Fitzmaurice, "Some Problems Regarding the Formal Sources of International Law," *Symbolae Verzijl* (La Haye: Martinus Nijhoff, 1958), p. 158; Grigori Tunkin, *Droit International Public* (Paris: Pedone, 1965), p. 139; Clive Parry, *op. cit., passim*.

79 "The records or *evidence* of international law are the documents or acts proving the consent of States to its rules. Among such records or *evidence*, treaties and *practice* play an essential part, though recourse must also be had to unilateral declarations, instructions to diplomatic agents, laws and ordnances, and, in a lesser degree, to the writings of authoritative jurists. Custom is merely that general practice which affords conclusive proof of a rule." Percy Corbett, "The Consent of States and the Sources of the Law of Nations," *BYIL*, Vol. VI (1925), p. 30. This statement originally made in 1925 still remains the basic authoritative doctrine on rules of evidence in international law.

80 This view is expressed by Judge Hudson in the International Law Commission. "Subheading (b) of Article 38 . . . was not very happily worded. It would have been better to say 'international practice, as evidence of a general custom, etc.'" *Yearbook of the International Law Commission*, Vol. II (1950), p. 4. For other criticisms of the wording of subparagraph (b) along the same lines indicated above, see Torsten Gihl, *op. cit.*, pp. 76-77; Wesley L. Gould, *An Introduction to International Law* (New York: Harper & Brothers, 1957), p. 137; Charles Rousseau, *op. cit*, p. 825; Max Sorensen, *op. cit.,* p. 84; Grigori Tunkin, "Coexistence and International Law," *RCADI*, Vol. 95 (1958-1959), pp. 12-13; Clive Parry, *op. cit.*, p. 56; and Karol Wolfke, *op. cit.*, pp. 26-27; also Georg Schwarzenberger, *International Law*; Vol. 1, 3rd ed., (London: Stevens, 1957), p. 39.

81 See Torsten Gihl, *op. cit.* pp. 76-77; Max Sorensen, *Les Sources du droit International*, p. 85; Paul Guggenheim, *Traite*, Vol. I, p. 46; Clive Parry, *op. cit.*, p. 61.

82 The traditional view was presented in a working paper prepared by Manley O. Hudson, which was to serve as a basis for the Commission's discussions on "ways and means of making the evidence of customary international law more readily available." *YILC*, Vol. II, p. 26.

83 Karol Wolfke, *op. cit.*, p. 45. For a complete account of the discussions in the International Law Commission and an analysis of it, see respectively, *YILC*, Vol. II (1950), pp. 367-372; and Karol Wolfke, *op. cit.*, p. 42ff.

84 Karol Wolfke, *op. cit.*, p. 129. See also Georg Schwarzenberger, *International Law*, pp. 302-308; and I. C. MacGibbon, "The Scope of Acquiescence in International Law," *BYIL* (1954), pp. 143-145, and I. C. MacGibbon, "Customary International Law and Acquiescence," *BYIL* (1957), pp. 115-145.

85 For a survey of the activities of the Court in ascertaining elements of customary rules of international law see Karol Wolfke, *op. cit.*, pp. 121-131. "In all cases indicated above of referring to proof of the element of acceptance, the Court took as a basis either circumstances of practice, or tacit toleration of the practice manifesting itself above all in absence of protest." *Ibid.*, p. 129. For

similar views see Georg Schwarzenberger, *op. cit.*, p. 552; and Max Sorensen, *Les Sources du droit International,* p. 110.

86 Karol Wolfke, *op. cit.*, p. 129.

87 Torsten Gihl, *op. cit.*, p. 74.

Notes to Chapter II

1 Most of the writers of that period seem to agree that the term "self-determination" was not in use until sometime during the war. However, while they claim that the expression itself was new at the time, the principle which it represents had a history which goes back to a much earlier period. As Sarah Wambaugh puts it, "The expression 'self-determination' is no older than the war, but the principle dates, as it logically should, from the end of the eighteenth century;" "frontiers by Plebiscite," *Century* (New York), Vol. 107, November 1923, p. 70.

There is less agreement on the origins of the principle. Most of the writers have taken the French Revolution to be the first manifestation of the principle; as Johannes Mattern asserts, " . . . the French Revolution proclaimed the dogma of *what we now term* national self-determination." *The Employment of the Plebiscite in the Determination of Sovereignty* (Baltimore: Johns Hopkins Press, 1921), p. 77. The italics are mine. For other expressions of this view, see Raymond L. Buell, International Relations. Rev. ed. (New York: Henry Holt & Co., 1929), p. 32; Erno Wittman, Past and Future of the Right of National Self-Determination, pp. 39-58; Theodore S. Woolsey, "Self-Determination," AJIL, Vol. 13 (1919), p. 302; Carlton J. H. Hayes, The Historical Evolution of Modern Nationalism (New York: The Macmillan Co., 1931), p. 38.

Many writers also see the principle of self-determination as being manifested in "Our Declaration of Independence and the American Revolution which sealed that independence stands high among the monuments of human freedom." R. Murphy, "The Principle of Self-Determination in International Relations." U. S. Department of State Bulletin, Vol. XXXIII (1955), p. 889. See also, Arnold J. Toynbee, "Self-Determination," Quarterly Review, (London), Vol. 243, (April 1925), p. 317; Alfred Cobban, op. cit., p. 53; Walworth Barbour, "The Concept of Self-Determination in American Thought," U. S. Department of State Bulletin, Vol. XXXII, (1954), p. 576; Benjamin Rivlin, "Self-Determination and Dependent Areas," 501 I.C., p. 195.

Some writers have gone as far as to suggest that the principle of self-determination was applied as early as 1526, when an attempted cession of Burgundy was opposed because "according to law no cities or provinces can be transferred to another power against the wishes of the inhabitants or subjects, but only with their expressed consent." H. Hauser, *Le Principe des Nationalites ses Origines Historiques* (Paris: Alcan, 1916), p. 5; Also Raymond L. Buell, *op. cit.*, p. 32; Muhammed A. Shukri, *The Concept of Self-Determination in the United Nations*, p. 19. Mattern disagrees with this interpretation. From his point of view, the incident referred to was no more than "a policy of opportunism which recognized, or even insisted upon, the principle of popular self-determination in the transfer of cities and territories if such self-assertion was favorable or could be forcedinto an expression favorable to France. . . ," *op. cit.*,

p. 53. See also, E. Rouard de Card, *Les Annexions et les Plébiscites dans l'Histoire Contemporaine. Etudes de Droit International* (Paris: G. Pedone-Lauriel, 1890), p. 42. The above disagreement suggests that the use of the term "self-determination" by writers to describe historical phenomena which occurred before the term came into use are products of the way in which such writers define the term. Therefore, the validity of such descriptions depend on the validity of their definitions of self-determination. Since the generally accepted definition of self-determination has been undergoing change, such descriptions are likely to be open to serious question. In any case, such descriptions should be validated case by case, not accepted *a priori*.

2 G. Murray, "Self-Determination of Nationalities." *Journals of the British Institute of International Affairs*, Vol. I (January 1922) p. 6.

3 The relevant resolution of the London International Congress reads as follows: "The congress declares that it upholds the full *"Selbstbestimmungsrecht"* of all nations and expresses its sympathy for the workers of every country now suffering under the yoke of military, national or other absolutism; the congress calls on the workers of all these countries to join the ranks of the class-conscious workers of the whole world in order to fight shoulder to shoulder with them for the defeat of international capitalism and for the achievement of the aims of international Social-Democracy." V. I. Lenin, *Critical Remarks on the National Question. The Right of Nations to Self-Determination* (Moscow: Foreign Languages Publishing House, 1954), p. 126.

4 According to Alfred D. Low, the *"selbstbestimmungrecht"* resolution of the Second International triggered a debate among three factions of Eastern European Social-Democratic groups centered "on national self-determination and its interpretation; the leftist, internationalist wing of the Party simply tended to disregard the Party's national program, while both the Right and Lenin upheld the right to self-determination, though they sharply differed in their interpretations of it." In his rather arbitrary classification, he put among the Rightists such groups as the Bund; among the Leftists he put such persons as Rosa Luxemburg and Nikolai Bukharin; and he identified as Centrist, the position advocated by Lenin and endorsed by the Russian Social Democratic Labor Party (RSDLP) at its Second Party Congress in 1903. *Lenin and the Question of Nationality* (New York: Record Press, 1958), p. 26. Actually, as Lenin rightly asserts, the dispute started on the eve of the 1896 Congress, perhaps in anticipation of the heated discussions there, with the articles of Rosa Luxemburg, Karl Kautsky and the Polish *"Niepodleglosciewcy"* in the German Marxist Journal *Die Neue Zeit*. Lenin, *op. cit.*, p. 195. Apart from the polemics in *Die Neue Zeit,* perhaps the two best known of which are Karl Kautsky's "Nationality and Internationality," No. 1 (supplement), 1907-1908, and Rosa Luxemburg's "The National Question and Autonomy," No. 2, 1908-1090, others appeared continuously in the *Sotsial-Democrat*, the organ of the RSDLP; illegally published from February 1908 to January 1917, and the *Gazeta Rabotinicza*, the organ of the Warsaw Committee of the Social-Democracy of Poland and Lithuania also illegally published from May to October 1906 and from January 1912 to January 1916. Lenin, *op. cit.*, pp. 170-194. Some of the best known products of this debate are Lenin's own work referred to above which appeared as separate articles; "Critical Remarks on the National Question," and "The Rights of Nations to Self-Determination," in different issues of the Bolshevik monthly theoretical journal *Prosveshchenive* (Enlightenment) was published in

St. Petersburgh from December 1911 to 11 June 1914 and Josef Stalin's *Marxism and the National and Colonial Question* (London: Martin Lawrence, Ltd., 1935), published in 1913 with Lenin's encouragement. Other works which had a great effect on the debate were those of the Austrian Social-Democrats. Otto Bauer, *Die Nationalitatenfrage und die Oesterreichische Sozialdemokratie* (Vienna: 1907); and Karl Renner *Das Nationale Problem* (Leipzig & Vienna: 1902). Most of these works were unknown outside the area of East-Central Europe, at that time. The treatment of the subject which received the widest attention in those days, was the discussion in the April 1916 (No. 2) issue of the Marxist journal *Vorbote*, published by the Zimmerwald Left, a goup of left-wing socialist internationalists organized by Lenin after the famous Zimmerwald Conference of September 1915. V. I. Lenin, op. cit., p. 195.

5 See Robert Lansing, *Self-Determination: Discussion of a Phrase*, p. 5; cf. Alfred Cobban, *National Self-Determination*, p. 12; Rupert Emerson, *From Empire to Nation*, p. 295; Frank Golder, "Will Unrestricted Self-Determination of all National Groups bring World Peace and Order?" p. 285; C. A. Macartney, *National States and National*, minorities pp. 185-6; Sarah Wambaugh, *op. cit.*, p. 69.

6 One of President Wilson's famous statements in which he outlined his conception of the principles of the settlement, was: "Peoples are not to be handed about from one sovereignty to another by an international conference or an undertaking between rivals and antagonists. National aspirations must be respected; peoples may now be dominated and governed only by their own consent. 'Self-Determination' is not a mere phrase. It is an imperative principle of action, which statesmen will hence forth ignore at their peril." Ray S. Baker & William E. Dodd, eds., *The Public Papers of Woodrow Wilson, Vol. I* (New York: Harper Brothers Publishers, 1927), p. 180.

It is doubtful that self-determination would have emerged as the leading principle of the peace settlement, and the proclaimed policy of the victorious allies had not President Wilson prepared it as a coherent body of political doctrine and forced it on the allies. For more than two years of the war, both the Allied and Central Powers had exploited the desires of the minority nationalities for selfish reasons, encouraging it where it could help them with the war and repressing it ruthlessly when it was directed at them. Even when the Russian Revolution made it more ecpedient for the Allies to fully endorse the principle, they hesitated until 1916, when Wilson made it categorically clear that the United States was committed to the principle and asked them to state their war aims. For a fuller discussion of President Wilson's role see Alfred Cobban, *National Self-Determination*, pp. 13-15; C. A. Macartney, *op. cit.*, pp. 184-185; Harold V. Temperley, (ed.) *History of the Peace Conference*, Vol. I (London: Henry Frowde and Hodder & Stoughton, 1921), p. 123ff.

7 In the words of Alfred Cobban, "self-determination was already, early in 1917, turning from a mere phrase into what Wilson later called 'an imperative principle of action.' " *op. cit.*, p. 13. "One of the first steps of the Russian Provisional Government was to announce, in March 1917, that its aim was the establishment of peace on the basis 'of the right of the nations to decide their own destinies.' With this declaration the ice broke, and the dammed-up waters of nationality began a wild rush which was to sweep onward until the end of the war and beyond, in an incrfasingly powerful and ultimately uncontrollable torrent." Cobban *Op. cit.*, p. 12. Of course this dammed-up force of nationality

which was realsed so dramatically towards the end of the war, had already begun to trickle into international affairs before the war, and in fact was a chief precipitant of the war. C. A. Macartney *Op. cit.*, pp. 180-181; cf. Raymond Aron, *The Century of Total War* (Boston: Beacon Press, 1954), p. 17.

8 C. A. Macartney, op. cit., pp. 95-96; cf. Jozef Sulkowski, "The Principle of Self-Determination," *New Europe*, Monthly Review of International Affairs, Vol. II, no. 8, (July, 1942), p. 230.

9 For a discussion of the rise of nationalities in East and Central Europe, see C. A. Macartney, *National States and National Minorities*, pp. 50-156; Hans Kohn, *Nationalism, Its Meaning and History* (New York: D. Van Nostrand & Co., Inc., 1955), pp. 38-64; Carlton J. H. Hayes, *Essays on Nationalism* (New York: Russell and Russell, 1966), p. 58 *et passim*, and Oscar Janowsky, *Nationalities and National Minorities (with Special Reference to East-Central Europe)* New York: The Macmillan Co., 1945), pp. 19-36. 19-36.

10 Raymond L. Buell, *op. cit.,* pp. 47-48. Also see note 15, *infra.*

11 Within the area of East and Central Europe, there was a great deal of borrowing of ideas across political boundaries. For instance, the ideas and writings of the two Austrian Social-Democrats, Karl Renner and Otto Bauer, who advocated exterritorial national-cultural autonomy had a great influence among some groups within the Russian empire. Organizations such as the Jewish Bund, the White Russian Socialist *Hromada,* the Georgian Socialist Federalist Party *Sakartvelo,* and the Armenian *Dashnakstutin* had become ardent proponents of it. It must be noted, however, that the Bruenn Conference of the Austrian Social Democratic Party held in 1899 was primarily concerned with finding a solution to the complex problem of national movements *within* the Austro-Hungarian Dual Empire, and so were the subsequent famous works of Karl Renner, Otto Bauer (R. Springer). Similarly, the famous 1903 Program of the Second Party Congress of the R.S.D.L.P. and subsequent debate between Lenin and the Bundists were directed at the nationality problems *within* the Russian empire.

12 Alfred Cobban ascribes to the Bolshevik revolution much of the credit for bringing the expression into general European discourse. "At Brest-Litovsk, for the first time in the war, self-determination becomes a dominant interest. The Soviets in their peace declaration of 8 November 1917 had brought it into the centre of the stage, and there ever since, for weal or woe, it has obstinately clung." *op. cit.,* p. 12. The subject nationalities were not far behind the Bolsheviks. Towards the end of the war, many of the subject nationalities held several international conferences to assert their claims and publicize their resolve. But even more significantly, some of the subject nationalities were already organizing governments and raising armies to help along the collapse of the empires and to secure some territory for themselves. By the time of the Peace Conference some of these nationalities had already achieved independence and presented the Allies with a *fait accompli.* Alfred Cobban, op. cit., p. 15; Harold Temperley (ed.) *A History of the Peace Conference*, 1920-1924, Vol. IV, p. 204. The groups which were working for the establishment of Yugoslavia and Czechoslovakia were the most active in this regard. As early as 1915 a Yugoslav Committee was formed in London and on July 20, 1917 the President of the Yugoslav Committee, Dr. Trumbic, and the Prime Minister of Serbia, Mr. Pasic, issued the famous Manifesto of Corfu which laid down the basis of a

future "Kingdom of the Serbs, Croats and Slovenes." The activities of this group was crowned by the use of Serbian troops in the Allied offensive on the Salonica Front in the autumn of 1918 "which profoundly affected the Southern Slav lands and brought on their complete break with the Dual Monarchy." Harold W. Temperley, *op. cit.*, p. 194. Similarly the activities of the National Council of Czechoslovakia under the leadership of Dr. Benes and Jan Masaryk, and especially the work of the Czech armies had led Great Britain on 9 August 1918 to recognize "the Czecho-Slovaks as an allied nation, their armies as regular belligerents and the National Council as the present trustee of the future Czecho-Slovak Government." *Ibid.*, p. 262. For complete accounts of the activities of the Yugoslav and Czechoslovak nationalists, see Harold W. Temperley, *op. cit.*, pp. 171-207; pp. 256-266 respectively.

13 When the International Conference of Nationalities met in Paris in June of 1915, they adopted *The Declaration of the Rights of Minorities* which said *inter alia* that "Nationalities, whether they are founded in a community of origin, language, or tradition, or whether they result from an association freely entered into by different ethnic groups have the right to dispose of themselves." Raymond Buell, *op. cit.,* p. 34; and on April 11, 1918, the "Congress of Oppressed Nationalities" at which were represented Italian, Rumanian, Czecho-Slovak, Polish and Southern Slav groups "resolved to proclaim completely independent national states, and to carry on in common the war of liberation against the monarchy." C. A. Macartney, *op. cit.*, p. 191, cf. Harold Temperley, *op. cit.*, p. 258.

14 C. A. Macartney notes "that during the past century, and particularly during the past twenty years, the units which have attempted to achieve 'self-determination' have been almost exclusively 'nations.'" He goes on to report that perhaps the only exception to this was "the case of 10,000 inhabitants of Holmes County, Ohio, who in 1926 requested that their county should be made into a free and independent state to be known hereafter as Holmes County, America which shall forever be the home of Liberty, geographical intelligence and democrats." *op. cit.*, p. 15; cf. Jozef Sulkowski, *op. cit.*, p. 320.

15 In perhaps the most authoritative statement on this subject in the interwar period, the Committee of Jurists appointed by the League Council to see into the Asland Islands dispute stated in their report that "Positive International Law no more recognizes the right of national groups, as such, to separate themselves from the state of which they are part, by the simple expression of a wish, than it recognized the right of another state to demand secession from it," League of Nations, *Official Journal*, suppl. No. 104 (1920), p. 47. See also Raymond L. Buell, *International Relations*, p. 33; Johannes Mattern, *Employment of the Plebiscite in the Determination of Sovereignty*, pp. 202-203. The statement made by Philip M. Brown in his article "Self-Determination in Central Europe," *AJIL*, Vol. 14 (1920), p. 235 that the right of self-determination was a "fundamental principle in international law and order," was quite contrary to the consensus among the publicists as well as to state practice.

16 Much of the literature about self-determination which evolved after the war was more political than legal, and some were even polemical. Some of the more political commentaries that appeared right after the war are the following: Frank Golder, "Will the Unrestricted Self-Determination of all National Groups Bring World Peace and Order?" *Journal of International Relations* (Worcester,

Mass.), Vol. 10, January 1920, pp. 278-288; Henri Lambert, "National Self-Determination," *North American Review* (New York), Vol. 207, April 1918, pp. 541-548; Robert Lansing, *Self-Determination: The Discussion of a Phrase,* reprinted from the *Saturday Evening Post,* New York, May 1921; Arnold J. Toynbee, "Self-Determination," *Quarterly Review* (London), Vol. 243, April 1925, pp. 317-338; and Theodore S. Woolsey, "Self-Determination," *AJIL*, Vol. 13 (1919), pp. 302-305.

17 It was due to Erno Wittman's acceptance of the contention that the right of self-determination implied the right of secession which led him to make the following statement: "Self-Determination would lead to saturnalia, rulers would change places with the ruled; and this, in truth, would not denote remedy. For tomorrow's discontent would lead to the same evils as those to which the discontent of yesterday had." *Past and Future of the Right of National Self-Determination*, p. 116, *ex passim*. See also Raymond Buell, *op. cit.*, pp. 45-46; Henri Lambert, *op. cit.*, p. 545; and especially Frank Golder, *op. cit.*, p. 282.

18 C. A. Macartney, *Op. cit.*, p. 395.

19 Raymond Buell, *Op. cit.*, p. 45.

20 In pointing out the importance of this problem, 'Erno Wittman quoted the following passage from a report presented by Carnot to the French National Assembly on February 14, 1973: "If it were otherwise, and any community whatever had the right to proclaim its will and separate from the main body under the influence of rebels, etc. every country, every town, every village, every farmstead might declare itself independent," *op. cit.*, p. 53. For a household to claim the right to independence would, of course, be a *reductio ad absurdum*. However, for this very reason, it points up the necessity of establishing some criteria on the basis of which a line can be drawn between those units which are large enough and those which are not. Nor was the problem purely academic. In the spring of 1934 the Ile Saint Louis which is situated in the river Seine at Paris appealed to the League of Nations for the right to self-determination in the following words: "High Magistrates of the Pact of Nations, Protectors of all Small oppressed peoples forgotten or wronged, L'Ile Saint-Louis hurls toward you a cry of appeal and protestation." Raymond Buell, *op. cit.*, p. 45, n. 1.

21 See Raymond Buell, *op. cit.*, p. 45; cf. C. A. Macartney, *op. cit.*, p. 4; Arnold J. Toynbee, *op. cit.*, pp. 319-322.

22 C. A. Macartney, *op. cit.*, p. 4; cf. Carlton J. H. Hayes, *Essays on Nationalism*, p. 3; Harry E. Barnes, *op. cit.*, p. 163; Alfred Cobban, *op. cit.*, p. 48.

23 See, for instance, Alfred Cobban, *op. cit.*, pp. 44-72.

24 See Chapter IV, *infra*.

25 See Carlton J. H. Hayes, *op. cit.*, pp. 4-5; Oscar Janowsky, *op. cit.*, p. 17; Oscar Jaszi, *The Dissolution of the Hapsburg Monarchy* (Chicago: Chicago University Press, 1929), p. 26, n. 1; C. A. Macartney, *op. cit.,* pp. 4ff.

26 C. A. Macartney, *Op. cit.*, p. 96. For an analysis of the development of this theory see C. A. MAcartney, *op. cit.*, 96-104; and especially C. J. H. Hayes, *The Historical Evolution of Modern Nationalism* (New York: The Macmillan Co., 1931), pp. 44ff.

27 J. G. Fichte, *Reden an die deutsche Nation* (Samtliche Werke, vii. 432), quoted in C. A. Macartney, *op. cit.*, p. 99.

28 See C. A. Macartney, *op. cit*, pp. 6-10; also C. J. H. Hayes, *Essays in Nationalism*, p. 5ff.

29 Otto Bauer, *Die Nationalitatenfrage und die Sozialdemokratie* (Vienna: 1907; second edition, 1924), p. 135.

30 C. A. Macartney, *op. cit.*, p. 7; C. J. H. Hayes, *op. cit.*, p. 4; Alfred Cobban, *op. cit.*, p. 24; Arnold J. Toynbee, *The World After the Peace Conference* (London: Oxford University Press, 1925), p. 18.

31 Josef Stalin, *Marxism and the National and Colonial Question* (London: Martin Lawrence, Ltd., 1936), p. 8. This was probably the only theoretical statement on the nature of nationality in Bolshevik Literature. But its authority as the statement of the Bolshevik position is unimpeachable. The book was written at the instigation of Lenin for the express purpose of producing an official Bolshevik doctrine to rebut the arguments of Otto Bauer and the Austrian Social-Democrats and groups in Russia such as the Jewish Bund which had come under their influence. Demetrio Boersner, *The Bolsheviks and the National and Colonial Question, 1917-1928* (Geneve: Librarie E. Droz, 1957), p. 30; Alfred D. Low, *Lenin and the Question of Nationality* (New York: Bookman Associates, 1958), p. 29. Furthermore, this statement represents the theoretical posture of Stalin during his term of office as the Commissar for Nationalities (November 1917-July 1923).

32 Alfred D. Low recognizes, of course, that there was a difference between the positions of Stalin and the Austrian Social-Democrats. However, exception must be taken to his statement that "while Otto Bauer had offered a novel and arresting interpretation of nationality—seeing in it a group tied together by common character traits which resulted from common historical expreiences— Stalin reverted from this dynamic to a rather static conception of nationality, to a pedestrian listing of a number of criteria generally found in an ethnic group. . .it contained little which set it apart from the 'bourgeois' theories of nationality, except perhaps the emphasis on its temporary, changing character." *Op. cit.*, p. 29-30. Apart from his requirement of a community of language, Stalin's characteristics of nationality are clearly not ethnographic, and most important, as Demetrio Boersner has noted: "He is certainly closer than Bauer to Marx's materialist thought, when he states that a nation is not a permanent unit, but simply a symptom of a certain phase of historical evolution, namely the phase of rising capitalism." *Op. cit.*, p. 11.

33 Josef Stalin, *op. cit.*, p. 11.

34 *Ibid.*, p. 12.

35 *Ibid.*, p. 8.

36 *Ibid.*, p. 5.

37 *Ibid.*, p. 11. Due partly to this community of territory, he denies Bauer's contention that the Jews are a nationality. "For, I repeat, what sort of nation, for instance, is a Jewish nation that consists of Georgian, Daghestanian, Russian, American and other Jews, the members of which do not understand each other (since they speak different languages), inhabit different parts of the globe, will never see each other, will never act together, . . ." *Ibid.*, p. 12.

38 V. I. Lenin, *op. cit.*, pp. 183-185.

39 *Ibid.*, p. 185 italics are mine. Lenin also specifically refers to the people in the colonies as nations. Commenting on the Western European countries and the United States, he asserts: "Every one of these 'great' nations oppresses other nations in the colonies and within its own country." *Ibid.*, p. 184.

40 *Ibid.*, p. 185.

41 In his essay "The Discussion of Self-Determination Summed-up" published in October 1916 in *Sbornik Sotsial-Demokrata,* Lenin denounced "The Polish comrades" for attempting to draw a distinction between the European nationalities and the colonies and advocating the right of secession in only the latter. Lenin argued that the main distinction between the colonies and the European nations was an economic distinction which "formerly consisted in that colonies were drawn into *commodity* exchange but not yet into capitalist production." He went on to assert, however, that "Imperialism changed that." Thus, "In Europe most of the dependent nations are capitalistically more highly developed (most, not all: Albanians, many national minorities in Russia) than in the colonies." But that only meant that " . . . revolutionary movements of *all* types—including also national—are more possible, feasible, persistent, class conscious and difficult to defeat in European situations than in the colonies." He therefore concluded by asserting that "In singling out the colonies and contrasting them with Europe the Polish comrades have lapsed into a contradiction which at once upsets all their erroneous arguments." See V. I. Lenin, *op. cit.*, pp. 223-228. For a discussion of the whole debate see Demetrio Boersner, *op. cit.*, pp. 49-56.

42 For a good short discussion of the development of the theory of popular sovereignty from the Glorious Revolution, the American Revolution and the French Revolution and especially the application of the doctrine to external relations, see C. A. Macartney, *op. cit.*, pp. 44-49; Johannes Mattern, *op. cit.*, pp. 76-79; Carlton J. H. Hayes, *Essays on Nationalism*, pp. 44-49.

43 C. A. Macartney, *op. cit.*, p. 46.

44 *Ibid.*, p. 6. So complete has been the equation of nation and state in Western European and American usage that the word "nation" is frequently used to mean "state" and *vice-versa.* For instance, " . . . The American Institute of International Law at a meeting to draw up a declaration of the rights and duties of nations in 1916, used the words 'nation' and 'state' interchangeably." Alfred Cobban, *op. cit.*, p. 59.

45 Johannes Mattern, *op. cit.*, p. 77.

46 See C. A. Macartney, *op. cit.*, p. 13; Alfred Cobban, *op. cit.*, p. 59; Oskar Janowsky, *op. cit.*, p. 17.

47 Alfred Cobban, *op. cit.*, p. 12.

48 Josef Stalin, *op. cit.*, p. 19.

49 For instance, one important reason why Stalin rejects Otto Bauer's contention that national-cultural autonomy is the same as national self-determination is that self-determination implies sovereign rights while national-cultural autonomy implies something less. "The first thing that strikes the eye is the entirely inexplicable and absolutely unjustifiable substitution of national autonomy for self-determination of nations. One or the other: either Bauer failed to understand the meaning of self-determination, or he did understand it but for some reason or other deliberately narrowed its meaning. For there is no doubt a) that national autonomy presupposes the integrity of the multi-national state, whereas self-determination transcends this integrity and b) *that self-determination endows a nation with sovereign rights*, whereas national autonomy endows it only with 'cultural' rights." *Op. cit.*, p. 31 italics are mine. Elsewhere, Stalin states, national self-determination deals not only with the question of combating national oppression but "the general question of

emancipating the oppressed nations, colonies, and semi-colonies from imperialism; . . ." *Ibid.*, p. 76; also p. 19. For Lenin's statements equating self-determination to national equality see V. I. Lenin, *op. cit.*, p. 94; pp. 98-99.

50 In his earlier writings, Lenin had stated that the " . . . self-determination of nations means the political secession of these nations from alien national communities; the formation of an independent national state." *Op. cit.*, p. 67. However, in his later writings, he consistently held the view, shared by Stalin, that the achievement of national equality was the aim of fighting for national self-determination and that the realization of this equality can be achieved by territorial autonomy, or federation just as well as secession.

In fact, as they frequently stated, the Bolsheviks were not at all in favor of encouraging secession and separatism. As Lenin puts it, "To accuse the supporters of freedom of self-determination, i.e., freedom to secede, of encouraging separatism, is as foolish and as hypocritical as accusing the advocates of freedom of divorce of encouraging the destruction of family ties." *Ibid.*, p. 112. According to them, it was precisely because they were against the formation of small states, and in favor of the "amalgamation" of nationalities in large multi-national states, that they advocated the right of national self-determination including the right of secession. As Lenin stated, "Just as mankind can achieve the aboliton of the classes only by passing through the transition period of the dictatorship of the oppressed class, so mankind can achieve the inevitable merging of nations only by passing through the transition period of complete liberation of all oppressed nations, i.e., their freedom to secede. *Ibid.*, p. 177.

Both Lenin and Stalin hoped that in the particular case of Russia the program of the party and the obvious economic advantages of large states would lead the subject natinalities to re-enter a multi-national soviet state on the basis of equality of all nationalities. Thus, Stalin states, "I believe that now, after the overthrow of tsarism, nine tenths of the peoples will not desire secession. The party, therefore, proposes to institute regional autonomy for regions which may not desire secession and which are distinguished by peculiarities of social life and language, as, for instance, Transcaucasia, Turkestan and the Ukraine." Stalin, *op. cit.*, p. 65; also Lenin, *op. cit.*, p. 97. To this end both Lenin and Stalin, while advocating that the proletariat of the *oppressing* nationalities should demand the right of the *oppressed* nationalities to secede, maintained that the proletariat of the *oppressed* nationalities should be fighting for "freedom of union" and the unification of the different nationalities into a multi-national state. V. I. Lenin, *op. cit.*, p. 179; Josef Stalin, *op. cit.*, p. 64. See also Demetrio Boersner, *op. cit.*, p. 53; Alfred D. Low, *op. cit.*, p. 87.

51 V. I. Lenin, *op. cit.*, pp. 114, 116 *et passim.* Lenin's definition of "oppressed nationality" which is, a nationality which lacks political independence, is the one that is generally used. For instance, J. Carlton Hayes states: "A nationality which is not politically independent and united is metaphorically styled an 'oppressed' or 'subject' or even 'enslaved' nationality." *Op. cit.*, p. 5;

52 The Bolsheviks themselves considered this unification of the status of the "oppressed nationalities" and the colonies as ectremely significant. Thus, Stalin states that Leninism "broke down the wall between Europeans and Asiatics, between the 'civilized' and 'uncivilized' slaves of imperialism and thus linked the national problem with the problem of colonies." *Problemy Leninizma*, 1952, 11th edition, p. 54, quoted in Alfred D. Low, *op. cit.*, p. 160, n. 125.

53 Josef Stalin, *Marxism and the National and Colonial Question*, pp. 58, 65, *et passim*.

54 One interesting point about the theory advocated by Otto Bauer and the Austrian Marxists is its extra-territorial definition of national self-determination. Following their idea that "nationality is not essentially connected with territory" (Rudolf Springer, *Das Nationale Problem*, p. 15.), they defined national self-determination in terms of national-cultural autonomy, according to which "Every nation living in Austria, irrespective of the territory inhabited by its members, constitutes an autonomous group which quite independently manages all its national (language and cultural) affairs." (quoted in V. I. Lenin, *op. cit.*, p. 42.) As Rudolf Springer explains the application of the theory, all the people in one nationality, would elect a National Council which "is the cultural Parliament of the Nation, empowered to establish the principles and approve the methods of, that is, to assume guardianship over, national education, national literature, art and science, the formation of academies, museums, galleries, theatres, etc.," *op. cit.*, p. 200. "Thus, national autonomy, the self-determination of nations, will necessarily become the constitutional programme of the proletariat of all nations in a multi-national state." *op. cit.*, p. 319. The Austrian empire collapsed before this theory could be put into practice and, therefore, it never received any attention on the international level. For discussions of this theory in the English language, see Demetrio Boersner, *op. cit.*, pp. 32-41; Alfred D. Low, *op. cit.*, p. 53ff.; V. I. Lenin, *op. cit.*, pp. 32ff.; Josef Stalin, *op. cit.*, pp. 26-35.

55 Erich Hula, *op. cit.*, p. 8.

56 C. A. Macartney, op. cit., p. 102.

57 Cf. Sarah Wambaugh, *A. Monograph on Plebiscites* (New York: Oxford University Press, 1920), p. 2, *et passim*. J. Mattern notes, "The mental and logical process was simple. The people are the state and the nation; the people are sovereign. As such they have the right to decide, as the *ultima ratio*, by popular vote and simple majority, all the matters affecting the state and the nation." Erich Hula, *op. cit.*, p. 7.

58 Sarah Wambaugh, *op. cit.*, p. 1; Johannes Mattern, *op. cit.*, p. 77; Erich Hula, "National Self-Determination Reconsidered," *Social Research*, Vol. 10, No. 1 (1943), p. 6. See p. 1, n. 1, *supra*.

59 C. A. Macartney, *op. cit.*, p. 100. See also Alfred Cobban, *op. cit.*, p. 53, *et passim*.

60 C. A. Macartney, *op. cit.*, p. 101. See also Frank Golder, *op. cit.*, p. 284; Robert Lansing, *op. cit.*, p. 6.

61 Sarah Wambaugh, *op. cit.*, p. 2. See also Johannes Mattern, *op. cit.,* p. 77; Erich Hula, *op. cit.,* p. 7.

62 Erich Hula, *op. cit.*, pp. 6-7. Hula describes the right of option as a "device of individual self-determination." The right of option has a long history in the law of cession. For some time it has been inserted in treaties of cession to overcome as far as possible the objection of the persons who are forced into allegiance to another sovereign by that cession. The right of option usually stipulated that within a specified period of time, each person affected by the treaty could opt to retain his original nationality, and usually to emigrate into the territory held by his original nationality. However, to describe it as individual self-determination is to stretch the meaning of both principles beyond all recognition. For a discussion of the history as well as the theory of the right of

option see Johannes Mattern, *op. cit.,* pp. 163-167.

63 Erich Hula, *op. cit.,* p. 7. This point is demonstrated by the fact that although most Alsatians are German in terms of language and culture, they have continually resisted the efforts of Germany to incorporate them into the German empire, and bitterly opposed the German annexation of Alsace. See Alfred Cobban, *op. cit.,* p. 142.

64 *Nationalism,* A Report by a Study Group of Members of the Royal Institute of International Affairs. (London: Oxford University Press, 1939), p. 4, also p. 249ff.; Erich Hula, *op. cit.,* p. 12.

65 As Alfred Cobban notes, an example of this theory of national-determinism "was provided by the German attitude towards the annexation of Alsace, which was justified on grounds of nationality, yet grounds far removed from anything that the West could have recognized as self-determination. 'We Germans who know both Germany and France,' wrote Treitschke, 'know better what is for the good of the Alsatians than do those unhappy people themselves ...We desire, even against their will, to restore them to themselves.'" *Op. cit.,* p. 53.

66 V. I. Lenin, *op. cit.,* pp. 82-83, *et passim*; Josef Stalin, *op. cit.,* pp. 12-15, *et passim.* For commentary, see Alfred Low, *op. cit.,* p. 30; Demetrio Boersner, *op. cit.,* p. 30.

67 V. I. Lenin, *op. cit.,* p. 83.

68 It is important to distinguish between the requirement of "common language" as a mark of nationality in the sense used by the advocates of the principle of national equality and the adherents of the principle of national determinism. In the case of the latter, "common language" is used to mean the language spoken by people of the same ethnic stock. In this sense "common language" is meant to be an indicator of common ethnicity. In the case of the Bolsheviks and the oppressed nationalities, however, "common language" is not meant to imply common ethnicity. Although the point is not explicitly made, from their definition by the other characteristics of nationality, it seems that they might describe as having a common language, people who have lived together so long that they have mutually intelligible languages, or a lingua-franca, or are people who live in multi-lingual communities, such as those described by C. A. Macartney as "racially mixed, bilingual and indeterminate." *Op. cit.,* p. 101; or people living together in the border districts of Poland, Lithuania and Russia described by Frand A. Golder, as having "a 'common speech' which is different from either one of the three languages." *Op. cit.,* p. 284.

69 Erich Hula, *op. cit.,* p. 10.

70 It was not until after the turn of the century, during World War I, that some writers began to apply the expression "self-determination" to the principle of "no annexation without consultation" due to the fact that the plebiscite which had been advocated in the nineteenth century as the means of consulting the inhabitants of a territory to be ceded was also the logical instrument for determining the will of the population to belong to the state which they defined as the test of nationality. It is significant to note that in all the nineteenth century literature on the subject the principle of "no annexation without consultation" was referred to as the plebiscite principle and never as the principle of self-determination. For a list of the most prominent works on the plebiscite principle see Sarah Wambaugh, *op. cit.,* pp. 20-23.

71 Sarah Wambaugh, *op. cit.*, p. 32. For a general discussion of the theoretical and practical problems concerning the institution of the plebiscite in matters concerning the change of sovereignty. see *Ibid.*, pp. 27-33; and Johannes Mattern, *op. cit.*, pp. 151-170.

72 Sarah Wambaugh, "Frontiers by Plebiscite," *Century* (New York), November 1923, Vol. 107, p. 82.

73 Sir Ivor Jennings, *The Approach to Self-Government*, p. 56.

74 This point is illustrated by Johannes Mattern in his discussion of the cases of ". . . .the secession of the Southern states from the North American Union, the secession of West Virginia from the State of Virginia, and the dissolution of the union of Norway and Sweden. In the last two cases the result of the plebiscites were recognized by Virginia and by Sweden. In the first case, the secessions, in spite of popular, direct or indirect votes, were opposed by the sword, and the seceding states forced to rescind their decisions. In both instances, however, the motive for the difference of attitude towards the seceding units was based on state policy and considerations of the legality on the principles of international law of the secession movements as such rather than on favorable or unfavorable opinions regarding the plebiscites as justifying the demand for secession." *Op. cit.*, pp. 167-168.

75 Hanri Lambert, *op. cit.*, p. 545.

76 Erno Wittman, *op. cit.*, p. 53; Johannes Mattern, *op. cit.*, p. 169.

77 Commenting on the Bolsheviks, who were the most outspoken advocates of the principle of national equality, Alfred Cobban notes in his *National Self-Determination*, that their definition of nationality "is probably as true a definition as one could reach for Central and Eastern European conditions, . . ." p. 104; and also that "their theory was better balanced," than the others, p. 106.

78 The problem of having to develop criteria for establishing the difference between those nationalities which may achieve independence and those to be granted territorial autonomy is by-passed by the Bolsheviks because of their clear stand against secessions and their preference for the reorganization of nationalities in large multi-national states on the basis of national equality. However, they insist that whatever their preference is, as Bolsheviks, the final decision as to secession dwells with the nationality concerned. Josef Stalin notes the following in the discussion of one specific case. "For instance, I personally would be opposed to the secession of Transcaucasia, bearing in mind the general level of development in Transcaucasia and in Russia, the conditions of the struggle for the proletariat, and so forth. But if, nevertheless, the peoples of Transcaucasia were to demand secession, they would, of course, secede, and would not encounter opposition on our part." *Op. cit.*, p. 64. Of course, the fact that Transcaucasia is a border region still leaves open the question of what would happen if a group in the interior of Russia wished to secede.

Notes to Chapter III

1 Rupert Emerson, *From Empire to Nation*, p. 27.

2 Mohammed A Shukri, *The Principle of Self-Determination in the United Nations*, p. 44. See also Ruth Russessl, *A History of the United Nations Charter* (Washington, D.C.: The Brookings Institute, 1958), p. 811.

3 Hans Kelsen, "General International Law and the Law of the United Na-

tions," in *The United Nations Ten Years' Legal Progress*, eds. G. H. J. Van Der Molen, W. P. J. Pompe and J. H. W. Verzyl (The Hague: Kijman, 1956), p. 1.

4 See Mohammed A. Shukri, *Op. Cit.*, p. 46. See also, Benjamin Rivlin, *Op. Cit.*, p. 199; Rupert Emerson, Self-Determination Revisited in the Era *of Decolonization*. Harvard: Center for International Affairs, 1964), p. 27.

5 Just as the writers during the inter-war period, the publicists of the United Nations era decided that the important point on which the definition of the principle of self-determination rested, was the determination of the nature of the group which would be entitled to the right. As Rupert Emerson noted, "The inescapable heart of the matter is the necessity of establishing what 'self' it is to which the right attaches." Rupert Emerson, *loc. cit.*

6 Rupert Emerson *From Empire to Nation,* p. 298; also, Benjamin Rivlin, *op. cit.*, pp. 199-200; Clyde Eagleton, "The Excesses of Self-Determination," p. 595; Rosalyn Higgins, *op. cit.*, p. 104.

7 For instance, Professor B. V. A. Roling asserts that "The principle of self-determination is so vague with regard to both the subject that can appeal to it and the circumstances under which it can become a claimable right, that there is little question of any positive legal content." *International Law in an Expanded World* (Amsterdam: Djambatan N.V., 1960), p. 78.

8 See, for instance, Obed Y. Asamoah, *The Legal Significance of the Declarations of the General Assembly of the United Nations* (The Hague: Nijhoff, 1966), p. 181.

9 See, for instance, Benjamin Rivlin, *Self-Determination and Dependent Areas,* 501 I.C. (1955), p. 198; Clyde Eagleton, "The Excesses of Self-Determination," *Foreign Affairs*, Vol. 31, No. 4 (July 1953), p. 595; Mohammed A. Shukri, *op. cit.*, p. 44ff.; Rosalyn Higgins, op. cit., p. 91; J. G. Starke, *An Introduction to International Law*, 4th edition (London: Butterworth & Co., Ltd., 1958), p. 102.

10 Benjamin Rivlin, *op. cit.*, p. 198. See also J. G. Starke, *op. cit.*, p. 102; Mohammed A. Shukri, *op. cit.*, p. 46; B. V. A. Roling, *op. cit.*, p. 78.

11 An example of an implied denunciation of the *national determinism principle* is found in the report of the discussions in Committee 1 of Commission I of the San Francisco Conference concerning the principle of self-determination. In presenting the report, Mr. Zeinedienne, the rapporteur of the committee, stated that, according to the understanding of the Committee, " . . . the essential element of the principle in question is a free and genuine expression of the will of the people, which avoids cases of alleged expression of the popular will, such as those used for their own ends by Germany and Italy in later years. . . ." *UNCIO Documents*, Vol. 6, Doc. No. 944 I/1/34(1), (June 13, 1945).

12 For other statements of Dr. Kelsen's interpretation of the principle of self-determination see, P. N. Drost, *Human Rights as Legal Rights* (Leyden: Sijthoff, 1951), pp. 28-31; C. G. Fenwick, *International Law*, 4th edition (New York: Appleton-Century-Crofts, 1965), p. 178; R. Brunet, *La Garantie Internationale des Droit de l'Homme d'apres la Chartre de San Francisco* (Geneve: Charles Grasset, 1947), p. 164.

13 Hans Kelsen, *The Law of the United Nations* (London: Stevens & Sons, Ltd., 1950), pp. 51-52.

14 Rosalyn Higgins, *op. cit.*, p. 104.

15 *Ibid.*, p. 105.

16 *Ibid.*, pp. 104-105.

17 *Loc. cit.*

18 Mohammed A. Shukri, p. 132. See also, ibid., p. 90, p. 110.

19 Harold S. Johnson, *Self-Determination within the Community of Nations*, p. 200.

20 Mohammed A. Shukri, *op. cit.*, p. 66.

21 *Ibid.*, p. 5.

22 *Ibid.*, p. 57, p. 125. According to Shukri, the two important criteria are those of territoriality, and single authority. For him the issue of whether the authority in question is alien or not is irrelevant. See *ibid.*, p. 57. Harold S. Johnson asserts that: "The first dimension in self-determination is territorial. Control over the activities within a particular area is a *sine qua non.*" *Op. cit.*, p. 112. He goes on to say that "Not only is it necessary to identify the territorial extent of the unit of self-determination, but it is also necessary to identify as its second dimension the people who are to speak for the unit." *Op. cit.*, p. 123. Presumably, then, the group entitled to the right of self-determination is the people in that territory, represented by their democratically elected government.

23 Huntington Gilchrist, "Colonial Questions at the San Francisco Conference," *APSR*, Vol. 39, No. 5 (1945), p. 986.

24 *Ibid.*, p. 987. See also Sergio Armando Frazao, "International Responsibility for Non-Self-Governing Peoples," *Annals*, Vol. 296, No. 58 (November 1954), p. 58; Alf Ross, *The Constitution of the United Nations* (Copenhagen: Munksgaard, 1950), p. 185ff.

25 Clyde Eagleton, *op. cit.*, p. 598.

26 *Loc. cit.*

27 G. B. Starushenko, *The Principle of Self-Determination of Peoples and Nations in the Foreign Policy of the Soviet State*, trans. by Ivanov Munjiev (Moscow: Foreign Language Publishing House, 1963), p. 143. For a list of other Soviet writers who subscribe to this view, see George Ginsburgs, " 'Wars of National Liberation' and the Modern Law of Nations—The Soviet Thesis," in Hans W. Baade (ed.) *The Soviet Impact on International Law* (Dobbs Ferry, N.Y.: Oceana Publications, 1965), p. 68ff.

28 Baratashvili, "Printsip samoopredeleniya Narodov v Ustave OON," The Principle of Self-Determination of Peoples in the U.N. Charter, in G. J. Tunkin (ed.), *Voprosy Mezhdunarodnogo Prava Questions of International Law* (Uchenye Zapiski, Institut Mezhdunarodnykh Otnoshenii, 1960), vyp. 2, p. 65 italics are mine.

29 See George Ginsburgs, *op. cit.*, pp. 79-80 for list of Soviet writers with this viewpoint, including the following: Baratashvili, *op. cit.*, pp. 57ff.; Speranskaya, *Printsip Samoopredeleniya v Mezhdunarodnom Prave The Principle of Self-Determination in International Law* (1961), pp. 72; Starushenko, *Protiv Izvrashcheniya Printsipa Samoopredeleniya Narodov i Natsii Against the Distortion of the Principle of Self-Determination of Peoples and Nations* (Sovetskoe Gosudarstvo i Pravo, No. 1, 1958), pp. 63-66, *et passim;* Korovin, *Mezhdunarodnoe Pravo na Soviemennom Etape International Law at the Present Stage* (Mezhdunarodnaya Zhizn, 1961), p. 24ff.; Onitskaya, "The Downfall of Colonialism and International Law," *International Affairs*, Vol. 1 (Moscow, 1961), p. 39, *et passim*.

30 Sharmanazashvili, *Kolonialnayya voina—gruboe Narushenie Mezhdunarodnogo Prava, Colonial War—A serious Violation of International*

Law (Sovetskoe Gosudarstvo i Pravo, No. 10, 1957), p. 60, quoted in George Ginsburgs, *op. cit.*, p. 82.

31 *Ibid.*, p. 76. As in other cases, this passage is reminiscent of a statement that Lenin made in his 1915 article *Socialism and War: The Attitude of the R.S.D.L.P. Towards the War* (Moscow: Foreign Languages Publishing House, 1952), pp. 15-16, " . . . if tomorrow Morocco were to declare war on France, India on England, Persia or China on Russia, and so forth, those would be 'just,' 'defensive' wars, irrespective of who attacked first; and every Socialist would sympathize with the victory of the oppressed, dependent, un-equal states against the oppressing, slave-owning, predatory 'great' powers."

32 George Ginsburg, *op. cit.*, p. 69.

33 *Ibid.*, p. 76.

34 *Loc. cit.*

35 Baratashvili, *op. cit.*, p. 60, quoted in George Ginsburgs, *op. cit.*, p. 82; also Sharmanazashvili, *op. cit.*, p. 60, and Tuzmukhamedov, *op. cit.*, p. 90, both quoted in George Ginsburgs, *op. cit.*, p. 84.

36 "National liberation wars can be equated with one of the forms of international sanctions, the application of which on the basis of the UNO Charter is being demanded ever more insistently by the peoples toward colonial powers persisting in their illegal policy of barring the self-determination of dependent peoples." Tuzmukhamedov, *op. cit.*, p. 91, quoted in George Ginsburgs, *loc. cit.*

37 See Inis L. Claude, Jr., *Swords into Ploughshares* (New York: Random House, 1964), p. 166. Cf. Quincy Wright, *Problems of Stability and Progress in International Relations* (Berkeley: University of California Press, 1954), p. 32.

38 Georg Schwarzenberger, *The Inductive Approach to International Law*, p. 76. In illustrating this point, Professor Schwarzenberger uses the principle of diplomatic immunity as an example: "The principle itself can tell us precisely nothing on any of the controversial issues beyond what can be ascertained without its assistance; for, in such instances, one principle clashes with other legal principles as, in this case, with that of unlimited territorial State jurisdiction. The problem remains how to balance such conflicting principles and the underlying legal rules." *Loc. cit.*

39 *UNCIO Documents,* Vol. 6, No. 723 I/1/A19, p. 704.

40 Harold S. Johnson, *op. cit.*, p. 201. Also see *ibid.*, p. 134; p. 198. See Mohammed A. Shukri, *op. cit.*, p. 7.

41 Mohammed A. Shukri, *op. cit.,* pp. 117-127.

42 *Ibid.*, pp. 143-151.

43 *Ibid.*, p. 127.

44 Harold S. Johnson, *op. cit.*, p. 204.

45 *Ibid.*, p. 200.

46 *Ibid.*, p. 200.

47 "The plebiscites which have been possible under the auspices of the United Nations have, in the main, been confined to assistance in the termination of trusteeship status." Harold S. Johnson, *op. cit.*, p. 202.

48 *Ibid.,* p. 111; also, p. 112.

49 As one of these theorists states, "It is striking that although the three chapters of the Charter (XI, XII, and XIII) pertaining to dependent peoples contain no mention of the principle of self-determination *per se*, it is through them primarily that practical application of the idea of self-determination has been incorporated into the United Nations system. . . .The entire tone of Chapters

XI, XII and XIII reflects the spirit of self-determination." Benjamin Rivlin, *op. cit.*, pp. 219-220. See also Sergio Armando Frazao, *op. cit.*, p. 58; Huntington Gilchrist, *op. cit.*, p. 986; Quincy Wright, *op. cit.*, p. 30.

50 Clyde Eagleton, *op. cit.*, p. 597.

51 *Ibid.*, p. 596.

52 *Loc. cit.*

53 *Ibid.*, p. 600.

54 *Ibid.*, p. 601.

55 As Florent Peeters notes, the question then becomes one of determining " . . . whether a national group has a right to conquer, though it be by revolution, (this) de facto status. In positive law the question amounts to asking if the right to revolt exists. This is, of course, a nonsensical question;—the answer is in the negative." Florent Peeters, "The Right of Nations to Autodeterminism," *World Justice*, Vol. III (December, 1961), p. 168.

56 The controversy seems to revolve around whether Article 51 should be read to mean that the plea of self-defense is permissible *only* "if an armed attack occurs . . . " or whether it leaves essentially unimpaired a recognized 'inherent right' of a state to use force in self-defense against infringements on rights it considers essential. Some writers, like D. W. Bowett, *Self-Defense in International Law* (Manchester: University Press, 1958), p. 24, *et passim,* argue in favor of a broad interpretation of Article 51 which would include the use of force in self-defense against "economic or ideological aggression . . . " or in anticipation of an attack. The more accepted view is an interpretation which would allow a plea of self-defense only if the force is used against an armed attack. For examples of this view, see, J. Brownlie, "The Use of Force in Self-Defense," 37 *BYIL* 183 (1961); also, Louis Henkin, "Force, Intervention and Neutrality in Contemporary International Law," Proceedings, *ASIL*, (April 26, 1963).

57 Max Sorensen, *ed. Manual of Public International Law*, p. 772. In Resolution 1514(XV), and in subsequent resolutions, the General Assembly has declared that "all armed action . . . directed against dependent peoples should cease." However, it has not made explicit its position on the place which wars of national liberation has in the law of the use of force.

58 See Rupert Emerson, *From Empire to Nations*, pp. 41-42.

59 " . . . the Geneva agreements recognized that national-liberation wars, by which peoples realize their right to self-determination, as just wars are from the standpoint of law legitimate wars. Recognizing the international legal character of national-liberation wars, they coincidentally recognized that questions of self-determination cannot be regarded as internal legal processes of the metropolitan country or the empire, that the hands of the colonial powers are not free to pacify and suppress national-liberation movements." Manfred Lachs, *Zhenevskie Soglasheniya 1954G. OB Indo-Kitae* The 1954 Geneva Agreements on Indo-China 189 quoted in George Ginsburgs, *op. cit.*, p. 71.

60 Of course, the Bolsheviks have consistently proposed their own criterion for determining the legitimacy of a claim by any national liberation movement. This criterion was always, the requirements of the socialist revolution and "the interests of the proletariat." Alfred D. Low, *Lenin and the Question of Nationality*, p. 104.

As a theory of the principle of self-determination, the Bolshevik position suffers from the same basic shortcoming as the *national determinism principle.*

They both make the wishes of the peoples irrelevant as far as their citizenship is concerned. While the *national determinism principle* relegates a person to membership in a state solely on the basis of his ethnicity and without regard to his own preference, this Soviet theory of national liberation wars relegates a person to membership in a state solely on the basis of the requirements of the revolution, equally without regard to his own preferences. One is tempted to disqualify this theory by naming it the *revolutionary determinism principle*.

61 Hans Kelsen, *The Law of the United Nations*, p. 51. See also R. Brunet, *La Garantie International des Droit de L'homme D'aspres la Chartre de San Francisco* (1947), p. 164; P. N. Drost, *Human Rights as Legal Rights* (1951), pp. 28-31.

62 Clyde Eagleton, *op. cit.*, p. 593; See also George Ginsburgs, *op. cit.*, p. 85;

63 Clyde Eagleton, *op. cit.*, p. 594.

64 Clyde Eagleton, *Op. cit.*, p. 594.

65 See, for instance, Benjamin Rivlin, *op. cit.*, p. 198.

66 Quincy Wright, "Recognition and Self-Determination," Proceedings of the *ASIL*, 48th Annual Meeting (April 22-24, 1954), p. 29; see also, Sergio Armando Frazao, *op. cit.*, p. 60; Huntington Gilchrist, *op. cit.*, p. 986.

67 Quincy Wright, *op. cit.*, p. 27.

68 *Ibid.*, p. 29. For a statement of this basic principle of international law, see, for instance, Georg Schwarzenberger, *International Law as Applied by International Tribunals,* p. 45.

69 *Loc. cit.*

70 *Ibid.*, p. 30. See also Hungtington Gilchrist, *op. cit.*, p. 986; Benjamin Rivlin, *op. cit.*, p. 219.

71 Quincy Wright, *op. cit.*, p. 32.

72 *Ibid.*, p. 33.

73 *Loc. it.*

74 For instance, after reviewing the claims made by the representatives of the United States of America and Chile he concluded that, "With such aims, self-determination loses all meaning, for it is extended to cover everything. Anything a 'people' or a 'nation' (provided it is a colony), whether already independent or not, may desire it is entitled to have. It would include the right to the protection of collective security, and full protection for all nationalistic economic actions." Clyde Eagleton, *op. cit.*, p. 598.

75 "Thus self-determination is to be applied only to colonies, and is identified with anti-colonialism—a sad comedown for a great principle once thought applicable to all mankind. . . ." *Ibid.*, p. 597.

76 Benjamin Rivlin, *op. cit.*, p. 207.

77 Rupert Emerson, *op. cit.*, p. 303.

78 Rupert Emerson, *Self-Determination Revisited in the Era of Decolonization*, p. 25.

79 Mohammed Aziz Shukri, *op. cit.*, p. 346.

80 Rosalyn Higgins, *op. cit.*, p. 104.

81 Baratashvili, *op. cit.*, p. 57, *et passim*. See also, G. B. Starushenko, *op. cit.*, p. 135; Tuzmukhamedov, *op. cit.*, pp. 87, 121, *et passim*.

82 George Ginsburgs, *op. cit.*, p. 81.

83 Harold S. Johnson, *op. cit.*, p. 111.

84 Rosalyn Higgins, *op. cit.*, p. 102.

85 *Ibid.*, p. 104.

86 *Loc. cit.*
87 Chapter III, n. 16, *supra.*
88 United Nations Document A/2428, 4 August, 1953.
89 Mohammed Aziz Shukri, *op. cit.*, p. 7, *et passim.*

Notes to Chapter IV

1 As Alfred Cobban notes in his *National Self-Determination*, p. 12, it was the Soviets who "in their peace declaration of 8 November, 1917 had brought it into the center of the stage...." See also C. A. Macartney, *op. cit.*, p. 187; Sarah Wambaugh, *Plesbiscites Since the World War*, Vol. 1 (Washington, D.C.: Carnegie Endowment for International Peace, 1933), p. 6. For a full text of the Soviet decree see C.·K. Cumming and Walter W. Petit, *Russian American Relations, March 1917-March 1920* (New York, 1920), No. 25, pp. 41-42.
2 A Macartney, *op. cit.*, p. 189.
3 J. W. Wheeler-Bennet, *Brest-Litovsk: The Forgotten Peace, March, 1918* (1938), p. 366. Also, Alfred Cobban, *op. cit.*, p. 12; Sarah Wambaugh, *op. cit.*, p. 10.
4 See C. A. Macartney, *op. cit.*, p. 187; Sarah Wambaugh, *op. cit.*, p. 8.
5 President Woodrow Wilson made four important speeches which are considered as collectively comprising *in toto* the statement of the war aims of the Allies and the principles on which they expected the peace to be based. The most famous of these is, of course, the *Fourteen Points for Peace* acceptable to the United States, which he presented to Congress on January 8, 1918; the *Four Additional Points* presented in his famous Mount Vernon speech of July 4th, 1918; and the *Five Additional Points* presented in President Wilson's speech at the opening of the Fourth Liberty Loan Campaign on September 27th, 1918.
These four sets of principles formed the basis of the peacemaking between the Allies and the Central Powers, at least with Germany. See Harold V. Temperley, *op. cit.*, Vol. I, App. IV, p. 450. See also, the Reply of the Allied and Associated Powers to the Observations of the German Delegation on the Conditions of Peace, quoted in Sarah Wambaugh, *op. cit.*, p. 12.
6 C. A. Macartney, *op. cit.*, p. 152.
7 C. A. Macartney, *op. cit.*, p. 180-181.
8 Sarah Wambaugh asserts that "The principle of self-determination is not, as is commonly supposed, one of the Fourteen Points." She goes on to say, however, that "self-determination is given a clear statement... in Wilson's February 11, 1918 speech in which the Four Principles are presented" Wambaugh, *op. cit.*, p. 11. While it is true that the term "self-determination" is actually used in that speech, it is significant that it is not presented, except possibly in inference in the Four Principles. It seems reasonable to think that a principle of such over-riding importance would be formally presented among the other principles. Parenthetically, the clarity of the statement is questionable, especially in view of the subsequent development in attempts to use it.
9 Alfred Cobban, *op. cit.*, p. 17; Sarah Wambaugh, *op. cit.*, p. 12.
10 As early as November, 1914, Mr. Asquith had declared that "we shall not sheathe the sword... until the rights of the smaller nationalities of Europe are placed on an unassailable footing." There were other speeches, such as the one by Winston Churchill on September 11, 1914, and Lord Grey's speeches on

March 23, 1915 and October 23, 1916 all of which declared that "the Allies would fight to ensure the right of nations to develop freely under equal conditions." C. A. Macartney, *op. cit.*, p. 182.

11 As Macartney explains it, "Both sides, again, exploited the principle of nationality in individual cases, where they thought they could weaken their adversary by doing so." *Op. cit.*, p. 183; see also Alfred Cobban, *op. cit.*, p. 11.

12 The only groups to which the Central Powers could appeal to, outside of those within the Russian Empire were such groups as the Irish, the Boer Republics of South Africa, and other groups in North Africa and the Middle East. For a statement made by the Central Powers about such peoples see Alfred Cobban, *op. cit.*, p. 11.

13 See C. A. Macartney, *op. cit.*, p. 183.

14 *Ibid.*, p. 189.

15 Alfred Cobban, *op. cit.*, p. 11.

16 *Ibid.*, p. 13; also Sarah Wambaugh, *op. cit.*, p. 5. See also Chapter II, n. 6, *supra*.

17 As Macartney notes, "The first definite change (of Allied attitude to national self-determination) came at the end of 1916, when President Wilson asked the Allies to state their war aims." *Op. cit.*, p. 184. For the Allied reply of January 10, 1917 to President Wilson's request, see H. W. V. Temperley, *A History of the Peace Conference of Paris* (London: 1920-24), Vol. I, App. 1, p. 428.

18 This conviction for which President Wilson was well known even before the Conference began, is expressed here in a note which he addressed jointly to the Prime Ministers of France and Great Britain on February 24, 1920: " . . . the central principle fought for in the war that no government or group of governments has the right to dispose of the territory or to determine the political allegance of any free people." Sarah Wambaugh, *op. cit.*, p. 13.

19 There is no doubt that the subject nationalities took President Wilson as the leading spokesman of the Allied Powers, and based their belief that the principle of self-determination would be implemented at Paris, chiefly on the promise of the President. On that basis many of them went to Paris with petitions fully expecting the President's promise to be kept. As Sarah Wambaugh describes it, "It would be impossible to exaggerate the emotion felt throughout the world at this promise of the end of the right of conquest. . . .The President had fanned the flames of hope from Asia to the Andes. From three continents . . .petitions, letters, and appeals poured in on the Paris Conference. Already, before the Conference had assembled, numerous delegations from national groups throughout the world were converging on Paris, some to ask for outright change of sovereignty, some to bring informal votes already taken, some to demand formal plebiscites." *Op. cit.*, pp. 12-13.

20 Ray S. Baker and William E. Dodd, *eds., The Public Papers of Woodrow Wilson*, Vol. I (Harper Brothers Publishers, N.Y., 1927), p. 180.

21 *Loc. Cit.*

22 Alfred Cobban, *op. cit.*, p. 13; cf. n. 19, infra.

23 This passage appears in Part VIII of the Allied Statement, for a full text of which see Harold V. Temperley, *op. cit.*, Vol. I, Appendix I, p. 428. Italics are mine.

24 As Alfred Cobban *Op. cit.*, p. 13.

25 This Allied definition of "liberation" is reflected in the famous "Fourteen

Points." According to this document, what the Allies wanted on behalf of the subject nationalities within the Austro-Hungarian Empire was the "freest opportunity for autonomous development" while they at the same time gave an explicit assurance of their desire to see the Empire maintained (point 10). Similarly, the nationalities under Turkish rule were to be liberated by "undoubted security of life and an absolutely unmolested opportunity of autonomous development" (point 12). The same attitude is reflected in a speech delivered by David Lloyd George to the British Trade Union Conference, three days before Wilson's Fourteen Points Speech; in which he asserted that " . . . we agree with President Wilson that the breaking up of Austro-Hungary is no part of our war aims, . . ." Commenting on Woodrow Wilson's "Fourteen Points" speech and his own January 5, 1918 speech, David Lloyd George notes the following. "The two speeches covered the same ground and were applicable to the same areas: Alsace-Lorraine, Poland, the non-Turkish portions of the Turkish Empire, and the peoples of the Austrian Empire who sought freedom from the Hapsburg rule. But both speeches had another feature in common, that, with the one exception of Poland, they did not so much contemplate complete independence for the various nationalities held in subjection by the German, Austro-Hungarian, and Turkish Empires as some special arrangement which—to use President Wilson't phrase—'accorded to them the freest opportunity of autonomous development.' " Dabid Lloyd George, *Memoirs of the Peace Conference*, Vol. II (New Haven: Yale University Press, 1939), pp. 495-496. For other comments on this Allied definition of national liberation see Harold V. Temperley, *op. cit.*, Vol. I, pp. 172 and 190; also C. A. Macartney, *op. cit.*, pp. 190-191.

26 Sarah Wambaugh, *op. cit.*, p. 4. In his January 5, 1918 speech David Lloyd George stated that " . . . the consent of the Government must be the basis of any territorial settlement in this war." David Lloyd George, *op. cit.*, Vol. II, p. 495. This statement seems to indicate the awareness of the relation between national liberation and territorial settlement by consent of the population. But as he stated in the same speech their aim was not to dismember Empires but to grant nationalities. ". . .genuine self-government on true democratic principles." David Lloyd George, *op. cit.,* Vol. II, p. 496. also, Harold V. Temperley, *op. cit.*, Vol. I, p. 190.

27 On April 11, 1918, the Congress of Oppressed Nationalities, made up of most of the minorities within Austria-Hungary, resolved in their Rome Conference " . . . to proclaim completely independent states and to carry on in common the war of liberation against the Monarchy." C. A. Macartney, *op. cit.*, p. 191. But even long before that many of the national groups, particularly the Czecho-Slovaks and Yugo Slavs, had publicly declared their decision to achieve full independence. On July 20, 1917, the President of the Yugo Slav Committee, Dr. Trumbic, and the Prime Minister of Serbia jointly issued the Manifesto of Corfu in which they laid down the basis of a future "Kingdom of the Serbs, Croats and Slovenes." Harold V. Temperley, *op. cit.*, Vol. IV, p. 188. On January 6, 1918, just two days before President Wilson presented the Fourteen Points, "All the Czech deputies in the Reichsrat and the provincial Diets, reaffirmed the principle of self-determination and demanded a sovereign state of their own. . . ." *Op. cit.*, p. 258. See also C. A. Macartney *op. cit.*, p. 191.

28 For the activities of the Czecho-Slovak-Yugoslav National Committees and Provisional Governments, see Harold V. Temperley, *op. cit.*, Vol. IV, pp. 193-201; 260-267. The Czecho-Slovaks made the most spectacular advances in

the creation of the image and appurtennances of national existence. As Harold Temperley notes, "On December 16, 1917, Dr. Benes was able to secure from the French Government the recognition of an autonomous Czecho-Slovak army, fighting under its own flag against the Central Powers, and acknowledging the military authority of the French High Command, but the political control of the (Czech) National Council in Paris." Harold V. Temperley, *op. cit.*, Vol. IX, p. 261.

29 On October 7, 1918, the Foreign Minister of Sweden relayed to the U.S. Secretary of State the Austro-Hungarian Note requesting an armistice and peace negotiations on the basis of the Fourteen Points. In his note of October 18, 1918 replying to this request, President Wilson himself asserted that the situation had changed so drastically since he uttered those words that in effect the terms of the peace with regards to the maintenance of the integrity of the Empire was not in his hands but in the hands of the nationalities. In the words of the Note: "The President deems it his duty to say to the Austro-Hungarian Government that he cannot entertain the present suggestion of that Government because of certain events of the utmost importance which, occurring since the delivery of his Address of January 8th last, have necessarily altered the attitude and responsibility of the Government of the United States. . . .The President is, therefore, no longer at liberty to accept a mere 'autonomy' of these peoples as a basis of peace, but is obliged to insist that they, and not he, shall be the judges of what action on the part of the Austro-Hungarian Government will satisfy their aspirations and their conception of their rights and destiny as members of the family of nations." Harold V. Temperley, *op. cit.*, Vol. I, p. 452-453.

30 Harold V. Temperley, *op. cit.*, Vol. I, p. 174.

31 As Alfred Cobban notes, "Self-determination was to Wilson almost another word for popular sovereignty." *Op. cit.*, p. 20. For more discussion of the political philosophy of Woodrow Wilson, and its effects on his politics, see Harold V. Temperley, *op. cit.*, Vol. I, pp, 173-183.

32 U. S. Congressional Record, Vol. 54, Pt. 2, p. 1742.

33 *Ibid.*, Vol. 56, Pt. 9, p. 8671.

34 C. A. Macartney, *op. cit.*, p. 193. According to C. A. Macartney, "The only genuine ambition to form a state which might have been respected, and was not, was that of the Ruthenes." *Loc. cit.*

35 Sarah Wambaugh, *op. cit.*, p. 15. In order to settle the territorial claims, the Council of Ten set up five ad hoc expert commissions and a coordinating Territorial Commission to study the claims and make recommendations to it. In line with the instructions that they consult the people concerned, the very first recommendation which was made by a Territorial Commission was that "the frontier between Germany and Denmark shall be fixed in conformity with the wishes of the population." *Loc. cit.*

36 "Whether the view was originally held by British delegation, or whether it developed as the difficulties of the Conference multiplied, it appears to be a fact that from the first the British at Paris looked on the Wilson principles as requiring plebiscites far more than the American delegation, and during the Conference evinced a greater willingness to resort to them." *Ibid.*, p. 14.

37 David Hunter Miller, *My Diary at the Peace Conference*, Vol. II, Doc. 4, p. 13.

38 See "Official American Commentary on the Fourteen Points," David

Hunter Miller, *op. cit.*, Vol. II, Document 12; cf. Alfred Cobban, *op. cit.*, p. 25.

39 The Italian member of the Commission on Belgium and Danish Affairs made the following statement while voting for the recommendations of a plebiscite in Schleswig: "The Italian delegates, while entirely associating themselves with the conclusions arrived at by the Committee, feel that they must take this opportunity of making reservations of a general kind relative to the scope of the principle of the Plebiscite regarded as the sole method of solving territorial problems." David Hunter Miller, *op. cit.*, Vol. X, p. 150. Also see Alfred Cobban, *op. cit.*, p. 25-26.

40 Sarah Wambaugh, *op. cit.*, p. 42; cf. Alfred Cobban, *op. cit.*, p. 26.

41 Ibid, p. 26.

42 The Hungarian Peace Negotiations, Vol. II, Note c, quoted in Sarah Wambaugh, *op. cit.*, p. 30.

43 See the full text of the Allied Statement in H. W. Temperley, op. cit., Vol. IV, p. 422. See also Sarah Wambaugh, *op. cit.*, p. 20 for Allied statement that "Whenever the will of the people is in doubt, a plebiscite has been provided for."

44 Quoted in David Lloyd George, *op. cit.*, Vol. II, p. 889. See also Oscar Janowsky, *Nationalities and National Minorities*, p. 110. That the policy of the Allied Powers was to establish territorial boundaries on the basis of ethnography is further indicated in the following official Allied commentary on the German Treaty: "Every territorial settlement of the Treaty of Peace has been determined upon after the most careful and laboured consideration of all the religious, social and linguistic factors in each particular country." They explain their departure from this policy (in ceding territories inhabited by Germans to other states) as a special circumstance necessitated by "the inevitable fact that an appreciable portion of the territory of the German Empire consisted of districts which had in the past been wrongfully appropriated by Prussia or Germany." Quoted in C. A. Macartney, *op. cit.*, pp. 194-195.

45 David Lloyd George, *op. cit.*, p. 898.

46 *Ibid.*, p. 881. He goes on as follows: "Sometimes the various races were apt to form groups or little communities of their own. But not infrequently in the same town or village there were huddled together Czechs, Magyars, Germans, Poles, Slovaks, Lithuanians,—and everywhere Jews. Next-door neighbours in the same street might represent different nationalities. In the same household there was often a compound of races." *Loc. cit.*

47 David Lloyd George, *op. cit.*, p. 890.

48 See C. A. Macartney, *op. cit.*, pp. 212-220 for a short survey of some of the activities of nationalities and peace organizations with regard to the preparations leading to the drafting of the Minority Treaties.

49 The Smuts Plan declined to apply the principle of self-determination to territories previously belonging to Germany. Alsace-Lorraine was exempted because it represented a *restitutio in integrum* and the ex-German colonies in the Pacific and Africa were exempted on the grounds that they " . . . are inhabited by barbarians, who not only cannot possibly govern themselves, but to whom it would be impracticable to apply any idea of political self-determination in the European sense." David Hunter Miller, *The Drafting of the Covenant*, Vol. II, p. 28. For a full text of the Smuts Plan, see General Jan Smuts, *The League of Nations: A Practical Suggestion* (London, 1918), reprinted in David Hunter Miller, *op. cit.*, pp. 23-37.

50 For a discussion of the activities leading to the establishment of the Mandates System, see Quincy Wright, *Mandates under the League of Nations*, pp. 25-63, also David Hunter Miller, *op. cit.*, Vol. I, pp. 101-117.

51 For instance, the principle of the physical transfer of population was contemplated by the Allied Powers as a way by which some minorities could achieve self-determination. See Inis Claude, *National Minorities*, p. 12; Stephen P. Ladas, *The Exchange of Minorities: Bulgaria, Greece, and Turkey* (New York, 1932). See also Harry Psomiades, *The Eastern Question: The Last Phase, A Study in Greek-Turkish Diplomacy* (Thessaloniki: Center of Balkan Studies, 1968).

52 Oscar I. Janowsky, *op. cit.*, p. 107. As Macartney sees it, (*op. cit.*, p. 273), in establishing the system of minority guarantees, the Allied Powers were in fact asserting "that there is a proper respect for their rights and feelings, it is possible for them to forget their own natural determined nationalism in favour of a true 'self-determination' based on feelings of political loyalty." Note the similarity between this statement and the policy statements expressed by Allied Spokesmen in early 1918 defining self-determination for subject nationalities within Austria-Hungary as the acquisition of self-government and autonomy for these nationalities without breaking up the integrity of Austria-Hungary. See note 30, *supra*.

53 The system for the international guarantee of minority rights is embodied in a variety of legal instruments including five Minority Treaties, four provisions within the peace treaties which were signed with the defeated states, and five declarations made by new states to the Council of the League of Nations. For the text of these instruments, see League of Nations, *Protection of Linguistic, Racial and Religious Minorities by the League of Nations* (Geneva, 1927).

54 See for example, Article 8 of the Polish Minorities Treaty, in Harold V. Temperley, *op. cit.*, Vol. X, pp. 437-442.

55 Inis Claude, *op. cit.*, p. 17.

56 C. A. Macartney, *op. cit.*, p. 291.

57 Some attempts were made to define the qualifications of those minorities which would be entitled to protection within the meaning of the League guarantee system. For instance, M. de Mello-Franco stated in a report to the League Council that "A minority as defined by the Treaties assuming its protection is not only a racial group incorporated in the body of a nation of which the majority forms a different racial unit. There is also a psychological, social and historical attribute, constituting perhaps, for the purposes of the definition which we are seeking, its principal differential characteristic." *League of Nations Official Journal* (Minutes of the 37th Council), February, 1926, p. 141. However, this statement was vehemently opposed in the Council. Other statements of this nature also aroused general opposition. See, for instance, L.N.O.J., July, 1928, pp. 888ff.

58 Speech delivered by President Wilson to the Conference on May 31, 1919, quoted in David Lloyd George, *op. cit.*, Vol. II, p. 890.

59 This view is expressed in a statement by Clemenceau as follows: "What we have to ascertain is whether in view of the past history of several peoples it may not be necessary to give, I will not say additional guarantees, but such guarantees of a more complete nature as may be admitted to be necessary." Quoted in David Lloyd George, *op. cit.*, Vol. II, p. 885. See also C. A. Macartney, *op. cit.*, p. 286; Harold V. Temperley, *op. cit.*, Vol. V, p. 129.

60 Inis Claude, *op. cit.*, p. 19.

61 *Ibid.*, p. 32.

62 See, for instance, the speech of M. Bratiano, which he presented to the May 31st 1919 Plenary Session of the Conference, as the spokesman of the New States, quoted in David Loyd George, *op. cit.*, p. 884.

63 Inis Claude, *op. cit.*, pp. 32-33.

64 Alfred Cobban, *op. cit.*, p. 36; also Inis Claude, *op. cit.*, p. 42.

65 David Lloyd George was for instance, explicit in his endorsement of the application of the principle of self-determination to the ex-colonies. In his famous war-aims speech of January 5, 1918 he stated that "The natives live in their various tribal organizations under chiefs and councils who are competent to consult and speak for their tribes and members and thus to represent their wishes and interests in regard to their disposal. The general principle of national self-determination is, therefore, as applicable in their cases as in those of the occupied European territories." Harold V. Temperley, *op. cit.*, Vol. 2, pp. 226-227.

66 Since the mandated territories were ex-colonies with recognized territorial boundaries, the problem of establishing the territorial limits of the mandated territories did not arise. There were very few cases in which mandated territories were involved in boundary changes and all of these were special cases. One such case was the amendment of the British and Belgian mandates in East Africa on August 3, 1923 in conformity with an Anglo-Belgian agreement to change the boundary between those territories so as to restore the unity of the territory formerly under the rule of King Musinga of Ruanda. See Quincy Wright, *op. cit.*, pp. 119-120.

67 Quincy Wright, *op. cit.*, p. 27.

68 *Loc. cit.* See also, Harold V. Temperley, *op. cit.*, Vol. V, pp. 350-352.

69 Excerpt from Wilson's January 27, 1919 speech to the Council of Ten, quoted in Quincy Wright, *op. cit.*, p. 35.

70 David Hunter Miller, *op. cit.*, Vol. I, p. 101; Quincy Wright, *op. cit.*, p. 15. For a discussion of the origins of the theory of tutelage and trusteeship see the following: Luther H. Evans, "Some Legal and Historical Antecedents of the Mandatory system," *Southwestern Political Science Association,* Proceedings (5th annual convention, March, 1924); M. F. Lindley, The Acquisition and Government of Backward *Territory in International Law* (London, 1926); Sir Frederick Lugard, *The Dual Mandate in British Tropical Africa,* 2nd edition (London, 1923); D. H. Miller, "The Origin of the Mandates System," *Foreign Affairs,* (January, 1928), pp. 277ff.; A. H. Snow, *The Question of Aborigines in the Law and Practice of Nations* (Washington, 1919); J. Stoyanovsky, *La Theorie generale des mandats internationaux* (Paris, 1925).

71 As Quincy Wright notes (*op. cit.*, p. 15), "Thus the theory existed, though it was not universally accepted, and seldom applied, that every considerable people of distinct culture is potentially an independent state and that imperial powers can properly exercise only tutelage over them pending their maturity." David Hunter Miller also notes that " . . . the idea involved the principle that the control of uncivilized peoples ought to mean a trusteeship or wardship under which the interests of the natives themselves should be paramount, . . ." See also Alpheus H. Snow, *op. cit.*, p. 70.

72 David Hunter Miller makes the following comment about the Smuts Plan: "Smuts gave some passing acclaim to the formula of 'No Annexation;' but did

not think that this formula applied to the German colonies. Of course, he said, they should be separated from Germany and, as they were to be outside the Mandates system, the obvious inference of conclusion was that German South-West Africa should become a part of General Smuts' country and German New Guinea a part of Australia, and so on. The legal ability and political ingenuity of Smuts were strikingly shown in this program put forward in advocacy of 'No Annexations.'" *Op. cit.*, Vol. I, p. 36. See also Quincy Wright, *op. cit.*, p. 30; Harold V. Temperley, *op. cit.*, Vol. II, pp. 21-31; J. Stayanovsky, *op. cit.*, Chapter I.

73 For a survey of the negotiations and compromises which led to the establishment of the Mandates System, see David H. Miller, *op. cit.*, Vol. I, pp. 103-117; Quincy Wright, *op. cit.*, pp. 24-63.

74 Quincy Wright, *op. cit.*, pp. 498-499.

75 "General Smuts had modified the text by omitting the word 'yet' in the qualification of the peoples of the areas subject to mandate as 'not yet able to stand by themselves' thus applying this qualification only to the former Turkish territory, but the original text was subsequently re-established by the drafting committee." Quincy Wright, *op. cit.*, p. 42.

76 David Hunter Miller, *op. cit.*, Vol. I, p. 108.

77 *Op. cit.*, p. 499.

78 Permanent Mandates Commission, *Minutes*, VII, p. 202.

79 *Loc. cit.* Italics are mine.

80 A leading advocate of this view was the famous British colonial administrator, Sir Frederick Lugard. In his view (P.M.C., *Minutes*, VII, p. 196), "The time when the bulk of the population of Tropical Africa will be 'able to stand alone in the strenuous conditions of the modern world' may not be visible on the horizon, but the mandates impose upon the powers which have accepted them the obligation to conduct the people towards that goal." In *The Dual Mandate*, p. 86, he explains that to stand alone would require " ... in matters social and racial a separate path, each pursuing his own inherited traditions, preserving his own race-purity and race pride. ..."

81 This view was expressed by M. Freine d'Andrade. See P.M.C., *Minutes*, VII, p. 207.

82 "Article 22, as we have seen, has furnished the basis for the development by the Mandates Commission of certain policies for developing the territories and their peoples while in the condition of tutelage. It is clear that this policy goes further and contemplates an eventual change of that status." Quincy Wright, *op. cit.*, p. 530.

83 *Ibid.*, p. 506.

84 *Ibid.*, p. 459.

85 The use of the terms "communities," "peoples" and "territories" in reference to A, B and C Mandates respectively is probably indicative of the feeling among the draftees of the Covenant that the achievement of a "community" is in itself a development of the inhabitants of the territory towards maturity and the capacity to stand alone. See Quincy Wright, *op. cit.*, p. 235.

86 These four qualities may be considered as the attributes of the sovereign state in international law, as stated by the Montevideo Convention of 1933 on the Rights and Duties of States. They were also reflected in the requirements for membership of both the League of Nations and the United Nations. See R. J. Alfaro, "The Rights and Duties of States," 97 *RCADI*, 95 (1959).

87 "Thus if one of these communities asserted that it no longer needed tutelage and the states of the world expressly recognized that claim, the status of the community would seem to be legally changed. *Such a general recognition, however, is hardly conceivable without formal action of the League.*" Quincy Wright, *op. cit.*, p. 505. Italics are mine.

88 Alfred Cobban, *op. cit.*, p. 27.

89 These types of difficulties were particularly evident in the Minority Protection System. "The States which were compelled to assume obligations were never reconciled to the restrictions upon their freedom of action and rarely missed an opportunity to condemn with passion and indignation the idea, as well as the methods, of this international protection of minorities. The minorities, too, bitterly complained that the League regime failed to provide adequate safeguards against injustice." Oscar Janowsky, *op. cit.*, p. 122. See also Inis Claude, *op. cit.*, pp. 40-48;

90 Oscar Janowsky, *op. cit.*, pp. 129-134; Inis Claude, *op. cit.*, pp. 35-39.

91 There were some disagreements with regard to the implementation of the principle of self-determination, especially between the Allied Powers and Germany. However, they were all agreed that the principle of self-determination was aimed at the removal of a group or nationality from a condition of subjugation. See, Alfred Cobban, *op. cit.*, pp. 96ff.

92 For this reason, The Minority Treaties decline to use the term "nationality" or attempt to define it.

93 "But, it has been suggested, if the native communities have not been recognized as 'states' the A Communities at least, have been recognized as 'nations.' According to this theory, the peace treaties and the League of Nations have given a legal meaning to the term 'nation' which hitherto has had merely an ethnographic and political meaning. International law, according to this contention, which formerly began with states, now begins with nations and any farily considerable population with a desire for autonomy may be recognized as of that status. Such recognition of nationhood implies a right of the community to further recognition as a state only when it has a level of culture and a capacity for government rendering it 'able to stand alone.' If those conditions are not fulfilled, recognition of nationhood entitles the community to special international protection in case the incapacity results from geograpical distribution or inadequate size of the community, or the form of mandate protection in case the incapacity results only from the social or political immaturity of the community," Quincy Wright, *op. cit.*, p. 460.

Notes to Chapter V

1 In the early development of the principles on which to organize the peace, the principle of self-determination was almost never mentioned. Some of the issues that were considered important are indicated in the following statement made by Secretary of State Cordell Hull in 1941: "The Department is concerned with defining and formulating the broad objectives of desirable post war policies, comprising the restoration of order under law in international relations; the elimination of the crushing burden of competitive armaments; and the creation of the kind of international commercial and financial relations which are essential to the preservation of a stable peace...." U.S. Department

of State, *Postwar Foreign Policy Preparation,* 1939-1945, Publication 3580 (February 1950), p. 47. The Allies were particularly impressed by the fact that the war had been precipitated due to the unavailability of a machinery for dealing with blatant aggression. Therefore, one of the most important concerns they had was the creation of an international agency with "an international military force, which it could use to enforce the peace." Ruth B. Russell, *A History of the United Nations Charter,* p. 21.

2 Of particular concern to the British and American governments was the question of settling territorial boundaries among the Balkan states and the restoration of sovereignty to the areas being liberated from Nazi control. See Ruth B. Russell, *op. cit.,* pp. 180-183.

3 For some comments on the similarity between the principle of self-determination as enunciated in the Atlantic Charter and President Wilson's statements, see Józef Sulkowski, "The Atlantic Charter and the Principle of Self-Determination" *New Europe,* Vol. II, no. 9 (August, 1942). See also, Rupert Emerson, *From Empire to Nation* (Boston: Beacon Press, 1960), p. 296; Florent Peeters "The Right of Nations to Autodetermination," *World Justice,* Vol. III (December, 1961), p. 169ff.; Benjamin Rivlin, "Self-Determination and Dependent Areas" 501, *I.C.,* p. 197; Alfred Cobban, *op. cit.,* p. 2.

4 Memorandum to Myron C. Taylor. Sept. 1, 1941, *Papers of President Franklin D. Roosevelt,* Secretary's File (Box 76), Hyde Park Library. Quoted in Ruth B. Russell, *op. cit.,* p. 43. The idea of applying the principle of self-determination according to this formulation was shared by the Soviet Union, as Stalin indicates in the speech he delivered on November 6, 1943, the Twenty-sixth Anniversary of the Bolshevik Revolution, "The policy of our Government remains unchanged. In common with our allies we must restore to the liberated nations of Europe the undiminished right and freedom of self-determination as to their political organization."

5 Hans Kohn, "The United Nations and National Self-Determination," *Review of Politics,* Vol. XX, (October, 1958), p. 532.

6 Ernst B. Haas, *op. cit.,* p. 18.

7 Cordell Hull, *The Memoirs of cordell Hull,* Vol. II, p. 1600. See also, Ernst Haas, "The Attempt to Terminate Colonialism: Acceptance of the U.N. Trusteeship System." 7 *I.O.,* p. 5.

8 U. S. Department of State *Bulletin,* Vol. 6, (May 30, 1942), p. 488. See also Ruth Russell, *op. cit.,* p. 75.

9 *Ibid.,* Vol. 7, (July 25, 1942), p. 642.

10 Ernst Haas, *op. cit.,* p. 4; Ruth Russell, *op. cit.,* p. 83.

11 Cordell Hull, *The Memoirs of Cordell Hull,* pp. 1600-1.

12 For a full account of these efforts, see Ruth B. Russell, *op. cit.,* pp. 75-91.

13 For the complete text, see U.S. Department of State, *Postwar Foreign Policy Preparation,* 1939-1945, Publication 3580, (February, 1950), pp. 470-472.

14 Ernst B. Haas, *op. cit.,* p. 14.

15 For a summary of Chinese and Soviet views on colonial policy prior to and at the San Francisco Conference, see Ernst B. Haas, *op. cit.,* pp. 11-12; see also Elliot R. Goodman, "The Cry of National Liberation: Recent Soviet Attitudes towards National Self-Determination," 14, *I.O.,* (1960), *in toto.*

16 For an examination of British and Dutch colonial policy, see J. S. Bromley and E. H. Kossman, *eds., Britain and the Netherlands in Europe and Asia,* (New York: St. Martin's Press, 1968).

17 Cordell Hull, *op. cit.*, pp. 1237-8.

18 Ernst B. Haas, *op. cit.*, p. 15.

19 See Ruth B. Russell, *op. cit.*, pp. 573-589.

20 In the words of Ernst B. Haas, "Whether these new humanitarian considerations or British coolness toward the first drastic American trusteeship proposals brought about a changed approach cannot be ascertained. Certain it is that the Department of State advocated 'self-government' and not 'independence' for trust areas after July of 1943 and reduced the power of the proposed international colonial authority. In the 'Possible Plan' for international organization prepared for the Dumbarton Oaks Conference, the retreat is in full evidence." *Op. cit.*, p. 6.

21 Emil J. Sady, "The United Nations and Dependent Peoples," in Robert E. Asher and Associates, *The United Nations and Promotion of the General Welfare*, pp. 820-821.

22 *Ibid.*, p. 834.

23 *Ibid.*, p. 833. See also, Ruth B. Russell, *op. cit.*, p. 809.

24 For full text of the Declaration on Liberated Europe, see U. S. Dept. of State, *Foreign Relations of the United States: The Conferences at Malta and Yalta,* 1945, Publication 6199 (1955), pp. 977-978.

25 In a cablegram which Winston Churchill sent Franklin D. Roosevelt with regard to the interpretation of the Atlantic Charter, the Prime Minister noted: "I hope you will let me see beforehand the text of any message you are thinking of sending me upon the anniversary of the Atlantic Charter. We considered the wording of that famous document line by line together and *I should not be able, without mature consideration, to give it a wider interpretation than was agreed between us at the time.*" Winston Churchill, *The Hinge of Fate,* p. 890. [Italics are mine.]

26 Ruth B. Russell, *op. cit.*, p. 158.

27 Ernst B. Haas, *op. cit.*, p. 8. See also Benjamin Rivlin, *op. cit.*, p. 220. Although I agree with Rivlin, I disagree with his method of analysis. Unlike Haas, his conclusion that those chapters represent the principle of self-determination is based on his prior definition of self-determination as the consent of the governed. As I have stated in Chapters II and III of this work, this type of ideologically deduced definition of self-determination (in this case, the *plebiscite theory*) has been responsible in a large measure for the difficulties which have plagued attempts to define this phenomenon as it has operated in international practice and thus led to the serious lag between the international practice of self-determination and the theoretical writings on it.

28 Annette Baker Fox, "The United Nations and Colonial Development," 4, *I.O.*, (1950), pp. 203-206.

29 Quincy Wright, "Recognition and Self-Determination," *Proceedings of A.S.I.L.*, (1954), p. 27.

30 Emil J. Sady, *op. cit.*, p. 827, notes: " . . . the establishment and operation of the Mandates System of the League of Nations had by far the most direct influence on the development of United Nations' principles and machinery relating to dependent peoples." See also, *ibid.*, p. 823; Benjamin Rivlin, *op. cit.,* p. 238.

31 Huntington Gilchrist, *op. cit.,* p. 985; and Ruth B. Russell, *op. cit.,* pp. 814ff., for an account of the changes made in the text.

32 UNCIO Documents, Vol. III, pp. 126-7.

33 Benjamin Rivlin, *op. cit..*, pp. 219-221.

34 According to Article 73(b) of the Charter, the aim of administering these territories was, *"to develop self-government*, to take due account of the political aspirations of the peoples, and to assist them in the progressive development of their free political institutions, according to the particular circumstances of each territory and its peoples and their varying stages of advancement;" [italics are mine]. Although by compromise it was decided that there were cases in which self-government could be interpreted to include independence, the Conference was quite deliberate in rejecting independence as the normal goal of the colonial administration.

35 See Ruth B. Russell, *op. cit.,* p. 511.

36 *Ibid.*, p. 811.

37 *Ibid.*, p. 831.

38 UNCIO Document, Vol. 10, p. 515.

39 Ruth B. Russell, *op. cit.*, p. 817.

40 Statement by Soviet Foreign Minister Vyacheslav M. Molotov to the *New York Times*, May 8, 1945. [Italics are mine.]

41 As S. B. Krylov of the Soviet delegation noted, "respect for the principle of equal rights and self-determination of peoples follows the principles of the Stalin Constitution." Ruth B. Russell, *op. cit.*, p. 812.

42 "To strengthen international order on the basis of respect for the essential rights and equality of states, and of the peoples' right to self-determination." See UNCIO Document 374, I/1/17.

43 UNCIO, Doc. 723, I/1/A19.

44 UNCIO, Doc. 343, I/1/16.

45 UNCIO, Doc. 944, I/1/34.

46 See pp. 212-216.

47 Hungtington Gilchrist, *op. cit.*, p. 986. He notes that the category of peoples mentioned in article 73 of the Charter, " . . . is perhaps the most satisfactory definition of dependent peoples that has yet been found; . . ." The designation of a description of the territories mentioned in Chapter XI as a description of dependent peoples is to say that groups in article 73 exhaust all types of dependent peoples. It would probably be more correct to take the view that the territories listed under article 73 were meant to be included in a larger group of dependent territories.

48 Mohammed A. Shukri, *op. cit.*, p. 90.

49 See *Ibid.*, p. 57. Article 74 of the Charter which separates the dependent territories from "Their metropolitan areas" supports this view.

50 UNCIO, Documents, Vol. 3, pp. 615-8. See Emil J. Sady, *op. cit.*, p. 836.

51 C. E. Toussaint, *The Trusteeship System of the United Nations*, p. 184. See also, Mohammed A. Shukri, *op. cit.*, p. 91. For an account of the entire debate see Ruth B. Russell, *op. cit.*, pp. 815-824.

52 UNCIO, Documents, Vol. 10, p. 562.

53 Mohammed A. Shukri, *op. cit.*, p. 54.

54 Emil J. Sady, *op. cit.*, p. 877.

55 By Resolution 66(1), December 14, 1946, the General Assembly listed seventy-four non-self-governing territories concerning which eight governments had already transmitted or declared their intention of transmitting information in accordance with article 73(e) of the Charter. Objections which were raised by Brazil and Panama concerning the list were simply recorded without comment.

Furthermore, the General Assembly took no action when in 1947 some of the territories were dropped from the list by the states which had first provided the list. For a discussion of this resolution, see Emil J. Sady, *op. cit.*, p. 891-893.

56 For a discussion of this problem, see U. N. General Assembly, Third Session, Fourth Committee, *Official Records*, 52nd and 59th Meetings, (October 6 and 14, 1948), pp. 10-11, 59.

57 For instance, during the 1949 meetings of the Special Committee on Information, the Soviet Union challenged the claim by the Netherlands that Indonesia was under its sovereignty. See U.N. General Assembly, Non-Self-Governing Territories, Special Committee on Information, *Summary Record of Eighth Meeting, Doc.* A/AC.28/SR.8, (August 31, 1949).

58 For some good accounts of this process see, Mohammed A. Shukri, *op. cit.*, pp. 143-151; Emil J. Sady, *op. cit.*, pp. 888-901.

59 Resolution 334(IV), December 2, 1949 states *inter alia* that "it is within the responsibility of the General Assembly to express its opinions on the principles which have concerned or which may in the future guide the Members concerned in enumerating the territories for which the obligation exists to transmit information under article 73(e) of the Charter."

60 U. N. General Assembly, Resolution 1542(XV), December 15, 1960.

61 The following works have good accounts of the General Assembly's work in decolonization in the early period. Robert E. Asher and Associates, *The United Nations and Promotion of the General Welfare,* especially pp. 677-690, 754-758, 888-908; Benjamin Rivlin, "Self-Determination and Dependent Areas," 501, *I.C.*, (January, 1955), especially pp. 204-218. The most comprehensive, up-to-date and incisive analysis of the work of the General Assembly is Mohammed A. Shukri, *The Concept of Self-Determination in the United Nations,* especially pp. 101ff.; David W. Wainhouse, *Remnants of Empire: the United Nations and the End of Colonialism* is particularly useful for the decolonization of the smaller territories after 1961, as is United Nations, *The United Nations and Decolonization.*

62 U.N. General Assembly, Resolution 545(VI), February 8, 1952.

63 U.N. General Assembly, Resolution 567(VI), January 18, 1952.

64 U. N. General Assembly, Resolution 637(VII), December 16, 1952.

65 William Korey, "The Key to Human Rights Implementation," 507, *I.C.,* (November, 1968), p. 54. The incorporation of the right of self-determination into the two Human Rights Covenants was completed in 1953. The text of the entire Covenants was accepted by the General Assembly by Resolution 2200(XXI), December 16, 1966. The fact that almost no ratifications have been received has raised the question about the legal significance of the Covenants. As yet the debate is inconclusive. For some views on this, see Evan Luard, *ed., The International Protection of Human Rights*, (London: Thomas and Hudson, 1967); John Carey, *United Nations Protection of Civil and Political Rights*, (Syracuse: Syracuse University Press, 1970).

66 The first operative paragraph of the resolution is an affirmation of a general "principle of self-determination of peoples and nations." In the second operative paragraph, this principle is applied to the peoples of Non-Self-Governing and Trust Territories the realization of whose right of self-determination the administering members are obliged to recognize and promote.

67 United Nations General Assembly, Eighth Session Report of the Ad Hoc

Committee on Factors, Non-Self-Governing Territories, *Doc.*, A/2428.

68 Usha Sud, "Committee on Information from Non-Self-Governing Territories: It's Role in the Promotion on Self-Determination of Colonial Peoples," *International Studies*, (Quarterly Journal of the Indian School of International Studies), Vol. VII, no. 2, October, 1965; p. 324.

69 U.N. General Assembly, Resolution 1467(XIV).

70 Usha Sud, *op. cit.*, p. 327. See also Philip M. Allen, "Self-Determination in the Western Indian Ocean," 560 *I.C.*, November, 1966, p. 44.

71 The fact that the U.N. has to be satisfied that the Trust Territory has acquired the capacity for self-government before it may exercise self-determination is dramatically demonstrated in Resolution 65(I), December 14, 1946 in which the General Assembly refused to accept South Africa's contention that the people of South-West Africa had expressed a strong desire to be incorporated into South Africa on grounds that "the African inhabitants of South-West Africa have not yet secured political autonomy or reached a stage of political development enabling them to express a considered opinion which the Assembly could recognize on such an important question as incorporation of their territory."

72 Patricia Wohlgemuth, The Portuguese Territories and the United Nations, 545 *I.C.*, (November, 1963), p. 13. Also, David W. Wainhouse, *Remnants of Empire*, p. 9. For more detailed presentation of this position see United Nations Office of Public Information, *The United Nations and Decolonization* (U.N. Pub. Sales, No. 65.I.8.); Mohammed A. Shukri, *op. cit.*, pp. 333-356.

73 Resolution 289(I), November 21, 1949. For comments on this see, Philip M. Allen, *op. cit.*, p. 31; Emil J. Sady, *op. cit.*, p. 858.

74 U.N. General Assembly Resolution 944(IX), December 15, 1955.

75 U.N. General Assembly, Resolution 1350(XIII), March 13, 1959; Resolution 1352(XIV), October 16, 1959; Resolution 1473(XIV), December 12, 1959.

76 U.N. General Assembly, Resolution 748(VII), November 27, 1953.

77 Resolution 945(X), December 18, 1955.

78 Resolution 849(IX), November 22, 1954.

79 Resolution 1469(XIV), December 12, 1959.

80 Philip M. Allen, *op. cit.*, p. 34.

81 Resolution 1542(XV), December 15, 1960.

82 Resolution 1747(XVI), June 28, 1962.

83 See the case of Ruanda and Burundi. Resolution 1605(XV), April 21, 1961.

84 Margaret Broderick, "Associated Statehood—A New Form of Decolonization," *ICLQ*, Vol. 17, Part 2, (April, 1968), p. 368. For a general discussion, see Patricia W. Blair, *The Mini-State Dilemma*, Revised Edition, (New York: Carnegie Endowment for International Peace, 1968), and David W. Wainhouse, *Remnants of Empire*.

85 See Resolution 1569(XV), December 18, 1969, for instance.

86 In the case of the Cook Islands, the General Assembly accepted the validity of their status as Associated State, although some questions were raised about the possibility that their choice may have been unduly influenced by the administering power and, therefore, not entirely free. For a discussion of the Cook Island case, see Philip M. Allen, op. cit., pp. 390-392.

87 See Carnegie Endowment for International Peace, *Issues Before the Twenty-Third General Assembly*, p. 48, n. 1.

88 For a generel discussion of this topic see, F. B. Sloan, "The Binding Force of a 'Recommendation' of the General Assembly of the United Nations," 25 *BYIL*, (1942); D. H. N. Johnson, "The Effect of Resolutions of the General Assembly of the United Nations," 32 *BYIL*, (1955-56); Oscar Schachter, "The Quasi-Judicial Role of the Security Council and the General Assembly," 58 *AJIL*, (1964); Rosalyn Higgins, *The Development of International Law through the Political Organs of the United Nations* (1963). For discussions particularly related to the issue of self-determination see Mohammed A. Shukri, *op. cit.*, especially pp. 333-353; and Obed Y. Asamoah, *The Legal Significance of the Declarations of the General Assembly of the United Nations,* especially pp. 46-62, 161-185.

89 One such discrepancy in the voting behavior of a state occurred in the adoption of Resolution 1514(XV), December 15, 1960, "The Declaration on the Granting of Independence to Colonial Countries and Peoples." The United States abstained on the Declaration itself, while voting in favor of Resolution 1654(XVI), November 27, 1961, which established the Committee of 17 set up purposely to implement the Declaration. In explaining the U.S. vote, Senator Wayne Morse of Oregon, one of the delegates, asserted that the U.S. abstention was a deviation from the affirmative vote which would have been consistent to its voting pattern, but that the U.S. had abstained due to pressure from the British. "But for this pressure from the British Government the United States would have voted in favor of the resolution." Senator Wayne Morse, Oregon, *The United States in the United Nations: 1960—A Turning Point*, Supplementary Report, Committee on Foreign Relations, U.S. Senate, 87th Congress, 1st Session (Washington, D.C.: G.P.O., 1961), pp. 20-21.

90 Resolution 1541(XV) was adopted by a vote of 69 to 2 (Portugal, South Africa), with 21 absentions. It is important to note that many of the abstentions comprised " . . . East European states, which felt independence should be immediate." "Issues before the Sixteenth General Assembly," 534 *I.C.* (September, 1961), p. 91. Thus, these states which usually vote with the Afro-Asian anti-colonialist group abstained because they didn't think the resolution went far enough, not because they disagreed with it in any basic sense.

91 See reports on the activities of the Committee of 24 in United Nations, *The United Nations and Decolonization*, (New York: United Nations Office of Public Information, 1965).

92 Rupert Emerson, "Colonialism, Political Development and the U.N.," p. 122.

93 Clyde Eagleton, *op. cit.*, p. 597.

94 Benjamin Rivlin, *op. cit.*, p. 270.

95 It would be interesting to attempt to speculate how the principle of self-determination would have been applied or conceptualized if the major claimants of the right after World War II had not been overseas colonies, but, say, unassimilated minorities in the U.S.A. and the Soviet Union, and if the war had been won by Germany and Japan.

96 Kenneth Robinson, "World Opinion and Colonial Status" 8 *I.O.*, (1954), p. 476.

97 Obed Y. Asamoah, *op. cit.*, p. 171. See, for instance, General Assembly Resolutions 545(VI) and 637(VII).

CHAPTER VI NOTES

1 Obed Y Asamoah states the case completely as follows: "A vote for a resolution is a formal state act. A resolution, therefore, is a collective act resulting from individual acts and represents state acts. But in deciding whether a rule of custom has developed, state acts outside the United Nations are also important." *Op. cit.*, p. 54.

2 Inis Claude Jr., *The Changing United Nations*, pp. 52-53; David Wainhouse, *op. cit.*, p. 4.

3 Rupert Emerson, "Colonialism, Political Development and the United Nations," in Norman J. Padelford and Leland M. Goodrich, *The United Nations in the Balance*, (New York: Praeger Publishers, 1965), p. 127.

4 Report of the Inter-Imperial Relations Committee to the Imperial Conference of 1926, *British Command Paper*, 2768, quoted in U. O. Umozurike, *Self-Determination in International Law,* (Hamden, Connecticut: Archon Books, 1972), p. 140.

5 Hansard, 5th Series, Vol. 32, p. 1246.

6 Hansard Society, *Problems of Parliamentary Government in Colonies,* (1935), p. 130. For more official statements on this policy see Nicholas Mansergh, ed., *Documents and Speeches on British Commonwealth Affairs*, Vol. I, (Oxford University Press, 1953), p. 1286-7. Also, for a discussion of the policy see J. S. Furnivall, *Colonial Policy and Practice*, (Cambridge: Cambridge University Press, 1948), p. 315 ff.

7 Associated Statehood is the newest constitutional design in British colonial practice to handle the self-determination of mini-states like the West Indian Islands of Antigua, St. Kitts-Nevis-Anguilla, Dominica, St. Lucia, St. Vincent and Granada all associated with Britain. For a discussion of this arrangement see Margaret Broderick, "Associated Statehood—A New Form of Decolonization," *International and Comparative Law Quarterly*, Vol. 17 (1968), pp 396 ff.

8 Excerpt from speech delivered by Anthony Eden in the House of Commons, November 15, 1941, quoted in Kenneth Robinson, "World Opinion and Colonial Status," 8 I. O. (1954), p. 468.

9 See J. E. Fawcett, *The British Commonwealth in International Law,* (London: Stevens, 1963), p. 144 ff.

10 General Georges Catroux, *The French Union: Concept, Reality and Prospect*, 495 I.C. (Nov. 1953), p. 203.

11 Quoted in John Hatch, *A History of Post War Africa,* (New York: Praeger Publishing, 1965), p. 37. See also the statement of H. Deschamps a colonial governor in Waldemar A. Nielsen, *The Great Powers and Africa* (New York, Praeger Publishing, 1969), p. 79.

12 General Georges Catroux, *op. cit.*, p. 207.

13 Leopold Sedar Senghor, *African Socialism* (New York: American Society of African Culture, 1959), P. 9. For a summary account of this process see Thomas Hodgkin and Ruth Schachter, "French-Speaking West Africa in Transition," 528 I.C., (May, 1960). For a more general discussion of French colonial policy see Kenneth E. Robinson, *The Public Law of Overseas France since the War*, Rev. ed. (Oxford: Institute of Commonwealth Studies, 1954), and Hubert Deschamps. *Methodes et Doctrines coloniales de la France,* (Paris: Pedone, 1953).

14 Immediately after Guinea voted for independence, "France withdrew its

personnel and technicians as fast as possible; cut financial aid estimated at about $17,000,000 a year; ceased to buy Guinea's bananas at subsidized prices; removed or destroyed equipment including government records and maps, medicines in hospitals, and even plates in the Government palace." Thomas Hodgkin and Ruth Schachter, op. cit., p. 423.

15 See *Evian Accords, AJIL*, (1962), p. 716 ff.

16 Kenneth Robinson, *op. cit.*, p. 469.

17 U. N. Document A/PV.1177, p. 27.

18 The "Belgian Congo" was listed among the original 74 territories which were submitted voluntarily by the administering states. For the full list, see U. N. Document A/74, (October 12, 1946).

19 Quoted in Waldemar Nielsen, *op. cit.*, p. 132.

20 GAOR, Fourth Committee, (Ninth Session), p. 150. For a discussion of the Belgian Thesis see Mohammed A. Shukri, *op. cit.*, pp. 108-110; Uta Shud, *op. cit.*, pp. 322-324.

21 Watson W. Wise, "The Right of Peoples and Nations to Self-Determination, U. S. Department of State *Bulletin*, February 2, 1959, Vol. XI, p. 172. For other statements of the U. S. committment to the principle of self-determination see R. Murphy, "The Principle of Self-Determination in International Relations," U. S. Department of State *Bulletin*, Vol. XXXIII, November 1955, *in toto*; and Walworth Barbour, "The Concept of Self-Determination in American Thought," U. S. Department of State *Bulletin*, Vol. XXXII, October 1954.

22 Statement by Secretary of State Cordell Hull quoted in Leland M. Goodrich and Marie J. Carroll, eds., *Documents on American Foreign Relations* Vol. 5, July 1942-June 1943 (Boston: World Peace Foundation), p. 6. See also the preamble of the South East Asia Collective Defence Treaty of which the United States is a signatory.

23 See Waldemar Nielsen, *op. cit.*, pp. 245-334.

24 U. S. Department of State *Bulletin,* October 16, 1961, p. 632. This view has been consistently expressed by U. S. delegates to the United Nations. See for instance, Watson W. Wise, op. cit. p. 174, and R. Murphy, *op. cit.*, p. 894.

25 Quoted in U. N. Document A/5160, Aug. 15, 1962.

26 GAOR: 11th Session, 656th Plenary Meeting, February 20, 1957, par. 73.

27 William Minter, *Portuguese Africa and the West*, (New York: Monthly Review Press, 1972), p. 20.

28 GAOR:16th Session, 1065th Plenary Meeting, Nov. 27, 1961, par. 281. For discussion of these arguments see Mohammed A. Shukri, *op. cit.*, pp. 119-123; David W. Wainhouse, *op. cit.*, pp. 30-4; Patricia Wohlgemuth, *op. cit.*, pp. 21-27.

29 U. N. Document, A/9694, August 6, 1974.

30 Emil J. Sady, *op. cit.*, p. 822. See also Edward T. Rowe, *op. cit.*, p. 214.

31 The U. N. strategy in the South West Africa issue has been to induce South Africa to transform the territory into a trust territory, and failing that, to prevent South Africa from annexing it. However, annexation has not been the fundamental issue. (Annexation, as the General Assembly demonstrated in Resolution 2074 could be handled as a problem of aggression). The idea behind the strategy was that by preventing annexation, the U. N. could stop South Africa from implementing there the same system of *apartheid* which was being used to infringe on the right of the black people to self-determination. This is

made clear in Resolution 2145(XX) which terminated the mandate. It states, *inter alia*, that the assembly "(1) Reaffirms that the provisions of General Assembly Resolution 1514(XV) are fully applicable to the people of South West Africa and that, therefore, the people of South West Africa have the inalienable right to self-determination, freedom and independence in accordance with the Charter of the United Nations;"

32 U. N. Document, A/3625.

33 United Nations, *Apartheid in South Africa III*, (New York, U. N. Office of Public Information, 1966), p. 17.

34 United Nations, *Apartheid in South Africa*, (New York: U. N. Office of Public Information, 1963), p. 11.

35 For a discussion of the legal aspects of the South West Africa dispute see Richard Falk, "The South-West Africa Cases: An Appraisal," 21 I.O. (1967), p. 7 ff.; L. C. Green, "The United Nations, South-West Africa, and the World Court," 7 *Indian Journal of International Law* (1967), p. 491 ff.

36 UNGA Resolution 2145(XXI), 27th October 1966.

37 *Africa Report*, Vol. 20, no. 4 (July-August 1975), p. 22.

38 Benjamin Pogrund, "1975: The Year of Change?" *Africa Report*, Vol. 20, no. 4, p. 4.

39 Elliot I. Goodman, "The Cry of National Liberation: Recent Soviet Attitudes toward National Self-Determination," 14 I. C. (1960), pp. 92-94; also Edward T. Rowe, *op. cit.*, p. 217

40 "Disregarding temporary deviations, it always has been the Communist view that colonialism is illegitimate and that legitimacy rests with those who are struggling to achieve independence." Rupert Emerson, *Self-Determination Revisited in the Era of Decolonization*, p. 7.

41 M. M. Lasserson, "The Development of Soviet Foreign Policy in Europe, 1917-1942," I.C. (1943), p. 11.

42 Alfred D. Low, *Lenin and the Question of Nationality*, p. 130.

43 L. Shapiro, ed., *Soviet Treaty Series, Vol. I,* Washington D.C.: 1950).

44 *Ibid.*

45 U. O. Umozurike, *Self-Determination in International Law*, p. 157.

46 U. N. Document, A/4519.

47 Statement by the 22nd Congress of the Communist Party in October, 1961, quoted in Jan F. Triska, ed., *Soviet Communism: Programs and Rules,* (San Francisco: Chandler Publishing, 1962), p. 67.

48 Zdenek Cervenka, *The Organization of African Unity and Its Charter,* (New York: Praeger Publishers, 1968), p. 82, no. 19.

49 Rupert Emerson, *Self-Determination Revisited in the Era of Decolonization*, p. 21; Inis Claude, *The Changing United Nations*, p. 60.

50 *Le Monde*, October 25, 1962, quoted in Rupert Emerson, *op. cit.*, p. 10.

51 The fact that African states are at this point militarily unprepared to undertake such a committment, makes the implementation of the resolution on any major scale rather problematic. It is important to note, however, that the claim has been made, and the machinery—The Liberation Committee—has been activated and is functioning in a limited way. So that when the African states are able to mount an offensive, the world is likely to be faced with a serious threat to international peace with something of the rigidity and intransigence of the present Middle East conflict and the savagery of the Vietnam War.

52 Quoted in Zdenek Cervenka, *op. cit.*, p. 229.

53 Katanga was not recognized by a single state. Biafra was more fortunate with recognition from Tanzania, Gabon, the Ivory Coast, Zambia, Haiti and France. Apart from France and Gabon which took a position in favor of Biagra on the basis of the right of self-determination, the rest of those states avoided any references to that principle, and based their support mainly on grounds of humanitarian considerations, See debates in 23rd and 24th Sessions of the U.N. General Assembly, September 1968 and September 1969.

54 UNGA Verbatim Records, 23rd Session, September 1968.

55 Rupert Emerson, *op. cit.*, pp. 35-6. Also Clyde Eagleton, "The Excesses of Self-Determination," p. 603.

56 Statement by Mr. Eklo, delegate from Togo, UNGA Verbatim Records, 26th Session, September 1971.

57 Edward T. Rowe, *op. cit.*, p. 228.

58 On this point it is important to note that when the General Assembly terminated the South African mandate in South-West Africa, the territory was not declared independent, but it was put "under the direct responsibility of the United Nations". See U. N. Resolution 2145(XXI), October, 27, 1966.

59 U. N. Document, E/CN, 4?SR.500, April 21, 1955.

60 This was immediately apparent when the first list of possible non-self-governing territories was presented by Belgium. In that list and in subsequent lists the Belgians have named groups spread out all over the world: in Canada, Mexico, the U.S.A., Brazil, India, Ethiopia, South Africa, Australia, Chile and Liberia. See U. N. Documents A/AC.58?1, A/AC.35/L.30 Add. 1, E/CN.4S/4.252, GAOR, Fourth Committee (7th Session), par. 77; GAOR Fourth Committee (8th Session), par. 59; GAOR Fourth Committee (Tenth Session), par. 30.

61 The Soviets made a feeble attempt in 1952 to apply the right of self-determination to territories. The suggestion was dismissed on the basis of the explicit separation between administering powers and their dependent territories in Article 74 of the Charter. See U. N. Document, E/CN.4/L.21.

62 Inis Claude, The Changing United Nations, p. 61.

63 Edward T. Rowe, *op. cit.*, p. 228.

64 U. N. Document, A/AC.35/L.142, (August 18, 1953)

65 U. N. Document A/9694, (August 6, 1974), p. 2.

Notes to Chapter VII

1 Inis L. Claude, Jr., *The Changing United Nations*, p. 54.

2 See Mohammed A. Shukri, *op. cit.*, p. 346; Rosalyn Higgins, *op. cit.*, p. 104; G. B. Starushenko, *op. cit.*, p. 135; Baratashvili, *op. cit.*, p. 57; Tuzmukhamedov, *op. cit.*, pp. 87, 128; J. J. Lador-Lederer, *International Group Protection*, pp. 280ff.; Obed Y. Asamoah, *op. cit.*, pp. 177ff.; Quincy Wright, "Recognition and Self-Determination," p. 29; Sergio Armando Frazao, *op. cit.*, p. 60; Huntington Gilchrist, *op. cit.*, p. 986; Rupert Emerson, *Self-Determination Revisited in the Era of Decolonization*, p. 25; Max Sorensen, ed., *Manual Of Public International Law*, pp. 771-2; Harold S. Johnson, *Self-Determination within the Community of Nations*, p. 41ff.; Lino Di Qual, *Les Effets des Resolutions des Nations Unies*, (Paris, 1969), p. 146ff.

3 Inis L. Claude, Jr., *op. cit.*, pp. 96-97.

4 Obed Y. Asamoah, *op. cit.*, p. 181.

5 See O. Y. Asamoah, *loc. cit.*,

6 Obed Y. Asamoah, *op. cit.*, pp. 181-2.

7 See Georg Schwarzenberger, *The Inductive Approach to International Law*, pp. 75-77; Torsten Gihl, *op. cit.*, p. 91.

8 See, for instance, Clyde Eagleton, statements in Chapter III, p.p. 64, 65, 77.

9 See Chapter II, pp. 31-34, 38-39.

10 Chapter II, n. 35.

11 Chapter II, p. 35, n. 60.

12 "Like the minorities regimes, the mandates and trusteeship regimes were the result of premeditated, though temporary, withholding of the right of immediate self-determination." J. J. Lador-Lederer, *op. cit.*, p. 55.

13 Armando Frazao, *op. cit.*, p. 58.

14 For a discussion of these problems, see pp. 125ff.

15 J. J. Lador-Lederer, *op. cit.*, p. 14.

16 *Op. cit.*, p. 54.

17 See Chapter II, pp. 55ff.

18 Rupert Emerson, *From Empire to Nation*, p. 102, explains a nation in the following terms: "The simplest statement thatucan be made about a nation is that it is a body of people who feel that they are a nation; and it may be that when all the fine spun analysis is concluded this will be the ultimate statement as well."

19 J. J. Lador-Lederer, *op. cit.*, pp. 13-14. See also Chapter II, p. 189.

20 Quincy Wright, "Recognition and Self-Determination," p. 33.

21 In spite of the obvious differences between the colonial territories and the subject nationalities in the Eastern European Empires, their status under foreign domination is enough to put them jointly in this category. J. J. Lador-Lederer has suggested a broad category of communities which might be brought under the protection of international law which will include, " . . . vast groups still living in the shadows of the past, in slavery, under colonialism or various forms of hetero-ethnic domination—indigenous populations, populations under mandates, trusteeship or *Apartheid,* minorities and scattered communities." *Op. cit.*, p. 43.

22 This seems to be the way in which the claim of Katanga (1960) and "Biafra" (1967) to the right of self-determination were interpreted. They were seen as cases of impermissible secession, because their relationship with the central governments was not of the CColonial" type of subjugation. See Ernest W. Lefever, *Crisis in the Congo: A U.N. Force in Action* (Washington, D.C.: The Brookings Institution, 1965), p. 72; Zdenek Cervenka, *op. cit.*, pp. 219 and 224; Crawford Young, "The Politics of Separatism: Katanga, 1960-63," in Gwendolin Carter, *Politics in Africa: 7 Cases* (New York: Harcourt, Brace and World, Inc., 1966), pp. 189-190.

23 In attemtping to ascertain the status of a community as a dependent or subject group, the international community has depended on a multiplicity of evidence including the distinctness of one group from the other. It must be noted that this distinctness is, *per se,* enough to establish whether the group—based on their distinctness—enjoy less civil and political rights than the other inhabitants, and whether they are defined as somewhat less than full citizens according to the constitution. Austria, Hungary and Portugal found out that the constitutional fiction of pretending that the subjects are actually full citi-

zens, by the 1868 Hungarian Law of Nationalities and the abrogation by Portugal of the "Colonial Act" in 1951, were not enough to forestall jurisdiction.

24 See Chapter II, n. 59, *supra*.

25 See Chapter IV, p. 190.

26 See C. A. Macartney, *op. cit.*, p. 276.

27 For a general discussion, see Patricia Wohlgemuth Blair, *The Mini-State Dilemma, passim*.

28 Frank A. Golder, "Will the Unrestricted Self-Determination of all National Groups bring World Peace and Order," *Journal of International Relations* (Worcester, Mass.), Vol. 10, January 1920, p. 282. See also, Robert Lansing, *op. cit.*, p. 15. Also see Chapter II, *supra*.

29 See Chapter II, n. 64, *supra*.

30 Harold S. Johnson, *Self-Determination within the Community of Nations*, p. 200. See also, Evan Luard, *Conflict and Peace in the Modern International System* (Boston: Little, Brown and Company, 1968), pp. 109-111. Johnson's entire work is based on this definition.

31 See Chapter IV.

32 See Chapter IV, p. 162.

33 The attempted secession of the Confederate States of the U.S.A. might prove instructive in this respect. It would seem that if the secession had been successful that it would have occurred on the same lines as the state boundaries thus eliminating the entire issue of territorial settlement. The attempted secessions of Katanga in 1960 and "Biafra" might also have occurred on established state boundaries.

34 Sarah Wambaugh, *Plebiscites Since the World War*, Vol. I., pp. 32 and 35-37. For instance, Czechoslovakia claimed that the territorial limits of her already firm nation should be established on grounds of historic rights and geographic unity (Bohemia, Moravia and Austrain Silesia), ethnography (Prussian Silesia and Lower Austria), and right of self-determination (the decision of Slovakia to join the Czechs in an independent state). *Op. cit.*, p. 23.

35 In spite of the problems that plebiscites were having in defining the term "nationality" the States were generally able to recognize a nationality where one existed. As we have seen, one of the criteria usecd by the states was the ethnic or religious or "racial" distinction between the group and the dominant society. This is reasonably valid, because it was usually on the basis of these circumstances that these nationalities were "oppressed." In fact this general way of identifying these groups was stated in at least two important international instruments of the time—the Minority Treaties and the Report of the Committee of International Jurists appointed by the League Council to study the Asland Islands dispute. See Chapter IV, pp. 169ff.

36 Max Sorensen, ed., *Manual of Public International Law*, p. 267.

37 Hersch Lauterpacht, *Recognition in International Law*, p. 8ff.

38 Perhaps as early as the seventeenth century and certainly during the nineteenth century, there had developed some awareness of the international importance of minorities, and a few treaties had been concluded in which such groups were 'recognized" for the purpose of guaranteeing their protection. According to C. A. Macartney, (op. cit., p. 157), the existence of these treaties, such as the Treaty of Berlin " . . . provided both legal and historical precedents for extending the system . . . " in the European Peace Settlement.

39 Max Sorensen, *op. cit.*, p. 262.

40 See Inis Claude, *National Minorities*, pp. 40-48.

41 Chapter IV, n. 34.

42 Leland M. Goodrich, *The United Nations* (London: Stevens & Co., 1959), p. 295.

43 *Ibid.*, p. 294.

44 Max Sorensen, *op. cit.*, p. 262.

45 United Nations General Assembly Resolutions, 637(VII), 648(VII), 742(VIII), 1541(XV). See appendix VIII.

46 See, for instance, Resolution 1755(XVII), December, 1962.

47 J. J. Lador-Lederer, *op. cit.*, p. 13.

48 James N. Hyde, "Permanent Sovereignty Over Natural Wealth and Resources," 50, *AJIL* (1956), p. 855.

49 See H. Shawcross, "Some Problems of Nationalization in International Law," International Bar Association. 5th Conference. (Monte Carlo, 1954).

50 See the comments of Mr. Miguel Rafael Urquia of El Salvador who was Chairman of the Working Party in the Third Committee, GAOR, Official Records. 10th Session, Third Committee 674th Meeting, p. 248.

51 For a discussion of some of the arguments, see Max Sorensen, ed., *Manual of Public International Law.*, p. 764.

52 Ibid., pp. 765-772. Also Inis L. Claude, Jr., "The United Nations and the Use of Force," 532, *I.O.* (March 1961); D. W. Bowett, *Self-Defense in International Law* (Manchester: University Press, 1958), esp. pp. 23ff.

53 Max Sorensen, ed., *Manual of Public International Law,* p. 323-324.

54 J. J. Lador-Lederer, *op. cit.*, p. 53. "In this sense, 'trust' is a convenient short-hand term for the general regime of limitations to hetero-ethnic rule, it sic is a useful working hypothesis. It would relate *mutatis mutandis,* to colonialism, belligerent occupation, or minority status."

55 See William W. Bishop, Jr., *International Law: Cases and Materials* (Little Brown and Company, Inc., 1962), p. 349.

56 J. J. Lador-Lederer, *op. cit.*, p. 244. For a full discussion of the nature of Agents of Protection see especially pp. 338-373.

57 Rene LeMarchand, "The Limits of Self-Determination: The Case of Katanga," Vol. 56, No. 2, *AIJR*, 410ff.

58 For instance according to the practice of the United Nations, both Goa and Angola were considered as "having the right of self-determination irrespective of the vastly different sizes, or importance to Portugal.

59 Lador-Lederer, *op. cit.*, p. 204.

60 Ibid., p. 31.

61 Ibid., pp. 167-180.

62 Ibid., p. 181-2.

63 See Max Sorensen, ed. *Manual of Public International Law*, p. 217.

64 ICJ Reports, 1962, p. 331.

65 Lador-Lederer, *op. cit.*, p. 244.

66 Ibid., p. 57.

67 Ibid., p. 53.

Notes to Chapter VIII

1 H. Lauterpacht, *Recognition in International Law*, p. 55

2 Arnold Toynbee, op. cit., p. 323.

3 Linda B. Miller, op. cit., p. 34. Also Lador-Lederer, op. cit., p. 18

4 See p. 150 *supra*.

5 Rosalyn Higgins, op. cit. pp. 90-106.

6 Norman Meller, *The Congress of Micronesia: Development of Legislative Process in the Trust Territory of the Pacific Islands* (Honolulu: University Press, 1969), p. 530 ff. For a general discussion of this issue, see United Nations office of Public Information, *The United Nations and Decolonization* (U.N. Publ. Sales No. 65. I.8).

7 Inis Claude, Jr. The Changing United Nations, p. 58.

8 Nkambo Mugerwa, "Subjects of International Law." in Max Soresen (ed.) *Manual of Public International Law*. (New York: St. Martin's Press, 1968), p. 263.

9 See for instance, Erno Wittman, *op. cit.*, p. 116 and R. Buell, *op. cit.,* p. 46.

10 Locksley Edmondson, "Africa and the Diaspora: The Years Ahead," in Ali A. Mazrui and Hasu W. Patel, (eds.) *Africa in World Affairs*, (New York: The Third Press, 1973), p. 11.

11 Lador-Lederer, *op. cit.*, p. 19.

12 Lador-Lederer, *op. cit.*, p. 53.

218, 219, 221, 223, 224
Codding, George: 192
colonial peoples: *see* colonial territories
colonial policies (and self-determination): 129-138
colonial powers: 102, 144, 154, 170, 175
colonial territories: 30, 46, 47, 99-101, 104-106, 120-121, 126, 127, 171, 175, 177
Committee of Twenty-Four: 115, 123, 129, 117, 185
Commonwealth: 88, 131
Conakry: 142
Connor, Walker: 192
Congress of Oppressed Nationalities: 34, 45, 202, 217
Corbett, Percy: 195, 197
customary international law (and self-determination): 60, 66, 124, 178, 194-198
Cyprus: 62, 192
Czech National Committee: 166, 218
Czechoslovakia: 162, 202, 217

Dahomey: 142
de Card, E. Rouard: 198
Declaration of the Rights of the Peoples of Russia (1917): 138
Declaration of the United Nations: 98
Declaration on Liberated Europe: 103, 150, 225
Declaration on the Granting of Independence to Colonial Territories and Peoples (1960): 59, 61, 120, 121, 122, 178, 184, 188, 230
decolonization: 12, 50, 140, 145, 147, 154, 161, 168, 170, 177, 230
Decree of Peace (1917): 69
dependent peoples: 55, 57, 58, 113, 116
Deschamps, Hubert: 231
Deutsch, Karl: 192
Di Qual, Lino: 234
Dodd, William E.: 200, 216
Drost, P.N.: 194, 210, 214
Dumbarton Oaks: 226
Durham's Report (1839): 130

Eagleton, Clyde: 14, 45, 52, 56, 59, 191, 193, 194, 195, 210, 211, 213, 214, 230, 234
Eastern Europe: 186
economic self-determination: *see* permanent sovereignty over natural resources

Eden, Anthony: 102
Edinger, L.J.: 192
Edmondson, Locksley: 237
Emerson, Rupert: 59, 192, 193, 194, 200, 210, 213, 214, 226, 230, 232, 233, 234
Equatorial Guinea: 133
Eritrea: 122
Ethical Policy: 133
Ethiopia: 143
Evans, Luther: 221
extraterritorial cultural autonomy: 158

Falk, Richard: 232
Fawcett, J.E.: 231
Finland: 84
Fichte, Johann G.: 30, 203
Fitzmaurice, Sir Gerald: 197
Four Additional Principles: 76, 215
Four Supplementary Points: 72
Fourteen Points: 72, 215
Fourth Republic: 132
Fox, Annette Baker: 226
France: 107, 119, 147
Frazao, Armando: 211, 213, 214, 234
French Policy (and self-determination): 81, 131-133, 186
French Revolution: 12, 31
French Union: 132
Fulro: 192
Furnivall, J.S.: 230

Geertz, Clifford: 191
Geneva Accords (1954): 55
Germany: 4, 109, 159, 192, 219
Ghana: 122
Gihl, Torsten: 194, 196, 197, 198, 234
Gilchrist, Huntington: 14, 44, 211, 213, 214, 226, 234
Ginsburgs, George: 211, 212
Glorious Revolution: 12
Goa: 142, 146
Golder, Frank: 191, 193, 200, 202, 203, 208, 235
Goodman, Elliot: 225, 232
Goodrich, Leland: 230
Gould, Wesley: 197
Greater Germany: 12, 159, 192
Green, L.C.: 232
Greenland: 122
Guadaloupe: 114
Guggenheim, Paul: 197
Guyana: 114, 192
Guinea, Republic of: 133, 231

240

Guinea-Bissau: 146

Haas, Ernst: 224, 225
Hatch, John: 231
Hauser, H.: 198
Hayes, J. Carleton: 195, 198, 201, 203, 204, 205
Hawaii: 122, 135
Henkin, Louis: 213
Herder, Gottfried: 26
Higgins, Rosalyn: 12, 43, 49, 59, 61, 62, 63, 210, 214, 229, 234, 237
Hitler, Adolf: 149
Hodgkin, Thomas: 231
Holland, E.T.: 194
Holmes County, Ohio: 202
Hudson, Manley: 197
Hula, Erich: 3, 191, 207, 208
Hull, Cordell: 99, 100, 224, 225, 231
Human Rights Commission: 115, 117, 118
Human Rights Conventions: 15, 115, 149, 170, 188
Human Rights Covenants (1966): 115, 172, 228
Hungarian Crisis: 128
Hyde, James: 236

Ile Saint-Louis: 203
independence: 22, 37, 56, 62, 77, 80, 93, 106, 107, 110, 112, 118-125, 126, 139, 140, 159, 162, 183, 184
India: 142, 144, 146, 192
Indonesia: 103
instant nations: 159
integration: 126, 162, 164
interim protection: 165
International Commission of Jurists: 150, 177, 202
International Court of Justice: 17, 18
international law: 15-19, 23, 40, 55-65, 117, 130-135, 149, 150, 155, 167, 173, 178, 183
International Law Commission: 18, 197
international peace: 4, 7, 19, 23, 96, 183, 186-187
international practice: 15, 16, 42, 129-144, 149, 150-155, 161-164, 166-169, 173-176, 177-178
inter-temporal law: 176
Iraq: 112, 192
Ireland: 1, 4
Israel: 191
Italy: 109, 129

Janowsky, Oscar: 201, 219, 220, 223
Jessup, Philip: 194
Jennings, Ivor: 35, 49, 209
Johnson, D.N.N.: 229
Johnson, Harold S.: 12, 44, 51, 195, 211, 212, 214, 234

Kaplan, Morton: 195
Katanga: 143, 163, 235
Katzenback, Nicholas de B.: 195
Kautsky, Karl: 199
Kelsen, Hans: 9, 10, 42, 48, 56, 194, 197, 209, 214
Kennedy, John: 135
Kenya: 131, 143
Kohn, Hans: 14, 201, 224
Korey, William: 228
Korovin, E.A.: 211
Kossman, E.H.: 225
Krylov, S.B.: 226
Kunz, Joseph: 195, 197

Lachs, Manfred: 213
Ladas, Stephen P.: 220
Lador-Lederer, J.J.: 189, 234, 236, 237
Lambert, Henri: 191, 193, 203, 209
Lansing, Rovert: 3, 191, 200, 203
Lasserson, M.M.: 232
Lauterpacht, Hersch: 8, 193, 194, 236, 237
League of Nations: 7, 84-93, 103, 141, 166, 173-178, 202, 220, 223
    Covenant of: 88-90
    Minorities Commission of: 7
Lefevre, Ernest W.: 235
Lemarchand, Rene: 236
Lenin, V.I.: 27, 34, 44, 45, 46, 108, 147, 199, 200, 204, 205, 206, 207, 208
Lindley, M.F.: 221
Lloyd-George, David: 83, 217, 218, 219, 220, 221
loi-cadre: 132
Low, Alfred: 199, 203, 204, 206, 213
Luard, Evan: 228, 234
Lugard, Sir Frederick: 221, 222
Lukens, Donald: 191
Luxembourg, Rosa: 199
Lybia: 122

McCartney, A.C.: 12, 31, 196, 200, 201, 202, 203, 204, 205, 207, 208, 215, 216, 218, 219, 220, 235, 236
MacGibbon, I.C.: 195, 197
MacDonald, Malcom: 130

241

242

243

Toynbee, Arnold: 5, 193, 194, 198, 203, 237
Transkei: 137
Tricontinental Conference (1966): 9
Triska, Jan: 233
trusteeship (principle of): 87, 101, 103, 104, 107, 116, 121, 132, 133, 134, 141, 145, 171, 174, 176, 179, 221
Trusteeship System: 104, 158, 179
Trust territories: 106, 118, 170, 228
Tucker, ROBERT W.: 197
Tunkin, Grigory: 195, 197, 211
Turkey: 83
Turko-Soviet Treaty (1921): 139
Tuzmukhamedov: 212, 214, 234

Uganda: 192
Ukraine: 139
Umozurike, O.: 230, 232
United Nations: 3, 7, 10, 129, 136, 167, 175, 177, 232
  Charter of: 3, 9, 14, 15, 39-44, 57-62, 96, 98, 102, 104-113, 128, 150, 212
  Article 1: 10, 42, 48, 57, 106, 107, 111, 112, 161
  Article 2: 10, 48, 57, 146, 174
  Article 51: 54, 173
  Articles 55 & 56: 57, 106
  Article 73: 57, 58, 63, 111, 119, 120, 123, 124, 170
  Article 76: 111, 184
  Chapter XI: 51, 104, 105, 116, 117, 122, 128, 158, 175, 176
  Chapter XII: 104, 105, 128, 175
  practice of: 15, 50, 51, 58-60, 113-128
  General Assembly: 1, 58, 114-123, 129-134, 137, 167, 191, 227
  UNGA Resolutions 637-A (VII): 117, 228
    648 (VII): 115, 116, 118
    742 (VIII): 118, 124
    1514 (XV): 62, 120, 121, 139, 140, 145, 229
    1541 (XV): 50, 62, 115, 120-124, 157, 159, 229
    1573 (XV): 62
    1747 (XV): 62

1004 (ES-11): 128
1005 (ES-11): 128
3089 (XXVIII): 168
Security Council Resolution S/4835: 62
United States: 2, 73, 79, 81, 97, 99-101, 112, 134-135, 147, 191
Universal Declaration of Human Rights: 170

Versailles Treaty: 97
Verwoerd, Henrik F.: 136
Viet Cong: 191
Vietnam: 2, 191, 192
Virally, Michel: 196
Virginia: 79, 193

Wainhouse, David W.: 227, 228, 229, 230, 232
Wambaugh, Sarah: 13, 35, 81, 195, 198, 200, 207, 208, 209, 215, 216, 217, 218, 219, 235
Weiner, Myron: 191
West Virginia: 193
Western Samoah: 123
Wheeler-Bennet, J.W.: 215
Wilson, Woodrow: 2, 21, 35, 70, 72, 75, 76-82, 87-89, 98, 99, 125, 149, 184, 200, 215, 218, 220, 221
Wise, Watson: 231
Wittman, Erno: 193, 198, 203, 209, 237
Wolfke, Karol: 194, 195, 196, 197, 198
Wolgemuth, Patricia: 228, 232
Woolsley, Theodore S.: 198, 203
world order: 181-190
World War I: 6, 22, 69, 127, 156, 162, 163, 183, 193
World War II: 2, 43, 97, 127, 154
Wright, Quincy: 9, 57, 58, 89, 92, 194, 212, 213, 214, 220, 221, 222, 223, 234

Young, Crawford: 235
Yugoslav Committee: 29, 201-202, 217
Yugoslavia: 162, 192
Yalta Conference: 102

Zimmerwald Conference: 203